MANAGING TO MAKE IT

STUDIES ON SUCCESSFUL ADOLESCENT DEVELOPMENT

The John D. and Catherine T. MacArthur Foundation

SERIES ON MENTAL HEALTH AND DEVELOPMENT

Managing to Make It

Urban Families and Adolescent Success

Frank F. Furstenberg, Jr.

Thomas D. Cook

Jacquelynne Eccles

Glen H. Elder, Jr.

Arnold Sameroff

With the assistance of
MONIKA ARDELT
W. TODD BARTKO
WING-SHING CHAN
LYNNE MAZIARZ GEITZ
CYNTHIA HARPER
JEONG-RAN KIM
SARAH E. LORD
RICHARD A. SETTERSTEN
JULIEN O. TEITLER
KAREN WALKER
CHRISTOPHER C. WEISS

The University of Chicago Press • Chicago and London

The University of Chicago Press, Chicago 60637
The University of Chicago Press, Ltd., London
© 1999 by The University of Chicago
All rights reserved. Published 1999
Paperback edition 2000
09 08 07 06 05 04 03 02 01 00   2 3 4 5 6

ISBN 0-226-27391-1 (cloth)
ISBN 0-226-27393-8 (paperback)

The University of Chicago Press gratefully acknowledges a subvention from the John D.
and Catherine T. MacArthur Foundation in partial support of the costs of production of this
volume.

Library of Congress Cataloging-in-Publication Data

Managing to make it : urban families and adolescent success / [edited by] Frank F.
    Furstenberg, Jr. . . . [et al.].
        p. cm.—(John D. and Catherine T. MacArthur Foundation series on mental
health and development. Studies in successful; adolescent development
        Includes bibliographical references (p.) and index.
        ISBN 0-226-27391-1 (alk. paper)
        1. Urban youth—Pennsylvania—Philadelphia—Family relationships. 2. Urban
    youth—Pennsylvania—Philadelphia—Longitudinal studies. 3. Parenting—
    Pennsylvania—Philadelphia—Longitudinal studies. 4. Socially handicapped
    teenagers—Pennsylvania—Philadelphia—Longitudinal studies. 5. Success—
    Pennsylvania—Philadelphia—Longitudinal studies. I. Furstenberg, Frank F.,
    1940–   .
    II. Series.
    HQ796.M268   1999
    649'.125'0974811—dc21   98-27071
                                                                                  CIP

Contents

Illustrations

Preface

This book is the first of a series of research studies produced by a decade-long effort to reshape disciplinary studies on disadvantaged adolescents that was sponsored by the John D. and Catherine T. MacArthur Foundation. It is no easier to redraw academic boundaries than geographical ones. Though we often articulate the importance of doing research that breaches traditional disciplinary boundaries and lament the limited theoretical and methodological confines of respective fields, it is not easy to stray very far from familiar territory.

Our attempt to do so in this study and the volumes that follow may appear timid to some observers. We can assure you that our efforts to reach further were not for lack of will or good intentions. Getting out of one's disciplinary frame of mind is as difficult as stepping out of one's culture. It produces an inevitable feeling of nakedness and confusion.

To the extent that we have succeeded, we owe a tremendous debt of gratitude to Dick Jessor, who was our guide and interpreter. Dick's familiarity with diverse theories, methods, and discourses is truly astounding. His patience in imparting these to us and instilling a sense of shared mission cannot be underestimated. Dick's grand vision of a more integrated social science that presents real individuals encountering real conditions and contexts enabled us to build this study into something more ambitious and far-reaching than it would otherwise have been. Without his help, the book would simply not exist in its present form. He deserves much credit for its virtues; for its shortcomings, we willingly accept the blame.

On the way to completing this study, we have incurred a large number of debts to the many individuals who helped us conceive of the project, carry it through, and bring it to publication. We have two apprehensions in acknowledging these debts: first that we may forget to mention some of those who helped us, and second that this token of appreciation seriously understates our gratitude.

As in many studies, the idea behind this research cannot be claimed as genuinely original. It has been examined, more or less explicitly, by many of those who shared their ideas and research findings with the MacArthur Foundation Research Network on Successful Adolescent Development among Youth in High-Risk Settings. In particular, we recall the meeting with Sandy Jencks, who stimulated so much of our interest in neighborhood research, and the association of some of us with the activities and participants in the Social Science Research Council on the Underclass. Similarly, we are indebted to colleagues in other MacArthur networks who supported our interest in this topic.

We are grateful to the MacArthur Foundation for entrusting us for so long a period with the support that enabled us to carry out this study. Special thanks in this respect go to Dennis Praeger, Robert Rose, and Idy Gitelson, who expressed confidence in the enterprise when confidence was needed.

Other members of our network, Albert Bandura, James Comer, Del Elliott, Norman Garmezy, Robert Haggerty, Beatrix Hamburg, Marta Tienda, and William Julius Wilson, played a special role in nurturing this study by serving as sympathetic and insightful critics throughout. All listened to countless presentations and patiently nursed us through crises along the way. Most read and reread early drafts, and their countless contributions have made this a better book than it otherwise might have been. Del Elliott, Marta Tienda, and Bill Wilson all went to summer camp with us at the Center for Advanced Studies in the Behavioral Sciences, where they were exposed to still further demands on their time. We must thank Neal Smelser and Bob Scott as well as the staff of the Center for taking such good care of us in the summer of 1995 and for continuing that caregiving in 1997–98 for two of us, Frank Furstenberg and Tom Cook, as this final draft was being completed.

Patricia Miller, administrative aide to Furstenberg, must be singled out as the patron saint of this project. She kept the study going on a steady course and made us feel well taken care of along the way. Along with her counterparts, Marilyn Sena, Danelle Winship, and Aline Christoffelsz, Patricia must be credited with silent authorship.

Finally, we are also grateful to the many students who are not coauthors on the various chapters but who provided invaluable input. Cynthia Harper provided excellent editorial comments along with Beth Czosek,

Angela Jernigan, and Tobia Worth. Thanks also go to Annette Lareau, Sarah Lord, and Rob Sampson for reading earlier drafts of the manuscript. Amanda Nothaft read and fact-checked the manuscript and cheerfully supported us through the last phase of the work.

PART ONE

The Theory and Research Design

Parenting in the Inner City
The Problem

JJ Newman and his family live in a dilapidated house on a block dotted with abandoned structures. In this deteriorating neighborhood of southwest Philadelphia, about a quarter of the families are living in poverty. Many others are just above the poverty line. Although far from one of the worst neighborhoods in the city, the area where the Newmans live is typical of most distressed communities in inner-city Philadelphia. It suffers from physical neglect and crime. The schools are bad and the parks unsafe.

JJ Newman and Annie, his mother, were among nearly five hundred families we have been studying for seven years to learn how families living in inner-city neighborhoods are faring, and especially about ways in which adolescent development and well-being are affected by growing up in a disadvantaged community. Neither JJ nor his family was doing well. His mother, a single parent with two other children, both younger than JJ, supported the family on welfare. Occasionally she worked as a barmaid to provide extra cash for the family. The money was sorely needed because Annie Newman had recently become a grandmother twice over as first JJ and then his younger sister had children.

JJ dropped out of school in the eleventh grade. In the spring of 1993 he had been caught on school grounds with a knife. This incident resulted in his being sent to disciplinary school, which only contributed to his negative feelings about school. In January of 1994 he stopped attending altogether:

Q: When did you stop going [to school]?
A: I think it was January.
Q: Can you tell me why you decided to stop going?

A: I had got stuck up for my chain down there. It happened before ah, [a] whole bunch of times—three or four times.

Q: Can you tell me what happened?

A: I ain't know who did it. [He] wasn't from around here.

Although JJ claimed that he would transfer from the disciplinary school and return to a comprehensive high school in the fall, he did not. In November 1994, his son was born, and JJ's girlfriend returned to finish high school while JJ watched their baby during the day. JJ wasn't employed, although he reported some income from gambling at craps and pool.

JJ's story would hardly surprise the general public, which has been inundated with statistics about children in poverty, disadvantaged minorities, and the "urban underclass." Over the past decade, social scientists and journalists have chronicled the experiences of families like JJ's, pointing out the corrosive features of growing up in persistent poverty. These images have become part of our conventional wisdom about life in the inner city. In both professional and popular writings, we are constantly being reminded that a crisis exists in our families, our schools, our legal system, and our social services. These institutions are serving children poorly, especially children residing in the ghettos of our large cities. An ever-larger proportion of our young people, it is said, is undereducated and inadequately prepared to assume the more complex jobs in a postindustrial economy (Behrman 1997; Blank 1997; Carnegie Corporation 1995; National Academy of Sciences 1993). High levels of poverty, family instability, and increased demands from the workplace have all been implicated in reducing parental investment and adding to the burden carried by public institutions that are charged with providing youth services.

At the same time, it appears that public support for youth-serving institutions is on the wane. Taxpayers seem reluctant to fund health services, education, training, and recreational facilities, not to mention public assistance for the needy. We are placing more responsibility on parents and giving them fewer public resources to do their job. Families like JJ's have become familiar symbols in news stories, journal articles, and political discussions, evidence of the failure of our families to honor their obligations. And JJ is portrayed as the product of this failure. He and others like him are part of an unpromising future generation—socially maladjusted, unable to assume autonomy, economically dependent, and untutored in the responsibilities of citizenship. From this perspective, the JJs in our study seem to issue from a common sociological mold.

Just two blocks away from where JJ and his family reside, however, Robert James lives with his parents and three brothers and sisters. Robert couldn't be further from the stereotype of the young black male in the inner city. Soft-spoken, thoughtful, and possessing a wry sense of humor, Robert seems well on his way to fulfilling his dream of becoming an accountant. In his junior year, he is doing well in the accounting program of one of the city's business charter school programs. After school Robert works part-time, but still manages to play an active role in his church's social life.

Lakisha Wilkenson also lives in the same community as JJ and Robert. Despite growing up in unfavorable circumstances, Lakisha, the youngest daughter of a single mother whose income comes from caring for two foster children in her home, is a resourceful and determined young woman. She was doing poorly in school in our 1990 survey and had repeated two grades. By 1995 however, her academic performance had begun to improve. Now in the eleventh grade at a vocational school, Lakisha participated in a special business program for motivated students that is funded by local entrepreneurs. Although she occasionally received C's, most of her grades were A's and B's. Considering college, Lakisha had plans to take the SATs and had talked to several teachers and counselors about suitable college programs. She was working between twenty-seven and forty hours a week at a convenience store where she did both bookkeeping and ran a cash register. She also planned to get a summer internship at a local law firm, which was to be arranged by her school program. She was sexually active, and her boyfriend lived in her mother's home with her, but she was adamant about not wanting children until she was able to move out of her neighborhood. Before she ever had intercourse, she had a contraceptive implant placed in her arm.

Social scientists have recently begun to give as much attention to the processes that produce Robert James and Lakisha Wilkenson as to those that produce JJ Newman and his counterparts.[1] Investigating how individuals and families find pathways out of poverty is instructive for several reasons. First, it may help eradicate the stigmatizing idea, all too often present in popular discussions about the poor, that disadvantaged parents are indifferent about their children's futures or inept when it comes to promoting their life chances. Most social scientists do not subscribe to such a deterministic view of children's fate, but our work is often interpreted by the popular press, politicians, and lay people to convey that impression. Sometimes we bear the responsibility for these sociological stereotypes because our tendency has been to report crude aggregate differences between social categories (teenage mothers vs. older childbearers or blacks vs. whites) rather than pursuing sources of variation within groups. This book explores why and how variation occurs within inner-city neighborhoods.

An added dividend of examining successes is the information that they offer about what makes inner-city families resilient to stressful conditions and what leads them to be creative in finding ways to help their children thrive. These attributes often take the form of individual qualities of parent or child, who may possess special beliefs, competencies, temperament, or resources that contribute to success in the face of adversity. It is equally possible that some children living in disadvantage grow up in a milieu that is out of the ordinary. What distinguishes them, then, is the quality of their immediate environment. Families, schools, or neighborhoods may possess collective beliefs, support networks, or special resources that advance children's prospects, provide them access to economic resources, or put them in touch with social agencies that influence the course of their development. A focus on success under unfavorable conditions can provide useful clues about which public policies could be adopted to assist children and families to cope with these conditions, thereby reducing the handicaps imposed on those economically disadvantaged at birth.

This study, and the broader research program of which it is a part, was designed to investigate the process of successful adolescence among individuals who live in varying social contexts. Cases like those of Robert James and Lakisha Wilkenson and their families can inform us about both the individual components of successful development and the special features of environments that promote children's success. This volume devotes particular attention to selected aspects of those environments—specifically how families and communities contribute to processes of development, helping children defy the odds of remaining disadvantaged throughout their lives. This introductory chapter describes why we focus on the question of how parents manage risk and opportunity when raising their children in less than optimal circumstances. Readers are introduced to the central premise explored in this study: that parents provide a vital connection between the community beyond the household and the developing child. This theme is also explored in the companion volumes in this series sponsored by the MacArthur Foundation, which examine conditions that promote successful adolescence among youths who grow up in disadvantaged communities (Cook et al. forthcoming; Elder and Conger in press; Elliott et al. forthcoming).

SUCCESSFUL ADOLESCENT DEVELOPMENT

We think of development as a process during which youth come to formulate and to alter their self-conceptions and expectations. Development requires new skills and behavioral strategies in response to physical and biological changes, exposure to different environments, or changing social expectations. To understand how development is affected by organizational and cultural features of any society, researchers must depict the experiences and responses of youth in everyday situations encountered in their families, schools, peer groups, through mass media, or in political and civic institutions. They must show how these encounters in *local* settings—which in turn are affected by changing levels of resources, opportunities, and social standards—gradually come to shape adolescents' self-definitions and competencies.

Development results from an ongoing process of social exchange between individuals and their immediate milicus. Obviously, no single study can fully chart this process, because individuals encounter numerous formal and informal institutions in the course of growing up. The objective of our project is to identify a strategic site—the interface between the family and community—that influences the course of adolescent development for disadvantaged youth.

Our research project is especially aimed at understanding adolescents like Robert and Lakisha, who are well positioned to make a successful transition to adulthood and who are able to elude many of the obstacles that beset other youth in their communities. We do not hold the view that attaining success is the same as avoiding problems. Our study focuses both on the acquisition of social commitments and competencies and on abstention from behaviors that compromise future prospects.

Much evidence suggests that problem behavior frequently begins in early adolescence. By their mid- and late teens, many youth are mired in an array of related ills. In fact, over half of today's youth between the ages of ten and seventeen have engaged in two or more risk behaviors, including unsafe sex, intercourse leading to teenage pregnancy, drug or alcohol abuse, school failure, delinquency, and crime (Lerner, Entwisle, and Hauser 1994; Zill and Nord 1994), and 10 percent of these youth engage in all of these behaviors (Dryfoos 1990). In addition to behavioral risks, physical risks to young people are on the rise as well. Adolescence is the only age group for whom mortality rates have been increasing (Carnegie Corporation 1995). The demographic data on the heightened risk of health-compromising behaviors inevitably raise the question of what makes adolescence such a turbulent time for youth in this country.

In traditional cultures—even in earlier centuries in America—adolescence typically is marked by a relatively brief transition between childhood and adulthood (Elder 1980; Feldman and Elliott 1990; Kett 1977; Mead and Wolfenstein 1955; Modell 1989). This stage of life has become more culturally salient as it has become more extended in years (Hamburg and Takanishi 1989; Coleman 1961). At the early stage of adolescence, biological changes signaling puberty now begin sooner owing to changes in diet and nutrition (Lancaster and Hamburg 1986; Paikoff and Brooks-Gunn 1989). Rights and responsibilities usually associated with the later period of adolescence and with maturity—completion of schooling, full-time entrance into the labor force, family formation, and the establishment of an independent household—often do not occur until well into the third decade of life or later. Whereas a century ago nearly all the teens in our sample would have been out of school and in the labor force, today virtually no one is economically self-sufficient before age eighteen (Hareven 1994; Modell, Furstenberg, and Hershberg 1976).

Yet in many other respects teens today are more autonomous at sixteen and freer of social constraints than they were in previous centuries. Their ability to engage in adult behaviors (sexual intercourse, alcohol use, or delinquency) has increased as a result of earlier physical maturity and greater freedom from home and adult supervision. Moreover, an autonomous youth culture reinforced by a powerful popular culture now competes with family and school for the attention, if not the allegiance, of young people (Modell 1989).

These changes in the structure and meaning of adolescence are centrally related to our explorations of family management strategies. Parents have been forced to contend with the realities of an even longer period of their children's semi-autonomy. The characterization of adolescence as a period of Sturm und Drang is nearly as old as the scientific study of adolescence. G. Stanley Hall (1904) regarded turmoil as a natural characteristic of the age group and intrinsic to the individual. Later writings challenged this view; social scientists have come to regard problem behavior largely as emerging from an interaction or fit between adolescents and their environments rather than an intrinsic or fixed set of attributes of the adolescents themselves (Bronfenbrenner 1979, 1986; Eccles et al. 1993; Erikson 1963; Jessor and Jessor 1973). From this vantage point, adolescent problem behavior appears to result from a mismatch between the needs of the child and the opportunities provided by the social context.

Under ideal circumstances, children are granted greater opportunities for independence, accorded more responsibility, and gradually earn greater authority during adolescence. Unfortunately, a coherent cultural orchestration of the adolescent years has not been worked out in contemporary society. Such a response tends to emerge in stable societies, where developmental agendas have been perfected and repeated for generation after generation (Sameroff and Fiese 1992).

In modern society—perhaps especially in urban settings—responses to adolescence are organized as much by the absence of clear-cut norms as by their presence. Hence it falls to families and, to some extent, schools to define the developmental agenda for young people. To a larger extent than may have been true historically, adolescents themselves are active in setting the course of their own development. They often do so in less than ideal circumstances. Adolescent settings such as junior high school, researchers have argued, are actually counterdevelopmental in their institutional organization and behavior because, compared to elementary schools, they grant less autonomy and provide more anonymity to their students (Eccles et al. 1993).

Similarly, the family does not always respond sympathetically to the child's need for increasing autonomy in the adolescent years. While existing literature suggests a wide range of family adaptions to pubertal changes, some evidence indicates that more conflict and decreased warmth are common responses (Paikoff and Brooks-Gunn 1991). Parents vary considerably in their capacity to respond to the physical and psychological signs of maturity, and these variations may be conditioned to some extent by their perceptions about the potential risks of autonomy as compared to its benefits. The perceptions among inner-city parents are, not surprisingly, more likely to lean in the direction of perceiving risks than opportunities for growth (Spencer and Dornbusch 1990; Steinberg 1990).

Family, school, or community may therefore be unable to nourish the adolescent's growing needs for autonomy, competence, and participation (Eccles et al. 1993; Friedenberg 1964). This sort of interpretation locates the roots of conventional or problem behavior in transactions between individuals and environments. Causal explanations that reside exclusively in either child or context are likely to miss the mark. In such dynamic systems approaches (Sameroff 1983, 1995) individual differences and courses of development in adolescents both provoke and are provoked by changes in the social context. For example, when disobedient children provoke hostile, aggressive reactions from their parents, they tend to become aggressive themselves; when inattentive students provoke rejection from teachers, they become even less attentive (Patterson 1976). Communities may fail to provide opportunities for participation or fail to foster development along paths valued by the larger society.

Recognizing that notions of success are historically and culturally situated, we will leave open for empirical examination the question of whether the objectives of successful development vary among the populations in our study. Nevertheless, our research program is based on the premise (which some may argue is a middle-class value) that a successful adolescence involves acquisition of the skills and competencies that lead to physical and mental health, social involvement, and economic self-sufficiency and productivity in adulthood. To achieve these aims, youth in American society must be given a fair chance (1) to acquire the cognitive skills and resources to become educated to their highest potential; (2) to accumulate psychological and social skills that foster a positive identity, including a personal sense of well-being and self-efficacy; and (3) to participate in activities that foster a capacity to perform as family members, workers, and informed citizens in their communities.

The possibility of successful development under disadvantaged circumstances has long been an interest of social scientists, particularly among Chicago school criminologists (Lemert 1951; Sutherland 1939). More recently, this strand of inquiry has intrigued scholars who have examined the notion of "risk and resiliency." Beginning in the 1970s, scholars from several disciplines began to examine "protective" sources that buffered children who were growing up at risk of lifelong disadvantage due to personal disabilities, lack of family resources, or difficult social environments (Rutter and Madge 1976; Werner and Smith 1982). Resiliency sometimes resided in an individual's special cognitive or emotional qualities, athletic or musical skills, or even physical appearance. Sometimes, protective conditions were present in the children's family environment, or in their social network, or from informal or formal institutions that afforded them support or mentoring (Garmezy 1985).

Although we share an intellectual orientation that attracts us to this theoretical approach, we recognize some limitations to the risk and resiliency framework. Too often, complex social processes or interactions between person and environment are neglected in an effort to predict outcomes. Deeper understanding of developmental pathways is sometimes replaced by more mechanistic interpretations that ignore how individuals navigate in various ways in similar environments. Ironically, the enterprise of cumulating risks from many sources, intended to explain how individuals elude disadvantage, can convey a certain inevitability about the effects of disadvantage, which appear to be surmountable only by fate, fortune, or heroic efforts. Without denying the fundamental insight that disadvantages frequently come packaged together, we argue that effective interventions may require a clearer understanding of how the fabric of individual experience and social context is woven together. Too often, we fear, social scientists are divided over the question of whether development is a process that takes place within individuals or one that is regulated primarily by culture and social structure—a dichotomy we find as misleading as it is unproductive.

We are more comfortable with a theoretical perspective that allows greater room for individuals to be active agents in constructing their environments. Development, we have said, is the product of an iterative and ongoing process between children and the settings in which they grow up. When successful, it results in the acquisition of skills and beliefs that increase a child's ability to master future challenges. At the same time, individual constructions, whenever they are formed, invariably reflect and are limited by the availability of resources and the existence of constraints and opportunities, as well as by the ways individuals' worlds are defined by others in their immediate milieus. Thus, our theoretical orientation features individuals, not merely as bundles of fixed attributes, but as actors with more fluid and reflexive sensibilities that allow for discretion in how they respond to and create their social environments.

This position, no doubt, will seem elementary to many readers who share our conceptions. Much of what we have sketched above draws directly from the heritage of psychological and sociological theories developed by our predecessors. Over the past century, they have provided the foundations of our respective academic disciplines. We are reminded of these ideas in the writings of James, Lewin, Dewey, Buhler, Erikson, and Bronfenbrenner among others in psychology, or of Simmel, Cooley, Mead, W. I. Thomas, Parsons, Mills, and Goffman, to mention but a few sociologists who have thought deeply about the links between individuals and contexts.

At the same time it also seems clear to us that the fields of sociology and developmental psychology have to some extent lost touch with this rich heritage, owing in part to increasing disciplinary specialization and increasing segregation within the social sciences. Since the middle of this century, psychology, sociology, and anthropology—not to mention economics and history—have gone their separate ways. Each field has evolved a distinctive language, set of methods, and set of disciplinary practices, encouraging less and less dialogue and exchange across fields of study that once shared a common intellectual and theoretical agenda. One of our aims in this study, and in our more general program of research, is to revive this heritage. More specifically, our objective has been to examine ways in which developmental processes are constrained by neighborhood settings—a problem that has recently attracted attention in sociology, psychology, anthropology, and, to some extent, economics as well (Brooks-Gunn et al. 1993; Jencks and Mayer 1990; National Research Council 1993; Sampson, Raudenbush, and Earls 1997; Simcha-Fagan and Schwartz 1986; Steinberg, Darling, and Fletcher 1995; Sullivan 1989; Wilson 1991).

Implicitly, and sometimes explicitly, much of this work has accepted the idea that parents and children produce characteristic responses to constraints and opportunities present in their immediate environments in ways that create distinctive local cultures. This idea can be traced to the popular idea of the 1960s that developed from Robert Merton's reformulation of Durkheim's theory of anomie. Merton (1968) argued that anomie was produced by a disjuncture between culturally defined goals and the means available for realizing those goals, and he identified several potential responses available to those faced with this socially structured dilemma.

The problem Merton identified did not disappear. Indeed, a long tradition of research in criminology continued to test and refine his ideas (Cloward and Ohlin 1960; Sampson 1992; Sullivan 1989). However, much of the interest in responses to limited social and economic opportunities petered out in other disciplines and has only been revived in the past decade as attention has focused again on responses to concentrated poverty. Our study is rooted in this theoretical tradition but attempts to incorporate a new understanding of how parents may play a part in mediating their children's adaptation to growing up in disadvantaged circumstances.

FAMILY MANAGEMENT AND ADOLESCENT DEVELOPMENT

Parents typically supervise their children's behavior, though certain features of family management have been inadequately appreciated by both sociologists and psychologists who study socialization within the family. Generally speaking, the identification of parenting processes has been limited to what happens inside households and specifically to dyadic encounters between parents and children. Undeniably, dimensions of parent-child relations are powerful predictors of children's developmental trajectories (Maccoby and Martin 1983). The quality of communication, trust, understanding, and bonding, along with styles of regulation, control, and decision making, are important dimensions of parents' success in instilling their beliefs, cultivating skills, and fostering motivation in children (Baumrind 1989; Steinberg 1990).

Yet parents also play an essential role in managing the external world by monitoring, locating, and cultivating the social contacts in which their children engage outside the household. When children are young, parents may be able to control these encounters to a greater or lesser extent by limiting their access to unfavorable settings, either by selecting appropriate peers, or by accompanying children as they engage in social contacts. These practices become less possible as children grow up; even so, strategies of family management remain a central avenue of parental influence (Farber and Iverson 1998; Iverson and Farber 1996). Family management strategies include, but are not restricted to, decisions regarding the selection of neighborhood, the choice of schooling, and the garnering of resources and services both within and beyond the household.

How families manage the external world involves not only the ways in which parents directly regulate the child outside the home but also how they indirectly organize the child's life in ways that he or she may not even recognize. In important respects, family management is about the use of what sociologists, following James Coleman (1988), have come to call "social capital." Coleman uses the term to refer to social relationships that serve as resources that individuals can draw upon to implement their goals. He identifies three forms of social capital: norms, reciprocal obligations, and opportunities for sharing information. The neighborhood is clearly a potentially important reservoir of such social capital. Putnam (1995), a political scientist, uses the idea of social capital in an overlapping way to describe the building of social investment that comes from collective associations and participation. Although he is not explicitly interested in human development, he argues that disengagement from collective life has had profound effects on community and family.

Sampson (1992) has argued that the concept of social capital dovetails with social disorganization theory; the lack of social capital is one of the distinguishing features in socially disorganized communities. The presence or absence of social capital in a community thus may be an important link between the structure of communities and the development of children.

Just as parents' face-to-face interactions with their children inform and affect children's attitudes and behavior, we may reasonably assume that they may be able to select and regulate their children's behavior indirectly by their choice of environments, agencies, and individuals who enter the child's life. This study explores whether these indirect mechanisms of socialization have important consequences for children's development and long-term welfare. We might expect the indirect effects of family management to be especially powerful in inner-city communities where opportunities are sparse and dangers are great. Parental strategies of managing environments outside the home could help explain differences between children who do well and those who do poorly under comparable circumstances. In addition, we investigate the different strategies that parents employ in varying neighborhood niches that work to the advantage of children over the long term.

We think of family management, then, as a particular feature of parenting through which parents construct and construe social connections for their children. Family management is a process by which parents build, invest, and deploy social capital—drawing upon social knowledge, information, and resources—in the interest of protecting and providing for their children and fostering their long-term prospects. We speculate that parents who manage these tasks with energy, commitment, and skill increase their children's chances of doing well during the adolescent years and of successfully negotiating the passage to adulthood. Whether these capacities vary across communities or whether they assume a different form depending on features of the community are questions that are of special interest to us, issues that connect to the burgeoning interest among social scientists in how properties of neighborhoods affect children's life chances.

NEIGHBORHOODS, FAMILY MANAGEMENT, AND ADOLESCENT DEVELOPMENT

In the late 1980s, owing in part to the publication of William Julius Wilson's important book, *The Truly Disadvantaged* (1987), academics of various disciplinary stripes began to take a renewed interest in poverty and its effects on children (Duncan and Brooks-Gunn 1994; Gephart 1997; Huston 1991; Huston, McLoyd, and Garcia Coll 1994). We say renewed interest because Wilson's book began by recalling the unproductive debates of the 1960s over the causes of poverty and its consequences for the welfare of children. Wilson argues that ideological and disciplinary differences had a stifling effect on academic scholarship, diverting attention from the growing crisis occurring in many inner-city areas. He links the collapse of urban neighborhoods and social institutions to a configuration of economic, demographic, and cultural conditions that undermine the family's capacity to protect and nurture children.

Building on the theoretical insights and empirical tradition of the Chicago school of sociology, especially its focus on urban ecology, Wilson shows how the growing concentration of poverty is a by-product of deindustrialization. A declining labor market for unskilled workers and an exodus of highly educated, middle-income blacks has resulted in a rapid shift in the composition of many inner-city neighborhoods (see also Massey and Denton 1993). Increased segregation of the persistently poor in neighborhoods bereft of institutional resources, social connections, role models, and work routines all contributed to creating a "ghetto-specific culture" that, Wilson argues, undermines commitment to mainstream values and the acquisition of skills that permit social mobility (Wilson 1996). The prospect that poverty neighborhoods are increasing—even if they contain only a tiny percentage of poor minorities—has revived interest in community studies and research on the "urban underclass," a phrase that has proved to be as professionally problematic as it is popular (Gans 1990; Wilson 1991).

Wilson's book, and a series of theoretical and empirical studies following its publication, drew attention to the potential importance of neighborhoods and communities as immediate and salient contexts for adolescent socialization. The idea that neighborhoods might provide distinctively different subcultures that influence the course of adolescent development has a long tradition in sociological theories of crime and deviant behavior, as we noted earlier (Cloward and Ohlin 1960; Elliott et al. 1996; Sampson 1992; Shaw and McKay 1942; Sullivan 1989; Tannenbaum 1938; Thrasher 1927). Only recently, however, have urban neighborhoods again become a locus of attention for developmentalists and for policy makers and interventionists who are designing programs to improve the life chances of minority youth, as they did in the 1960s during the Kennedy and Johnson administrations (National Research Council 1996).

Several distinct mechanisms have been identified to explain how environments may influence the course of adolescent development. In their review of the evidence of neighborhood effects, Jencks and Mayer (1990) summarize the alternative explanations that have been invoked in prior studies: (1) normative environments among neighborhoods may differ, thus providing varying levels of support or toleration for mainstream or alternative belief systems; (2) adult role models or agents for socialization may be more or less abundant in different communities, affecting the degree of social control or enforcement of norms; and (3) communities may be relatively rich or impoverished in formal and informal resources and in institutions that provide access to adult roles. Obviously, these explanations are not mutually exclusive; we may see them as separate strands that come together in communities. As Del Elliott and colleagues (1996), among others, have argued, these features of neighborhoods provide a powerful blend of normative support, social networks, and resources that promote the life chances of children growing up in favorable circumstances; alternatively, their absence implies a toxic environment for children.

In the past few years, researchers have made vigorous efforts to demonstrate that links exist between community characteristics and youth outcomes, largely by relating demographic characteristics of census tracts to survey or census data on adolescent outcomes (Furstenberg and Hughes 1997). Though some studies have discovered intriguing associations, the body of existing research provides a rather mixed picture of support for these theories (Gephart 1997; Steinberg 1990). Certainly, evidence has been found showing that children who grow up in impoverished neighborhoods with high rates of family instability fare less well in late adolescence and early adulthood, but few studies have been able to demonstrate that features of the neighborhood such as those mentioned above account for these differences (Brooks-Gunn et al. 1993).

Moreover, some of the existing studies show rather modest associations, or none at all, between demographic features of neighborhoods and adolescent outcomes (Cook et al. forthcoming; Cook et al. 1997; Teitler 1996).

The presence of neighborhood effects has been consistently demonstrated by ethnographic and qualitative researchers (Jarrett 1992; MacLeod 1987; Stack 1974; Sullivan 1989; Suttles 1968). Many field studies have provided compelling accounts showing that individuals who grow up in highly disadvantaged settings hold mainstream values but, without the resources to realize them, are often forced to stretch their values or adopt alternative strategies in order to survive. Children accordingly may be exposed to different values, taught to adhere to different priorities, or prepared to use alternative means of survival in early adulthood that depart from mainstream ideals of success (Burton 1990; MacLeod 1987).

Compelling as these accounts are, they almost invariably show considerable variation within neighborhoods (Anderson 1990; Burton, Obeidallah, and Allison 1996; Jarrett 1992; MacLeod 1987). Many families differ in their responses to seemingly identical conditions in their immediate environments. The presence of these variations raises the question of whether families are responding to conditions in their neighborhood or are reflecting other personal or social attributes that may not be specific to their communities. Ethnographic research is not typically designed to distinguish whether neighborhoods actually differ or whether the observed differences have more to do with the types of families studied (Sullivan 1989 and MacLeod 1987 are exceptions). This leaves open the critical question of whether poor families are different because they reside in disadvantaged neighborhoods or whether the neighborhoods merely *appear* different because more of the residents are poor. Unless neighborhood researchers can demonstrate the former by showing that living in a poverty area creates distinctive responses among families who are otherwise alike, then contextual effects may be more apparent than real.

To show that neighborhoods affect the course of adolescent development, researchers ideally need to demonstrate that young people growing up in communities known to have different resources, opportunities, and normative climates experience systematically different courses of development. It might satisfy the claim that social processes within specific neighborhoods influence adolescent development if we discovered that different developmental trajectories emerge in different neighborhoods during the course of the adolescent years. Even when they do, however, we need to rule out the possibility that such differences result from migration of more successful and effective families who move out of impov-

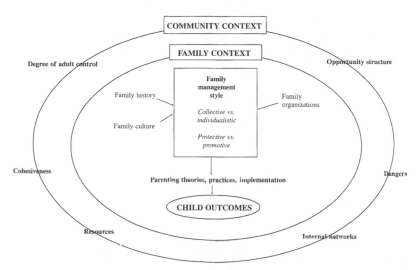

Figure 1.1 Conceptual Framework for Philadelphia Family Management Study

erished communities into those endowed with more resources (Tienda 1991). Those concerned with how neighborhoods influence the process of development might still ask for further evidence that directly links the process and course of development to distinctive features of the neighborhoods.

This study is a piece of a larger effort undertaken by the MacArthur Committee on Successful Adolescent Development in Disadvantaged Communities to discover pathways that link neighborhoods, families, and the developmental course of children. We focus on the extent to which families actually mediate the impact of neighborhoods through the management strategies that parents use to contend with local dangers and cultivate opportunities. A preliminary field study described in the next chapter gave us reason to suspect that parents' direction of their children's prospects by their actions (or inactions) might be a pathway through which neighborhoods exert influence on their children. However, the theoretical perspective discussed in this chapter also persuaded us that how families manage the external world might be an important mechanism mediating neighborhood effects.

A CONCEPTUAL FRAMEWORK FOR THE STUDY

Figure 1.1 provides a schematic representation of the theoretical perspective we have described so far. A fuller discussion of the methods and measures that will refer to this scheme follows in the next and subsequent chapters. The figure summarizes the broad framework of the study and provides a rationale for the analysis presented in later chapters.

We think of neighborhoods as geographically confined areas with distinctive social milieus, containing local resources in the form of services and social capital and providing varying levels of opportunity and dangers. Neighborhoods are not accidents. They are the products of systematic sorting processes. For families with sufficient economic resources, neighborhood choices reflect decisions about other families with whom they are willing to live, particularly in close proximity. Social class, race, and ethnic status are salient determinants of these sorting processes. Like Philadelphia, where our study was carried out, most American cities are heavily segregated along these demographic characteristics (Massey and Denton 1993). These compositional features are related variously to physical and social properties of neighborhoods.

Parents with the means to select their communities prefer physical settings that are safe, contain schools and services for youth, and include neighbors who support one another. In this sense, parents are looking for contexts in which their children are co-socialized according to their values and expectations, contexts in which other members of the community will look out for their children and let them know if they are misbehaving. They will often prefer neighbors of equal or slightly higher social class whose child-rearing practices are likely to be similar to theirs. They want to live near families with children who are suitable peers for their own offspring, who will directly and indirectly promote their standards of right and wrong. Local communities can be potential reservoirs of social capital, as Coleman uses the term, which parents can draw upon just as they may take advantage of the services and institutions in their immediate environments. Children growing up in social contexts with high levels of social capital and strong institutions are likely to learn norms about interpersonal behavior and self-regulation from the surrounding world that reinforce what they have acquired at home. This is what we mean when we say that communities co-socialize children.

In saying that parents select neighborhoods that provide this sort of co-socialization, we are leaving open the question of whether neighborhood "effects" are created in part or entirely by parents' choices and actions. Parents, especially in the families and communities we studied, were not always in an economic position to live where they might desire, and in some cases they were forced to make difficult tradeoffs in their choice of residence in order to remain near family or church, or to afford schooling. Similarly, parents may not move and hence give up these forms of institutional support in order to remain near kin or within their own ethnic community. Alternatively, if they are minorities, they may be forced to do so because of racial segregation.

Hence parents were forced to adopt other management strategies to shield their children from local dangers and connect them to sources of human and social capital. Parents exhibit a variety of techniques for sheltering their children and promoting opportunities. These efforts range from a high degree of vigilance that involves restricting or overseeing children's activities outside the home to directing children to protected niches within and beyond the community. These strategies, we will argue, are related to features of the community.

Whether these management strategies in turn influence children's development is a separate question that animates this study. We are not in a strong position to provide a definitive answer for reasons that we explain in chapter 2. Nonetheless, we will examine whether family management strategies are an important bridge between neighborhood contexts, as described above, and developmental trajectories. In truth, this cross-sectional study can only provide a varied set of indicators of children's developmental status. The measures we use were selected because they have proven to be rather potent predictors of success in later adolescence and early adulthood in previous studies (Elliott et al. forthcoming).

The approach followed in the study and represented in the diagram is not intended to consider the full range of neighborhood effects on children's development. We fully understand that neighborhoods exert potential and perhaps more powerful influences in other ways: through the school, on street corners, and, indirectly, by the absence of resources and social connections that might occur outside the household. Our objective is not to capture as much of the effects of neighborhoods as we might if we explored all of these mechanisms. Instead, we have elected to explore in more depth the part played by the family, parents in particular, as agents who broker social resources in ways that promote the child's welfare.

In our quest to expand traditional ideas of parenting to include strategies for managing the external world, we have tried not to neglect the core and well-established practices that parents employ to regulate their children's behavior. Indeed, it is important to know how various elements of family management relate to one another and to previously studied child-rearing techniques that capture styles of parent-child interaction.

We deliberately omitted from Figure 1.1 the traditional arrows signaling causal pathways, for two reasons. We have already referred to the first in pointing out that individuals select neighborhoods, and neighborhoods their residents, by virtue of the goods and services they offer and the characteristics of their residents. Even if this were not the case, we would be hard-put to make a strong case for causal connections in this cross-sectional study. We take pains not to adopt the language of causality, even as we recognize that falling into this practice is almost unavoidable when exploring "neighborhood effects" and "the part played by family management" on "life-course development." We will often remind readers that our findings rarely establish likely causal directions.

OUTLINE OF THE BOOK

This chapter has introduced the question of how families manage risk and opportunity in disadvantaged neighborhoods as a general problem related, we think, to the broader issue of how children living in disadvantage successfully negotiate the adolescent years. We have located our study in a long tradition of social science research that seeks to integrate approaches from sociology and psychology. The concept of family management—the package of beliefs and practices that families employ to protect their children and promote their chances of success—is, we argue, a strategic site for examining linkages between communities, families, and children's development.

The next chapter describes how the study was carried out, introducing the families and the communities where they reside in the city of Philadelphia. We also discuss some of the nuts and bolts of the research to familiarize readers with both the strengths and limitations of the project. The empirical work draws on qualitative as well as quantitative data collected over a period of some years. The substantive chapters that form the body of this study attempt to weave these results together in an effort to illuminate the role of family management in the development of youth at risk.

Chapters 3 through 9 describe the substantive results. Many of the findings are descriptive and can be easily grasped by readers unfamiliar with statistical techniques. Others require more technical training, but we try to explain the key findings in language that permits the general reader to follow the line of the argument and appreciate the key findings, while giving enough details to permit a full appraisal of the evidence. This is sometimes a difficult balance to achieve; whenever possible, we have relegated technical information either to appendices or footnotes in order to make this book as "reader friendly" as possible.

Following the diagram presented in this chapter, we work backward from indicators of how the children are faring to the reasons that they are doing well or poorly. Chapter 3 introduces the children and the key indicators of their well-being. Chapter 4 examines family practices, and

Chapter 5 looks at the relationship between children's behavior and parenting practices, especially different varieties of family management.

Chapters 6 and 7 can be read as a pair. Both consider whether the relationship between parenting practices and children's success is altered by the context. Chapter 6 examines whether key demographic features of the family—in particular, race, socioeconomic status, and the marital status of the household head—influence either the type of family management practices used by parents or the relationship between particular techniques and children's behavior. In short, we are raising the critical question of whether poor parents, blacks, or single parents have to be more adept to achieve high levels of success with their children or whether they must resort to different strategies to be effective. Chapter 7 asks the same sorts of questions about neighborhood contexts. It examines whether features of neighborhoods are linked to family management practices and whether parents, using similar or different strategies, have greater success in neighborhoods that are more or less endowed with resources and social support.

Chapters 8 and 9 approach the issue of family management from different vantage points. In Chapter 8, we look at risk cumulatively and see whether family management practices, especially when examined in combination, offer protection to the child at risk. In short, we are considering whether effective family management reduces the level of risk created by demographic, social, and environmental factors. Chapter 9 probes more extensively into the subtleties of family management, relying on the qualitative fieldwork. Because it relies on data collected more recently, it provides us with a glimpse of the future—what we might find when the children reach late adolescence and early adulthood. It lays the groundwork for a study now being undertaken that will follow up the families seven years after the initial interviews were completed.

Chapter 10, the final chapter, summarizes the key findings of the study and considers their implications for public policy initiatives. Although this study is exploratory, some of the findings strongly suggest programs and services that might assist parents as well as more general policies relating to institutions that attempt to improve the opportunities of low-income youth. We return to the question of how it may be possible to produce more Robert Jameses and Lakisha Wilkensons and fewer youth who turn out like JJ Newman.

Two

The Philadelphia Study

With the assistance of
JULIEN O. TEITLER AND LYNNE MAZIARZ GEITZ

Research projects are shaped by a peculiar blend of intention and opportunism. This enterprise is no exception. The Philadelphia Study is based on a 1991 survey that was carried out after a year spent visiting and observing families in five neighborhoods in the city. The ethnographic study exposed a rich and largely unexplored territory: how community conditions influence and are influenced by family and parenting processes, and the fieldwork provided a number of promising leads that could extend our understanding of how conditions in neighborhoods and families operate in tandem to affect the course of adolescent development.

Like all empirical studies, the design of the survey that followed the fieldwork was constrained by a series of decisions made along the way. Some of these were foreseen and simply were inevitable compromises struck because of the modest scope of the study; others were unforeseen and would not be repeated. We will try not to disguise the study's limitations, but we believe that the primary purpose of the project—to break new ground in understanding how inner-city parents respond and adapt to their immediate environments—was accomplished.

This chapter sets the stage by introducing the places and the faces: the neighborhood settings and the participants. Over a period of several years, the Philadelphia Study was transformed from an exploratory qualitative project into a survey of nearly five hundred families, and then refocused again into a fieldwork study. Each phase investigated how parents interpret, experience, and react to neighborhood settings in ways that might affect their children's chances of success. The task of translating the experiences of the fieldworkers from the qualitative study was complicated by our effort to uncover often-elusive processes of family management. And it was encumbered as well by the need to forge links in conceptualization and measurement between the Philadelphia Study and a set of kindred network projects, to which we will occasionally refer, undertaken in Denver, Chicago, Prince Georges County (Maryland), and rural Iowa. Across these sites, our committee used a number of different approaches to study the ways in which particular mixes of local conditions influence, facilitate, or impede successful adolescent development or stunt its course. Each study came at this problem from a slightly different angle and gave more or less attention to certain features of context. Our attempt to incorporate common measures in the multiple sites both posed problems and afforded opportunities for replication that we will mention from time to time.[1]

A METHODOLOGICAL PROLOGUE

Even prior to forming the joint enterprise sponsored by the MacArthur Foundation, each of us had come to value methodological pluralism, or the practice of using varied and often multiple methods of data collection that provide varied and potentially reinforcing vantage points for empirical investigation. This shared commitment made a small-scale, intensive study of how families manage risk and opportunity in inner-city neighborhoods seem an appropriate prelude to a population survey. We initially thought of the qualitative phase of the research as informing the quantitative study; as we became more deeply involved in analyzing the data, however, we came to regard these activities less as sequential or successive steps and more as complementary, mutually reinforcing, iterative steps toward understanding the reality of managing adolescent development in urban areas (Jessor, Colby, and Schweder 1996). Accordingly, we followed our survey with another qualitative investigation, during which we revisited a designated subset of thirty-five families in our sample. We think of these follow-up interviews as an example of "focused" fieldwork, a term first employed by Merton and his colleagues. Focused interviews are a method of data collection that is aimed at specifying, explicating, and extending survey research (Merton, Fiske, and Kendall 1990). Lagged qualitative case studies, if properly situated in a larger sample, offer the benefits of testing explanations, resolving anomalous findings, and suggesting leads for additional data analysis.

Qualitative research, when practiced by quantitative researchers, is often limited to ornamental applications, illustrating, as it were, what is demonstrated by the quantitative research. This is unfortunate. We believe that issues of measurement, sampling, inference, and generalizability pose similar problems regardless of method. Combining methods,

which one of us has labeled "critical multiplism," provides a way of esti-
mating and containing sources of error that are routine by-products of
any effort to collect and analyze empirical evidence (Cook 1985). Social
worlds are difficult to know and impossible to know fully, but appreciation of this fact only places a greater obligation on social researchers to
hedge their bets.

THE ETHNOGRAPHIC PRELUDE

As we said, the potential importance of family management emerged
from a small-scale qualitative study of five Philadelphia neighborhoods.
Each of the neighborhoods we came to know in detail were located within
a couple of miles of the gleaming new skyscrapers that define the heart
of what is known to Philadelphians as Center City. A vast social distance
extends between these areas and the restored colonials, genteel brown-
stones, and stately apartment houses that line Center City's most desirable streets. The five communities are as remote from the mostly affluent
residents of Center City as they are from the suburbanites who have
come to fear the city as a whole. They include a small, white ethnic en-
clave where many families have resided since the early part of the century; another working-class community feeling the threat of invasion by
new immigrants; a black neighborhood that had once been solidly middle
class and was now in decline; a housing project and surrounding neighborhood in one of the poorest sections of Philadelphia; and a nearby
Puerto Rican community struggling to protect itself from active drug
trade. All but one of these communities, and many neighborhoods like
them, were part of the catchment areas in which Furstenberg was conducting an evaluation of expanded family planning services (Hughes,
Furstenberg, and Teitler 1995). We selected the neighborhoods partly because, knowing their characteristics, we anticipated large differences in
parenting management styles.

   Five fieldworkers observed and interviewed repeatedly a small set of
families in each of the five neighborhoods to explore how families managed risk and opportunities in their communities. In the course of getting
to know the families, fieldworkers both discussed how parents perceived
their neighborhoods and observed family members' encounters with formal and informal institutions in each community. From the small, catch-
as-catch-can sample, it was not possible to form any secure generalization
about the link between community organization and styles of family
management. Nonetheless, there were strong indications of great variation in how parents responded both within and across communities.

   A more detailed summary of the fieldwork results has been published elsewhere (Furstenberg 1993). Here we highlight some of the important findings that guided the design of the survey we used to explore the links between features of neighborhoods and family management practices more systematically.

We discovered skilled and resourceful parents in all of the neighborhoods. Of course, it was impossible to infer the distribution of parental competence by neighborhood from the qualitative study, so that became an important objective of our subsequent survey. In all the communities we studied, parents were discontented with resources for their children and cognizant of the risks they faced. Hence many able parents considered or were in the process of moving out. Geographic mobility was a primary family management strategy once parents perceived high dangers, inadequate resources, and social disorganization. Nonetheless, many parents who wanted to escape were prevented from doing so because of limited economic resources. Residents of the transitional neighborhoods sometimes rued their decisions to remain, observing that many of the more stable families had migrated to greener pastures. Parents in the transitional areas felt deserted as families who shared a common sense of community abandoned the neighborhood.

In the poorest of the neighborhoods we studied, the Projects, parents were cut off altogether from sources of social support. Contrary to Carol Stack's (1974) finding of extensive exchange networks among the poor, we discovered that families often distrusted their neighbors and restricted their involvement and their children's involvement with residents of the surrounding community. Low social trust made community building difficult, hence reinforcing the belief that parents could not rely on neighbors. These jaundiced views about the immediate environment led parents to adopt highly individualistic styles of family management. At the extreme, some parents resorted to a "lock-up" strategy whereby children were confined to the household or only permitted to engage in the community if they were chaperoned. The most resourceful and energetic parents sometimes were able to locate safe niches within the community but more often ferried their children to opportunities outside their neighborhood.

Garrison Heights, a white ethnic neighborhood, provided a sharp contrast to the transitional neighborhoods and especially to the Projects. As residents of a tiny neighborhood surrounded on three sides by an impoverished black ghetto, Heighters retained a powerful sense of community and a deep suspicion of outsiders. Most residents had grown up in the community; many lived in or near the houses where their parents or even their grandparents had been raised. The dense kinship and friendship networks created a perception that neighbors shared their family values and could be counted upon for assistance. The relatively high degree of social trust encouraged Heighters to invest in local institutions and services for youth in the community. Accordingly, parents frequently delegated responsibility for their children to other adults in the community and likewise assumed responsibility for children outside the household. Parents served as both agents of social control and talent scouts, protecting and promoting children in the community. Thus, in stark contrast to the Projects, where parents reluctantly relied on local institutions or neighbors for child-rearing assistance, residents of Garrison Heights treated parenting more as an activity to be shared among parents and the community.

These observations suggest that characteristics of communities are indeed linked to styles of family management, especially to the ways that parents regard and relate to their immediate milieus. Parents' strategies of involvement and oversight appeared to be influenced by the cohesiveness of the neighborhood, the presence of drugs and violent crime, and the availability of youth services and community resources. These elements both affected and were affected by the willingness of parents to invest in local youth-serving institutions. The readiness of parents to delegate some responsibilities to the community produced a more collective style of family management in the stable neighborhoods like Garrison Heights. In contrast, individualistic strategies of management occur when institutional resources are lacking, social networks are restricted, and distrust of neighbors is high. Most of the parents in the most dangerous neighborhoods were preoccupied with protecting their children, and the restrictive measures they resorted to led them to limit their children's involvement in local community institutions. Parents in the more protected environments were not so constrained and could afford to entrust their children to local institutions. Of course, adept parents who live in high-risk neighborhoods might also reach out of the community for assistance, but the fieldwork revealed that many of these parents had neither the knowledge nor the resources to locate safe niches outside their neighborhoods.

We could only speculate whether these observations were particular to the families or communities involved in the pilot study. And, even if they were generally true, there was no basis for knowing whether parents' responses to opportunities in the neighborhood were likely to affect their children's long-term prospects of escaping disadvantage. But the ethnographic study encouraged us to proceed with plans for a longitudinal survey that would investigate these questions more systematically.

The ethnographic work suggested that parents might be resorting to different sorts of strategies in neighborhoods with varying levels of cohesiveness and with different access to community resources such as schools, social services, and informal networks connecting families to opportunities beyond the neighborhood. The fieldwork also led us to suspect that the presence or absence of these elements would influence parent's practices both within and outside the home. Specifically, we hypothesized that particular features of a neighborhood that generate *community-based* social capital would enhance the ability of parents to enforce their rules, assist one another, and monitor their children, which would in turn affect the process and pattern of adolescent development. We also anticipated, however, that differences in parent's competencies and household resources, which might be referred to as *family-based* social capital, would exert an effect on children's life chances independent of community location (see Furstenberg and Hughes 1995). A study of family management strategies required a design that would allow us to contrast family processes between and within neighborhoods and examine their relations to adolescents' behaviors.

Our interest was not confined to the question of how parents manage the external world. We also addressed how effectively urban parents, especially those who are disadvantaged minorities, manage their children inside the household as well. As the story unfolds, we see that parenting processes exhibited by families in our study resemble practices observed in other, more advantaged populations that we and others have studied.

WHY PHILADELPHIA?

Situating the study in Philadelphia was admittedly an opportunistic decision: convenience and cost considerations figured prominently in locating the study there.[2] Nonetheless, Philadelphia is an appropriate site for a study of how families respond to differences in risks and opportunities in disadvantaged settings. Like most other cities in the Northeastern United States, Philadelphia has experienced severe economic and social deterioration. Most of its neighborhoods are struggling with crime, blight, institutional collapse, and the out-migration of substantial numbers of middle-class residents.

One of the nation's oldest cities and still its fifth-largest city, Philadelphia has been a city of ethnically and socially diverse communities (Hershberg 1991). Philadelphia began to take its current shape in 1854 when a number of townships were consolidated, expanding the area of the city from two to one hundred square miles (Adams et al. 1991; Goode and Schneider 1994). Many small industrial towns, just beyond the old city boundaries, have remained physically and socially distinctive communities, retaining even to the present day something of their historic character. Other sections of the city have experienced tremendous flux as successive waves of immigrants have moved into declining neighborhoods and more prosperous residents have abandoned their communities to seek refuge in less-settled parts of the city and surrounding suburbs.

Throughout the early part of the twentieth century, Philadelphia maintained a robust and mixed industrial economy. Since World War II the city has witnessed, in company with other East Coast urban centers, a decentralization of its economy and an exodus of jobs and job-seekers to the surrounding suburbs and beyond (Yancey and Ericksen 1979). The sharp decline of manufacturing jobs, the aging of industrial plants, and the deterioration of the city's schools and services have all taken their toll. Corrupt and inept political leadership in the early decades of the century left Philadelphia ill-prepared to modernize and capitalize on its natural assets: its port, its historical attractions, and an abundance of colleges and universities.

A brief period of political reform in the 1950s during the administrations of Mayors Clark and Dilworth restored historic sections of the central city and held on to some middle-class residents in the inner city. The pace of gentrification picked up again in the 1980s, spurred by a boom in the professional and service sectors. But all the while, manufacturing jobs were disappearing, especially in the textile and apparel industries, which together had formed a core sector of Philadelphia's economy. The loss of 115,000 manufacturing jobs from 1947 to 1986 contributed to a destabilization of many of Philadelphia's neighborhoods. At the same time, many city residents were drawn to the suburbs as economic expansion in the region grew and as families sought relief from urban tax burdens and refuge from the growing number of urban social ills.

Overall, Philadelphia declined in population from 2.1 million to 1.7 million in the period from 1960 to 1980. In the following decade, it lost another 6.1 percent of its inhabitants, dropping to 1.6 million despite improved economic fortunes during most of the 1980s. A boom in the financial, insurance, real estate, and construction industries produced a surge of well-paid jobs, but the gain was offset by a manufacturing sector that continued to sag, forcing many families with modest education and working skills to leave the city. Center City flourished as new commercial buildings sprang up and gentrification of nearby historical neighborhoods spread. Communities on the periphery, however, found themselves struggling to maintain adequate schools and decent community services.

Early in this century, Philadelphia's African-American population remained a tiny fraction of the city's total habitancy, increasing only modestly from 4 percent in 1900 to 7 percent in 1920. By 1950, the proportion of black residents had risen to 18 percent, partly as a result of a more rapid pace of suburban out-migration by whites. This pattern accelerated after the 1950s as whites with resources and job skills fled the city, leaving behind an increasingly black population with ever-more-limited access to well-paid employment.

Despite their decreasing presence within city boundaries, whites maintained a hold on the better jobs and housing. As one chronicle of Philadelphia's economic growth tells it:

> Unlike the white ethnic communities whose neighborhoods were "ghettoes of opportunity," black communities tended to be "ghettoes of last resort"—residential areas that had been rejected or abandoned by other ethnic groups. (Adams et al. 1991)

In recent decades, the situation for African-Americans in Philadelphia has continued to deteriorate, while their proportion in the city has more than doubled. By 1990, nearly 40 percent of the city's residents were black. The erosion of industrial jobs in Philadelphia has dislocated employment opportunities for blacks, especially black men. Increased residential segregation has relegated all but the middle class (and even many of them) to racially homogeneous neighborhoods, many of which bear the signs of a shrinking population in the form of abandoned and dilapidated housing. A rising number of Puerto Ricans—more than 5 percent of the city's population in 1990—suffered the same, if not a worse, fate. Many of the poorest census tracts in the city are now predominantly Puerto Rican.

In short, the urban character of Philadelphia resembles a number of older U.S. cities whose economies have been eroded by the disappearance of manufacturing and skilled labor jobs in the 1970s and 1980s. These cities are increasingly characterized by what Douglas Massey (1996) has recently referred to as hypersegregation. The growing separation of rich and poor into spatially segregated geographic localities or neighborhoods, along with the presence of adverse conditions such as crime, drugs, teenage child-bearing, gangs, and the like, has stratified the level of institutional support available in the community. The consequences of this stratification for family functioning and adolescent development are topics explored in this book. As we noted in the previous chapter, many social scientists believe that neighborhoods have become highly differentiated systems of opportunity that promote or prevent children's chances of success in later life.

DEFINING NEIGHBORHOODS

Despite the widespread belief that neighborhoods influence opportunities, no general consensus exists among social scientists as to how to define a neighborhood, and no simple procedure exists for capturing the geographical boundaries of neighborhoods in social surveys. Neighborhood, like family, is an inherently fuzzy term that can be defined operationally but has no precise or consistent meaning among residents with a geographically defined community (Elliott et al. 1996; Furstenberg and Hughes 1995; Gephart 1997). For example, in this study residents of the same block often defined their neighborhood differently, and youth were especially vague when asked to specify the boundaries of their neighborhood.

Indeed, the definition of a neighborhood itself could be thought of as a neighborhood characteristic. High consensus existed in how locals referred to the surrounding community in some neighborhoods; in others, almost no one agreed, or they resorted to idiosyncratic referents, supplying the nearest corner to their house as the name of their neighborhood. Even within linguistically cohesive neighborhoods, youth and adults in the same household sometimes proposed dissimilar neighborhood boundaries. Among a small sample who were interviewed several months apart, we discovered that definitions of the size of neighborhoods among the same individuals were only modestly correlated.[3]

In much of the discussion that follows, we use a census tract as a proxy for a neighborhood, understanding full well that this operational indicator is a concession to convenience. Using census tract boundaries has the virtue of permitting us to supplement our survey data with census information, but the boundaries correspond only loosely to shared notions of neighborhoods, if such notions exist at all. Whether individual or aggregate conceptions of the neighborhood affect the ability of parents to regulate their children's behavior is a question that is taken up in chapter 7. Preliminary work made it apparent that we needed to take into account both geographically and socially defined neighborhoods (and the correspondence between the two) when addressing the question of how parenting practices are influenced by community contexts.

Determining whether or not neighborhoods influence the behaviors of families and individual residents requires more than merely demonstrating the existence of an association between where people live and how they live. It is essential to show that the motives and meaning that people ascribe to their actions are created and communicated collectively.

This means showing in this study that families who live in close proximity respond to their environs similarly and devise like strategies for supervising their children. Finally, we must demonstrate that features of the local environment lead to management practices that have consequences for the development and well-being of children. Designing a study that could reveal such a set of interrelated social patterns led us to sample densely in communities with differing social characteristics in order to detect whether distinctive family management practices exist across neighborhoods.

HOW THE SAMPLE WAS DRAWN

As a way of minimizing the considerable costs of sampling households with young adolescents within designated census tracts, this study was coupled with another ongoing survey of Philadelphia teens within specific neighborhoods that was designed to evaluate the impact of family-planning services on sexual practices. The screening for both studies was done at the same time, in the spring of 1990.

A sample of 65 census tracts (out of a total of 365) was drawn from four large sections of the city. These particular sections were selected because they surrounded the family-planning clinics that were part of the evaluation. However, the designated areas were sufficiently broad to include a large swath of the less affluent part of Philadelphia. Figure 2.1 shows a map of Philadelphia, locating the census tracts that fell into the catchment areas. With the exception of the northeastern and northwestern neighborhoods, much of the rest of the city was included in the sampling frame. The broad areas are generally understood as discrete communities in Philadelphia, though each consists of many smaller, locally defined neighborhoods, each of which comprises from one to three separate census tracts.

The western part of the city is home to mostly poor and near-poor African-Americans, though solidly working-class sections of homeowners survive in West Philadelphia. Long-time residents nostalgically recall an era when the community was thick with institutions and full of hope. They decry the menace of drugs and the exodus of the middle class, which have been accompanied by a decline in the public schools and the disappearance of civic and community associations.

South Philadelphia embraces some impoverished areas inhabited by black residents, but it also retains working-class white neighborhoods, a few of which recently had been gentrified. The white neighborhoods, stretching along a two-mile span that at times is as much as a mile

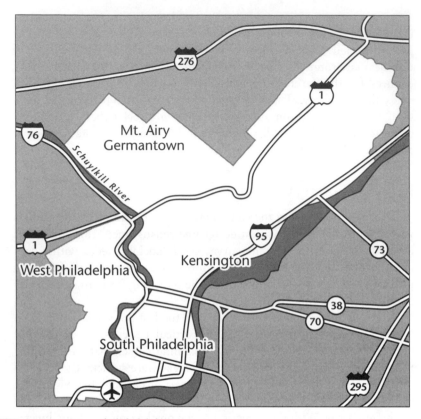

Figure 2.1 Map of Philadelphia

deep, look very much as they did at the middle of this century. So do many of the residents, whose families moved into these communities two generations ago. Many have seen their children move to the New Jersey suburbs, although younger families remain in these neighborhoods.

Another wide strip of neighborhoods that runs along the western bank of the Delaware River, generally referred to by outsiders as Kensington or Greater Kensington, includes a myriad of smaller neighborhoods. One of them, Port Richmond, is almost entirely white and mostly middle class. A relatively high proportion of residents grew up in the community and generally speak of their neighborhood in very positive terms. "I love living here," one participant volunteered, "I grew up here . . . around the corner practically, so this has always been my home. That's why I feel comfortable here, you know." Another participant highlighted the close relationships that long-term residence had fostered:

My neighbors next door—I feel we're friends, you know. We usually are involved with the kids when her—her children are all grown—but when they have a get-together, we were always invited, and they're invited to anything I had. And the man across the street, that was the same way. These are people, too, that I grew up with. I mean they have been here forever.

An adjacent neighborhood, Fishtown, is composed largely of ethnic, working-class white tracts; some of them are quite stable, and others are experiencing population changes. Nearby are other sections of Kensington, containing tracts where the poorest whites in the city reside. There, residents feel much less secure. One family moved away during the course of the study; the mother explains their decision: "Well, the neighborhood was really, really getting bad, and the kids in the neighborhood was taking over, destroying property. They threatened to fire bomb our house. Yes, because we're the only ones that said anything to them."

While some Kensington tracts are entirely contained within self-identified neighborhoods, others spill over into different communities. Also, residents—even those living on the same block—do not always locate themselves in the same "neighborhood." In a follow-up focus group conducted with adolescents who had participated in the survey, it immediately became apparent that interpretations of neighborhood boundaries varied. Marcia, one of the participants, said, "No one knows what neighborhood they live in: Kensington, Fishtown, Port Richmond." She located her neighborhood by saying she lived a few blocks from York Street, and added, "The girls I go to school with, the girls in Port Richmond, say that I live in Fishtown, [while] the girls in Fishtown say I live in Port Richmond." Another girl remarked, "I always thought it was anything before York Street was Port Richmond, anything after was Fishtown," to which Marcia responded, "Some of the Port Richmond girls say that anything below the bridge is Fishtown. Nobody really knows what it is."

Next to Kensington is an area of North Philadelphia that is mostly Puerto Rican and desperately poor, with no distinctive name, even among residents. The underground economy is particularly active here, and virtually every block has its share of youth hanging out on the street corners and openly peddling drugs to passers-by—outsiders in cars or locals on foot.

To the northwest of Kensington lies the fourth-largest area in our sample. It is composed of communities called Germantown and Mount Airy, each of which includes a number of different micro-neighborhoods. Some of these sections are mixed socioeconomically, some are solidly working class, and a few are primarily middle class. All are predominantly African-American. The same sort of diverse living conditions mark these communities as we found in Greater Kensington, where clusters of blocks or blocks themselves sometimes represent extraordinarily different micro-environments.

The four broad catchment areas, then, are different from one another, and each contains a varied set of small neighborhoods, only some of which are formally recognized by a name or subsumed within a single census tract. The areas themselves, though not distinctively different from many other sections of Philadelphia, are not entirely representative of the city. They seriously underrepresent higher-income, white areas of the city—the most upscale neighborhoods in Center City and the wealthier communities lying within the city boundaries, such as Chestnut Hill and Manayunk/Roxborough. By also excluding the northeastern part of the city—known as the "Greater Northeast"—we underrepresented many white families with moderate to higher incomes who fled from the declining industrial sectors of Philadelphia. Finally, our sample does not include most distressed areas of North Philadelphia, which contain the highest concentration of extremely poor blacks.

On the other hand, the sample has the singular virtue of encompassing some of the poorest white sections in Philadelphia and a large range of black neighborhoods, from very poor to solidly middle-income. Thus, it offers an unusual opportunity to make racial comparisons that disentangle, at least to some extent, race and social class.

Within each of the sixty-five census tracts in the sample, one- to three-block groups were randomly selected, depending on the population size of the tract. Within each of the selected block groups, the listed phone numbers were enumerated by use of a reverse phone directory.[4] In effect, then, our sample is representative of listed numbers—no doubt, the more stable residents—living within broad areas of Philadelphia's inner city.

The sample of households with listed numbers was screened by a group of interviewers at the University of Pennsylvania during the summer of 1990, yielding 805 potentially eligible families in which a youth between the ages of ten and fourteen resided with a parent (biological or surrogate).[5] In the fall of 1990, a letter was sent to all of these families describing the objectives of the research, encouraging parents to participate, and offering an incentive for taking part in the study. Shortly thereafter, families were called by an interviewer trained by the Institute for Behavioral Science at the University of Colorado, the agency that fielded the study, to conduct in-person interviews with parents and children. Completed interviews were obtained from 78 percent of either an eligible

Table 2.1

Characteristics of Persons in all Philadelphia Tracts, in MacArthur Study Tracts, and in MacArthur Study Sample

	Persons in all Philadelphia tracts[a] (%)	Persons in all tracts in the MacArthur Study[a] (%)	Parents in MacArthur Study (%)
African-American	39	61	64
White	52	31	31
Below poverty	16	24	—[c]
High school graduate[b]	63	57	70
College graduate[b]	15	9	9

a. Figures are from 1990 census data

b. Percentages indicated in the first two columns are based on all adults ages twenty-five and above.

c. The lack of detailed income measures in the survey prevented us from computing poverty rates.

teen or a parent, but it was not always possible to interview both. In all, 482 parent-and-teen pairs participated in the study.[6]

Nonparticipation typically resulted from the inability to contact the target family, even after repeated attempts. Despite the effort to trace eligible families that had moved, the average six-month interval between the screening process and the initiation of the study and the long process of completing the fieldwork resulted in some attrition. Among families successfully recontacted, only 14 percent of the parents refused to participate, and among parents successfully interviewed, only one refused permission to have the child participate in the study.

A DESCRIPTION OF THE SAMPLE

Obviously, the sample, while randomly drawn and representative of residents with listed phones, cannot be thought of as a random sample of inner-city Philadelphia, much less of the entire city. For this reason we devoted considerable time to looking at how closely the sample corresponded to the population of Philadelphia, especially the census tracts from which the sample was drawn. This process involved comparing our sample with data from the 1990 census, completed the year before most of the fieldwork in this study was carried out.

Table 2.1 compares the population of the entire city of Philadelphia as reported by the 1990 census figures, the subset of the population residing in the selected study tracts, and the population from which completed interviews were obtained. The tracts in the catchment areas from which our sample was drawn have a notably higher proportion of African-Americans, contain a larger proportion of poor families, and have fewer highly educated adults than the city of Philadelphia as a whole. These differences result from drawing our sample primarily from inner-city census tracts and excluding the affluent areas of the city as well as the predominantly, white, moderate-income sections of the Greater Northeast.

The exclusion of the poorest sections of North Philadelphia limits the number of tracts with a high proportion of families living in poverty (30 percent or more). Of the 350 census tracts in Philadelphia with at least one hundred families, 10 percent have 40 percent or more families with incomes below the poverty line, and 27 percent have at least 30 percent of families living in poverty. Our sample contains 13 tracts with poverty levels of 30 percent or higher (one-fifth of the sample) but only several tracts of the most extreme levels of poverty.

Although the selection of tracts in the sample is not representative of the city as a whole, individuals within selected tracts closely mirror the overall distribution of individuals residing there. The last two columns of table 2.1 compare the census data in the tracts to the study sample. The figures indicate that, apart from an overrepresentation of more-educated parents, most likely due to the exclusion of households without telephones, our study did an adequate job of obtaining a representative sample of the designated areas of Philadelphia.

We attempted to assess the effect of the phone screening on the composition of the sample by comparing the sample drawn from households listed in the Cole's reverse directory with a randomly selected list of 900 household addresses with unlisted or no phones. By screening those addresses in person, we identified 61 eligible households (with children in the appropriate age range) and successfully interviewed 47 of them. A comparison of the families that were screened in person with the rest of the sample confirms our suspicion that the phone screening resulted in an underrepresentation of the most disadvantaged households.[7]

Both the range of census tracts and of families within them were narrowed by excluding the richest and poorest tracts and failing to include a proper representation of families without phones. A likely consequence of our sampling procedure was to decrease variation both within and between neighborhoods. The results on neighborhood differences that we report in chapter 7 are the most affected by these sampling limitations. Readers should keep in mind that those findings provide a conservative estimate of neighborhood effects.

Still, substantial differences exist among the neighborhoods we sampled. When we compare the top and bottom quartiles of census tracts, arrayed by family poverty levels, for example, 28 percent received food stamps in at least one of the past five years in the top quartile compared

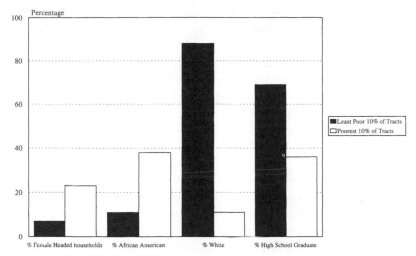

Figure 2.2 Neighborhood Characteristics

to 53 percent in the bottom quartile. Similar differences exist in the num ber of households headed by a married couple or a parent with at least some college. Thus the modal parent in the top quartile of neighborhoods is a married person with some college; in the bottom quartile, the modal parent is an unmarried, high school graduate. When we compare residents of the top and bottom decile tracts (the six least-poor tracts with the six poorest tracts), the range of our sampling frame is even more impressive. Figure 2.2 shows the distribution of female-headed households, race, and high school graduates in these extreme neighborhoods.

The physical characteristics of the top and bottom quartiles also are visible. At the high end, most families are living in comfortable if modest circumstances: single dwelling or attractive twin and row homes in well-kept neighborhoods with parks and urban amenities close by. Parents are content to have their children play on the streets or in the local parks. A visitor to the neighborhood is likely to get a friendly nod from residents during the day and a careful look at night. Neighbors are used to looking out for one another. They can be seen sharing news and gossip on street corners, in parks, or on stoops. In all but a tiny fraction of families living in these neighborhoods, parents are employed in middle-class jobs, teaching in the schools, in government, small businesses, or as skilled workers in union trades. Many of the families send their children to parochial schools.

At the other extreme, most areas are desperately poor. These neighborhoods are dotted with abandoned and burned-out houses, schools and convenience stores covered with graffiti, and corner lots littered with uncollected trash. Drugs are sold openly, and residents do not walk in their communities after dark without fearing for their safety. Relatively few families can afford to send their children to parochial or private schools, and parents typically worry about their children's safety when they are outside the home. Thus, the extremes in the sample should be large enough to capture important effects resulting from differences in the physical and social character of neighborhoods.

THE QUALITY OF THE DATA

Although we are reasonably confident that the Philadelphia sample contains sufficient variation to detect neighborhood differences of the kind predicted by social scientists, we still question whether the measures used in the survey are sensitive enough to capture existing differences. The problem of data quality is a vexing one, especially so because some of our most important constructs involved breaking new ground in measurement. We relied heavily both on qualitative fieldwork that preceded the survey and on research that had been conducted in other sites to guide us in the development of appropriate scales. Work already underway in Denver, Chicago, and Iowa provided us with a large array of existing measures and items that were relevant to examining the link between neighborhoods, families, and individuals. Inevitably, we were forced to balance our interest in collecting comprehensive and complete information about the contexts that we were examining, the need to use measures with known psychometric properties, and the desire to match our data with the parallel ongoing studies. In the end, about two-thirds of the measures were taken from existing studies, and the rest were newly constructed for this project.

We used a combination of in-person interviews and self-administered questionnaires to collect data from parents and children.[8] Information was also obtained from interviewer observations of the home and, when available, of parent-child interactions.[9] Following the survey, we spent nearly a year in building reliable scales and assessing the validity of the data to the extent that we had ways of ascertaining whether the information provided was accurate (see the appendix for a more detailed discussion of measurement quality). The details of scale construction for particular measures are introduced in later chapters. In general, scale reliabilities reached conventional standards of acceptability—at least .6 and typically .7 and above. (For interested readers, the scales and reliability measures are listed in appendix tables A.2.2 and A.2.3)

In addition to requiring internal consistency of the measures, we also adopted two other approaches to checking the data, both of which involved the use of reinterviews. As mentioned before, an evaluation of a family planning program was fielded at about the same time as a parallel study of older children, ages fourteen to eighteen, was being conducted. As it happened, nearly a fifth of the sample—ninety-two families—were interviewed in the two surveys that on average occurred only several months apart. Appendix table A.2.1 arrays the items asked in both surveys along with cross-study correlations and the percent of the same response that was provided in the two surveys. The status characteristics and demographic data are quite reliable, with most correlations in the range of .9 or higher. Predictably, much lower correspondence occurs for more subjective items or measures that could change over time, such as neighborhood features, child-rearing practices, and participation in neighborhood services. For most of these items, correlations range between .3 and .6, with a few falling outside that band.[10] Items that could be scaled show somewhat higher levels of concordance. The scales with reasonable levels of reliability (.8 or more) revealed respectable correlations of .6 and above across the two studies. The reliability of items across the surveys is about as high as the association of separate items within each study. These results are very reassuring.

As mentioned earlier in this chapter, we started reinterviewing thirty-five of the families in the study two years after the interview was completed as a way of exploring puzzles emerging in the analysis as well as checking the validity of findings supplied in the survey. Key constructs were coded from the open-ended interviews corresponding to the survey's most important scales relating to family management practices and adolescent outcomes. Using this quite different procedure, we find at least moderate correlations (between .3 and .6) between the data collected in the survey and those in open-ended interviews. These results, described in more detail in chapter 9, led us to conclude that the survey detected consistent and meaningful differences among families, especially so because they reappeared in open-ended conversations that occurred two years after the survey was completed.

Still, the measurement fluctuation at the same point in time and over time is great enough to be of concern. We are not spared from the problem familiar to all social science research: the necessity of relying on imprecise measures. The results reported in the chapters to follow are likely to understate the linkages between neighborhood, family, and adolescent behavior. In this respect, however, we are no different from other behavior researchers who must discern social patterns through the haze of imperfect measurement.

PART TWO

The Findings

Three

How They Fared

Measuring Adolescent Success

With the assistance of
SARAH E. LORD, W. TODD BARTKO, AND KAREN WALKER

Tracking successful development in children requires the ability to follow a moving target. During early adolescence this target moves a bit more rapidly as the meaning of success and the value placed on particular competencies are often recast. Definitions of success among parents and youth sometimes begin to diverge as children increasingly divide their loyalties between parents and peers. Most of the Philadelphia youth were still a few years away from the exploration of adultlike roles that becomes such a prominent feature of middle and late adolescence. Nonetheless, we are catching youth in the early stages of a critical passage to autonomy.

The general focus in this volume is on how that passage is managed by parents, but our exploration begins with a descriptive portrait of how the youth were faring on important dimensions of success. These findings lay the groundwork for the analysis in the following chapters, investigating the links to parenting processes and family management techniques inside and outside the household.

DOMAINS OF SUCCESS

Chapter 1 provided a broad rationale for our approach to measuring success. It relied on a long history of developmental and sociological research on adolescence that has explored the criteria of success and how to measure it. Because our objective was to investigate how success is managed by families in different ecological settings, we mostly relied on tried-and-true indicators: academic competence, self-competence and psychological adjustment, problem behavior, and prosocial involvement. All these measures, save the last one, which has been a relatively neglected strand of development compared to the other four criteria of doing well, are conventional in the literature and have been investigated in countless studies (Bornstein 1995a; Eccles et al. 1997; Elliott, Huizinga, and Ageton 1985; Feldman and Elliott 1990). They are widely accepted benchmarks for gauging whether youths are achieving goals and acquiring competencies in areas important to attaining and enacting appropriate roles related to work, family, and citizenship adulthood (Elliott 1983).

We were reassured to discover that the criteria of success used by researchers closely match the standards articulated by parents and youth in our follow-up study of thirty-five families. Predictably, we learned from those interviews that precise meanings of success are embedded in local situations and contexts; standards are sometimes differently interpreted and understood by parents and children; and they are unevenly acted upon. Nonetheless, the parents and children in our study have adopted mainstream notions of what it means to do well. Virtually all acknowledge the importance of academic success and staying out of trouble. As one of the parents told us about her son: "For some reason, I'm fairly lucky, he's not a problem child. You know, school attendance is regular and there's never ever been a police at the door for anything."

These rather modest goals of finishing high school and staying out of trouble are the universal, essential ingredients of success. It was much less common to hear the message of another parent: "Your children have to be well rounded. So you (have to) expose them to archery and programs and girl scouts. Certain things to build a better character." Instead, most parents set the bar at a level not so high as to invite disappointment. Yet, virtually all held out the hope that their children would exceed these minimal goals and "get some kind of degree."

"I'm always telling her that I don't want her getting married at eighteen," another parent recounted wistfully as if reflecting back on her own experience. "I want her to go to college. I want her to get a good job. I want her to travel and, you know, have fun before she gets married."

It does not necessarily follow from this commonality of aspirations that we will find no variation in the behavior of youth across neighborhoods. A large body of research suggests that parents possess different capacities and resources to shape and direct their children's ambitions and behaviors (Bornstein 1995a, 1995b; Bugental and Goodnow 1998; Eccles et al. 1997; Grolnick and Ryan 1989; Parke and Buriel 1998). It follows that their children may possess different levels of commitment and capability in realizing their parents' aspirations or in tailoring their own objectives as they face constraints imposed by the opportunities and resources available to them. So when we collected our data, we expected to find that youth in poorer neighborhoods, less endowed with institutional resources, would not be doing as well as those in better-off communities. In the aggregate, more JJs would exist in the poorer communities than Roberts.

On the basis of prior studies, we also expected to find pronounced differences by gender and age of the children—at least for some of the criteria of success. The possibility that race might be linked to the level of success was also considered, although a reading of existing studies produces ambiguous impressions if only because race is so often confounded with socioeconomic status. One of the advantages of our study is that it was designed to minimize the association between race and class by including a disproportionate share of low-income white and middle-income black neighborhoods in our sampling frame.

MEASURING SUCCESS

Before turning to the findings, we should say something about our general approach to constructing the measures. We rely on multi-item scales designed to ensure that respondents give consistent answers to similar questions. Researchers refer to this property as reliability.[1] As noted in the preceding chapter, these scales were generally drawn from preexisting measures that were known to have good psychometric properties.[2]

After the initial wave of the focused interviews was completed in 1994, we coded all the interviews with parents and youth to build measures from the open-ended interviews regarding the success measures. Happily, the global measures of performance derived from open-ended questions correlated at fairly high levels with the items that we have reported in this chapter.[3] Given the time gap between the survey and fieldwork, and the very different procedures used for assessment, these correlations increased our confidence that the quantitative scales do a good job of capturing the youths' performance.

The following section of this chapter describes the measures; their links to gender, age, and race are described in the next section. Then we address the central question of this chapter: whether differences in adolescents' performance vary systematically across neighborhoods. To answer that question, we first consider each measure separately and then turn to a more global approach that clusters patterns of success among the youth. The clustering technique allows us to see whether demographic differences emerge when we consider individuals as entities rather than breaking them into discrete properties. Clustering characteristics in this way more nearly approximates the case studies that we present.[4] Throughout the book we alternate these different approaches to examining the link between successful development and parenting processes.

Measures of Successful Development

The domains of success combine scales and items culled from existing surveys that we occasionally had to adapt to our purposes. Standard techniques, item-correlation matrices, and factor analyses were used to build measures that typically combined a set of related subscales. Readers interested in the details of scale construction and the sample items included should consult appendix tables A.2.2 and A.2.3. A general description of the four measures is provided below:

ACADEMIC COMPETENCE. Among the most frequently employed measures of success in the literature on adolescent development is academic performance or mastery of skills necessary to do well in school (Eccles et al. 1997; Schneider and Coleman 1993; Weston 1989). School skills become a source of positive self-esteem for youth. As early as the first grade, doing well in school predicts long-term educational success (Alexander, Dauber, and Entwisle 1993; Alexander, Entwisle, and Dauber 1994; Entwisle, Alexander, and Olson 1997), and educational failure is linked to a host of problem behaviors in late adolescence and early adulthood (Entwisle, Alexander, and Olson 1997; Roeser and Eccles in press; Roeser, Eccles, and Sameroff in press). School success in the adolescent years is one of the best predictors of occupational attainment in later life (Featherman and Hauser 1978).

Various measures, including self-reported grades, test scores, behavioral problems, and teacher evaluations, have been used as indicators of a child's success in school. They all tend to be highly interrelated by early adolescence (Dornbusch et al. 1987; Weston 1989). Therefore, we drew measures from parent, youth, and interviewer into a broad scale of academic competence that measured both cognitive performance and school adjustment.

Parents and youths were both asked to report various dimensions of school success: grades, school problem behavior, and grade failure. Self-reports of students and parents usually correlate well with records from school (.70 or higher), suggesting that a combination of reports from parents and youth should provide a reasonably good gauge of school success (Dornbusch et al. 1987). In addition, the subscales of reports from parents and youths on school performance were highly correlated with each other (.62 or higher).

We found substantial variability on all of these measures. Academic success is well distributed within the sample: a third of the students overall were doing remedial work, and a third were enrolled in advanced course work. Grades were distributed evenly among students getting mostly A's, mostly B's, and mostly C's or below. More than a third of the sample had failed at least one course in the past year. A third of the boys, for example, and a quarter of the girls had been held back a grade in school.

Despite this varied performance, relatively few students had disengaged from school by the time of the interview. Virtually all were currently enrolled and most were attending classes on a regular basis (78 percent said that they never skipped school; 10 percent said they hardly ever did). Yet the early symptoms of disengagement were present in a substantial minority. Although the vast majority of students had not experienced any serious behavioral problems in school and even said they liked going to school, nearly a third had been expelled or suspended at least once in the previous year.

A comparison of these results with findings from other studies using items similar to ours shows that these distributions of academic performance are fairly typical of the school performance of early adolescents. We are assessing school success *before* the ninth and tenth grades—the time when students begin to drop out in large numbers.

As an independent measure of the adolescent's cognitive ability, we asked the interviewers for their impressions of the adolescents during the interview session. The six-item scale was designed to allow the interviewer an opportunity to rate the cognitive ability of the youth in the study. Surprisingly, interviewer evaluations of cognitive ability have proven to be a remarkably good predictor of test scores in previous studies (Baldwin et al. 1993). This subscale was strongly related to both parents' and youths' scales of academic performance. We therefore felt justified in creating a macro-construct of academic competence that combined the reports of parents and youth regarding grades, school problem behaviors (such as expulsion and suspension), and retention with the interviewer's reports of cognitive competence.

ACTIVITY INVOLVEMENT. School performance, the customary arena of adolescent success, is often contrasted with problem behaviors as if these are the only dimensions relevant to adolescent success or failure. Confining their focus to the narrowly academic, researchers have paid far too little attention to other prosocial activities that engage the time and energy of children. Several recent research reports have stressed the importance of involvement in after-school activities both for protecting students from adverse influences and for cultivating social competencies, leadership skills, and self-esteem. Whether activities are devoted to sports, clubs, youth groups, or community service, we are beginning to learn that involvement in organizations may do much to foster success in later life. Younger adolescents who are involved in prosocial activities are more likely to graduate from high school and attend college and less likely to become involved in serious problem behavior. They feel better about themselves and develop a stronger sense of self-efficacy regarding tasks in late adolescence and early adulthood (Carnegie Corporation 1992).

This study uses involvement in positive, organized activities as one of the primary indicators of successful adolescent development. Parents and youth were asked a series of questions about whether the adolescent participated in a list of after-school activities, including athletics, extracurricular activities at school, organized sports in the community, church activities, and summer recreational programs. These reports were summed to get a picture of the breadth of participation in such activities. We then combined the summed reports of both parents and children into a single indicator of the breadth of activity involvement.

Like our indicator of academic competence, participation in organized extracurricular activities showed good variation within the sample. Thirty-six percent were not involved in any after-school or summer program, while 40 percent were involved in two or more organized activities. Later in this chapter, we examine how the availability of resources for youth is distributed across neighborhoods. Several previous studies suggest that after-school activity and summer activities may differ sharply by locality (Medrich et al. 1982; National Commission on Children 1991; Wynn et al. 1988).

PROBLEM BEHAVIOR. The domain of problem behavior is one of the most popular areas for research on younger adolescents. Specialists on delinquency, substance abuse, and sexuality have all explored the incidence of risky behavior in early adolescence (Carnegie Corporation 1992; Elliott, Huizinga, and Ageton 1985; Jessor 1992). Youths who engage in such behaviors do not inevitably experience problems in later adolescence or adulthood, because experimentation with adult behaviors is a common if not normative part of growing up in American society. Nonetheless, risk-taking behavior, especially when it occurs very early in life, is associated with lower prospects of economic and emotional adjustment in later life (Elliott 1983).

A substantial literature reports that so-called problem behaviors, while discrete acts, are highly interrelated (Haggerty et al. 1994; Jessor in press). Substance abuse is related to many forms of delinquent behavior and similarly to early onset of sexual activity. Consequently, we created a global indicator of problem behaviors based primarily on the youth's reports. Unlike parents' reports on school performance and prosocial involvement, their reports were assumed to be of limited use, since most parents are not likely to know of their children's risk-taking behavior unless someone reports it to them. However, we did include parents' reports of aggressive behavior, since this type of behavior is easily observed in the home.

Our global measure tapped adolescent involvement in risky behaviors from five different categories. Three of these, based on a conceptual scheme outlined by Elliott and his colleagues (Elliott, Huizinga, and Ageton 1985) involved youths' reports of their frequency of engaging in the following sets of behaviors: *delinquent behavior* (e.g., theft, prostitution, drug dealing, vandalism); *risky behavior* (e.g., going to court, running away, engaging in sex); and *substance abuse* (e.g., drinking alcohol, smoking cigarettes, using street drugs). We also included indicators of the frequency of *aggressive behavior* based on both parent and youth reports (e.g., physically aggressive behavior like hitting or pushing someone), and *school truancy* (based on adolescent self-reports).

In general, our adolescents reported low levels of problem behavior. Of the twenty-three delinquent activities, for example, the sample average was barely more than one, indicating that many youth are either underreporting unlawful activities or generally staying out of trouble. Similarly, low scores appeared on the other subscales, with few youths engaging in health-compromising or aggressive behaviors.

Although some readers may doubt that these self-reports provide an accurate account of problem behavior among the sample youth, our findings are consistent with other studies of early adolescents (Elliott, Huizinga, and Ageton 1985). The incidence of problem behavior rises sharply with age; the picture would have been markedly different had we examined the same youth three or four years later.

Even when we acknowledge that most of our teens are still too young to register on the measures of serious problem behavior, the results also suggest that our notions of the number of teens who engage in serious problem behaviors are somewhat exaggerated, partly because of the tremendous amount of attention given these behaviors by the media (Males 1996). Most adolescents pass through the teen years committing only minor acts of delinquency and engaging in experimental use of drugs and alcohol. Many adolescents have sex but typically do not begin until in their middle or later teens.

Even in an urban population of Philadelphia youth, no more than 7 percent could be classified as having serious trouble based on any of the separate indices that we used to tap problem behavior. Combining all five measures into a single, global measure revealed that only 5 percent might be considered seriously troubled. This is consistent with the findings of many criminologists that a relatively small proportion of youth are involved in a very substantial proportion of the serious acts of delinquency (Sampson and Laub 1993; Elliott, Huizinga, and Menard 1989).

SELF-COMPETENCE AND PSYCHOLOGICAL ADJUSTMENT. Social scientists, especially psychologists, have demonstrated that success in later life depends on the acquisition of psychological as well as social and economic resources. In fact, some are convinced that psychological resources are the primary influences on success (Bandura 1996; Eccles et al. 1983; Kazdin 1993) because they are the most proximal to the individual. We used both caregivers' and adolescents' reports of several different aspects of positive and negative mental health as our indicators of psychological resources and adjustment.

Adolescents' psychological functioning was reported by both youth and their parents. This dual-report method was used for several reasons. First, mothers have long been relied on as a principal source of information about their children (Achenbach, McConaughy, and Howell 1987). Parents provide an alternative perspective on the child's well-being, supplying a perspective that adolescents themselves may have difficulty reporting. Results that are obtained from one informant and confirmed by the other can be considered more valid than those without dual-informant confirmation.[5]

Unlike the scales for academic performance and positive activity described earlier, which yielded single, composite scores for each indicator based on both informants, psychological adjustment scales did not.[6] Factor analyses indicated that the adolescent and the parent reports should be treated as separate constructs. Like other researchers, we found a discrepancy between the parents' and youth's reports of the youth's psychological functioning (Achenbach, McConaughy, and Howell 1987). Since the youth's report included mostly positive aspects of psychological functioning, we labeled this indicator *self-competence.* Since the mothers' report was dominated by scales assessing emotional problems, we labeled this indicator *psychological adjustment.*

We were interested in measuring both positive and negative aspects of self-competence in the youth. We therefore included three types of positive psychological characteristics widely recognized as key indicators of psychological well-being/adjustment: self-esteem, self-efficacy, and resourcefulness. Self-esteem—that is, how satisfied a person is with him or herself—is the most general of these characteristics. The second indicator, self-efficacy, taps a person's belief in his or her ability to accomplish important tasks such as doing well in school or getting other people to help when assistance is necessary to accomplish some goal. Similar to self-efficacy, resourcefulness represents a capacity to cope with difficult situations and bounce back from negative experiences. Abundant evidence exists to show that individuals high on each of these three characteristics do better at a variety of life tasks, including school and work, and cope better with problems when they arise in many life arenas (Bandura 1996; Eccles et al. 1983; Harter 1983).

On average, the young adolescents in this study expressed moderate to high levels on each of these measures, with mean levels indicating that most felt good about themselves and their ability to cope with challenging demands. Only 5 to 10 percent reported experiencing serious problems on any of these three indicators. For example, only 5 percent of the adolescents reported feeling not very happy with the kind of person they were and with their relationships with others.

On the negative side, we considered the adolescents' reports of depressive emotional states, because such states are known to undermine a person's ability to manage difficult situations or even to summon up sufficient motivation to meet the requirements of daily living (Brent and Moritz 1997; Gjerde and Block 1996). We asked the adolescents how often in the last couple of months they had felt various depressive emotions such as being unhappy, sad, or hopeless. The mean reported frequency on this scale was low (2.33, on a 5-point scale with 1 representing almost never, 3 indicating sometimes, and 5 almost always). Again, a relatively small percentage (8 percent) reported experiencing depressive symptoms often or almost always.

Parents were asked to rate their children's behavior on two of these dimensions: depression and resourcefulness. In addition they provided evaluation of the child's level of anger, anxiety, and ability to concentrate on tasks. Like the results for the adolescents' self-reports, most caregivers indicated that their adolescents were functioning well. Only one in ten parents indicated that their children had serious psychological problems on any of these dimensions.

As already reported, parents and adolescents in the same family did not necessarily offer similar assessments. Scale correlations of depression and resourcefulness measured only .25, indicating that children used different criteria to form judgments about their well-being than did their parents. The youth, no doubt, relied on internal states of mind, while parents relied on external signs of their children's psychological health. Children's emotional lives become increasingly diverse, and their moods may accordingly become increasingly situation-dependent. The sulky, embarrassed *daughter* may be a cheerful, compassionate *peer* with her friends.

To summarize our findings from the various domains of success, we have learned that adolescents vary tremendously in their skills and competencies. However, to make a broad generalization about the population, most are performing adequately. The majority are at grade level and not experiencing severe school problems. About two-thirds are involved in extracurricular activities, and mean levels of problem behaviors are low. The majority appear quite well adjusted according to both their own reports and those of their parents.

On the negative side, we observed that a significant minority of the youth had been held back a grade and were not doing well in school. About a third were involved in no activities outside of school. About one in fifteen had been involved in delinquent or problem behavior, and one in ten were experiencing psychological problems on one or more of our measures.

DEMOGRAPHIC DIFFERENCES IN ADOLESCENT SUCCESS

These findings in the aggregate ignore variability within the population related to demographic differences, household and family characteristics, and temperamental qualities of parents and children. Some of these sources of variation are explored in later chapters. To orient the reader to later analysis, however, we first consider several major demographic differences that account for considerable variation in the performance of adolescents. We cannot ignore these differences as we take up the question of whether parental management is linked to the success of youth differently by neighborhood settings.

In introducing the domains of success, we also raised the central question of whether main effects vary by neighborhood: are youth from neighborhoods that are more endowed with resources and more cohesive doing better than those in less-advantaged neighborhoods? This question is addressed primarily in chapter 7, but we offer a preview of our findings on neighborhood variation in the final part of this chapter.

Age

Age as a demographic marker of exposure to varying social experience, and hence of development itself, figures significantly in several of the domains of success. Most notably, a large literature shows that academic success declines with age and that problem behavior sharply increases as children move from the pre-teen years into the early and mid-teens (Eccles et al. 1993). Parents are less able to supervise their children as they move into middle school, and children usually are also granted more autonomy. As parents lose or relinquish the ability to monitor their children, peer and neighborhood influences may fill the vacuum.

A number of researchers have also traced a decline in institutional commitment and involvement during the teen years. School organization provides a less nurturing, more demanding, and more stratified environment that may produce greater alienation as youth shift allegiance in varying degrees from adult-organized to youth-organized reward systems (Eccles et al. 1983). Other researchers have noted that institutions serving youth become more scarce as children approach their teens, and this is perhaps especially true of urban areas. The scarcity of institutions may account for the high number of teens who are not involved in after-school or summer organized activities (Carnegie Corporation 1992; Wynn et al. 1988).

The relation between age and psychological adjustment is less clear-cut. There is some indication that self-esteem may decline and depression increase during the early teens, particularly for girls (Gjerde and Block 1996; Petersen et al 1993). Parents and youth are more likely to report more disputes as children enter adolescence. Consequently, it is entirely possible that we will see a decline in psychological adjustment with increasing age.

The results from Philadelphia are generally consistent with findings of previous investigations. Figure 3.1 plots the different domains by the age of the youth in the sample. It shows the expected relationships between age and several of the success indicators. Our global measure of academic performance declines with age, showing that parents have cause for being concerned about their children as they enter the early adolescent years.

A parallel but less strong decline occurs in the measure of after-school and summer organized activities. This shift reflects two patterns: First, there is a steady and statistically significant decrease in participation in church and service activities from pre-adolescence to mid-adolescence. This decline, however, is offset by a greater involvement of older youth (males especially) in organized sports; when sports are included, the age

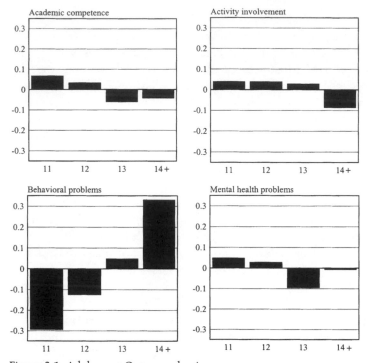

Figure 3.1 Adolescent Outcomes by Age

pattern disappears. Boys, particularly, appear to be engaging in more sex-segregated activities as they move beyond the pre-adolescent years.

As in the results of other studies, problem behavior in our sample of teens sharply increases with age. All the subcomponents of the scale show a marked rise in delinquency, substance abuse, risky behaviors, and aggressiveness. Figure 3.1 plots this change for the global index. The rise in behavioral problems is particularly evident as teens enter the high school years. Fifteen-year-olds are more than ten times more likely than twelve-year-olds (52 percent versus 5 percent) to be in the top quartile of the scale.

Age was largely unrelated to the global measure of mental health. An inspection of the components also turned up no systematic variation by age for any of the separate scales drawing on reports of youth or their parents.

Gender

Whatever the causes of gender differences (e.g., cultural, psychological, or biological), social scientists have long known that gender has a pro-

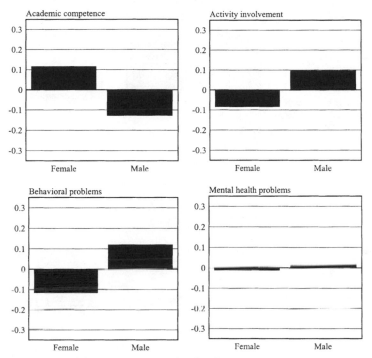

Figure 3.2 Adolescent Outcomes by Gender

found impact on the behaviors and competencies of boys and girls that leads to sizable differences in certain domains of success (see Ruble and Martin 1998). Differences in academic performance, problem behavior, and psychological adjustment are known to vary by gender during middle childhood. Behaviors can further diverge during the early adolescent years as gender becomes an even more salient source of differentiation. Researchers have observed that boys are more likely to exhibit aggressive forms of problem behaviors, while girls are more inclined to experience internal problems of anxiety and depression (Ruble and Martin 1998).

These findings are replicated among the Philadelphia youth in this study. Figure 3.2 displays the gender differences on four of the five global measures that revealed these trends (adolescent's self-report of psychological problems omitted). Girls scored significantly higher than boys on several components of our global measure of academic performance, including the interviewer rating of cognitive competence (not shown). Lower levels of acting-out in school also contributed to girl's higher standing.

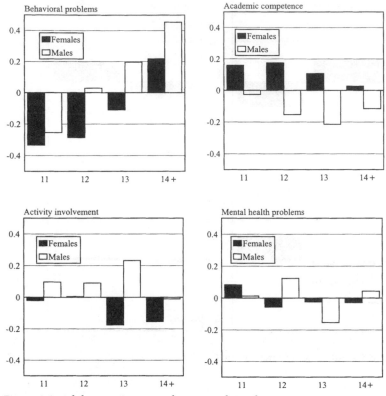

Figure 3.3 Adolescent Outcomes by Age and Gender

The gender difference was reversed in participation in after-school and summer activities. Predictably, boys had significantly higher involvement in sports, but they also had participated at somewhat higher levels in the scale of other activities at younger ages. Boys may be granted greater freedom, providing them access to summer and after-school activities, while heavier responsibilities for chores and childcare may fall upon girls in the household.

As expected, boys were also more likely to engage in problem behaviors. Large and significant gender differences occurred on all of the component scales of the global measure. Boys were generally one and a half times as likely as girls to be in the top quartile in the global measure of problem behavior. The global index rises sharply for older boys, especially (see figure 3.3).

While girls report higher levels of depression, they also have a greater sense of efficacy and self-satisfaction. Consequently, the global measure of the child's report of her or his psychological well-being does not differ by gender. Similarly the parent measure did not show consistent gender differences. On the subscales, boys were more likely to exhibit problems of concentration, and girls were marginally more likely to be rated as depressed by their parents.

Racial Differences in Performance

Researchers who have examined racial differences in adolescent development have not reached much consensus on the effect of race on different domains of success. Many studies have shown that black children, boys especially, are more likely to experience problems in school, black youth are much more likely to show up in the criminal justice system, and blacks report lower levels of tobacco, alcohol, and drug use (Condran and Furstenberg 1994; Johnston, O'Malley, and Bachman 1993). However, previous investigators have had difficulty in agreeing on why these differences occur. It is difficult to disentangle race and class effects even when the socioeconomic status of the family is taken into account, because African-Americans with comparable education and occupation are far more likely to have poverty backgrounds, live in poverty neighborhoods, have fewer assets, and reside in different family forms. The effects of race confound differences in resources, opportunities, history, and culture, and combinations of these elements.

Our sample was designed to permit examination of racial differences at different socioeconomic levels; thus, it included many more poor whites than might be expected by chance, and fewer poor blacks. One of the strengths of this study is that race is not strongly associated with educational level or income, as is typically the case in studies of adolescent development. Still, economic differences have not been completely eliminated by sampling design.

Consistent with other studies, we found that black children were not performing as well in the measure of academic competence as were European-Americans (Schneider and Coleman 1993). Finer-grained comparisons within socioeconomic groupings diminished the overall difference. On selected subscales such as school problems and placement in remedial classes, however, black children remained significantly higher. Of particular relevance to the academic futures of black and white children is their placement in public or private schools. European-American children were far more likely to be attending parochial or private schools than African-Americans. Although participation in extracurricular activities was not linked to race, whites were much more likely to be involved in organized teams and sports. This may be linked to the greater availabil-

ity of these activities in parochial schools and white ethnic neighborhoods.

Blacks were more likely to engage in risky behaviors, largely involving
unprotected intercourse at an early age. This finding is consistent with
many previous studies (Hayes 1987). Other investigators also report
lower levels of substance abuse among blacks than whites, in particular
smoking and marijuana use (Kandel 1991). Whites in our sample reported higher levels of aggressiveness. However, the summary score of
problem behavior was not significantly different by race. Mental health
differences by racial category were neither large nor significant. An
examination of the subscales did not reveal any consistent racial variation.

Overall, then, African-American children in Philadelphia were not
generally exhibiting lower levels of success than whites in early adolescence in terms of the five broad markers of success that we used in this
study. These findings are in stark contrast to the differences that appear
in school performance, involvement with the criminal justice system,
teenage parenthood, and employment patterns in late adolescence and
early adulthood. This paradox will be taken up in chapter 9.

NEIGHBORHOOD DIFFERENCES AND
ADOLESCENT SUCCESS

The evidence presented so far leads us to a much-discussed question: Is
there a link between the quality of neighborhoods and indicators of adolescent success? Most studies exploring this question have looked at demographic differences between tracts and various kinds of outcome measures from public records: the level of school dropout, delinquency, or
teenage childbearing (Furstenberg and Hughes 1997).

Ours is one of the few studies to examine whether and how features
of the neighborhood are linked to adolescent behaviors, using measures
of neighborhood characteristics based on reports of residents and measures of adolescent behaviors based on reports of parents and youth. This
chapter looks descriptively at the relation between where families live
and the developmental status of the youth. Chapter 7 delves more deeply
into the question of whether neighborhoods may actually affect the
course of development.

Rather than relying exclusively on information about localities from
census data, we asked a lengthy series of questions about the level of
resources, quality of social relationships, and perceived opportunities for

families and youth in their immediate localities (see appendix tables A.2.2 and A.2.3). These reports were combined into scales that tapped different features of neighborhoods. As is common practice in studies of ecological contexts, we developed measures of these features based on the aggregated reports of people living in close proximity (see the fuller discussion of the measures in chapter 7). These composite measures were derived both from the theoretical literature on neighborhoods and from ethnographic studies of how neighborhoods influence adolescent behaviors.

The ethnographic study of Philadelphia neighborhoods discovered that families deployed different strategies, depending on the level of institutional resources, the social networks, and the degree of trust and cohesiveness in the community. However, we could only speculate whether particular management strategies produced more successful development.

The first step in examining this proposition is to consider whether adolescent behaviors vary across neighborhoods. Using scores from a composite of different scales, we developed a typology of forty-five census tracts with differing levels of resources, cohesion, and social control. To draw the sharpest distinction between neighborhoods of differing quality, we restricted the top 20 percent to the favorable category and the lowest 20 percent to the unfavorable category; the remaining 60 percent were put in the middle. Accordingly, the highest group can be thought of as communities with relatively strong social networks, abundant and accessible organizations and programs, low prevalence of social problems, and high levels of social cohesion and trust. The lowest group of communities, in contrast, typically lacked most or all of these attributes. Despite our efforts to balance the racial sample by including poor whites and middle-income blacks, the lowest group consisted primarily of very poor African-American and Puerto Rican areas, and the highest areas were primarily white—a strong testimony to the different living conditions encountered by the varied groups even when individual socioeconomic status is more or less taken into account.

By and large, the classification that we developed based on residents' reports corresponded closely to the perceptions of Philadelphia locals and to data from the socioeconomic and housing information derived from the census. We had previously learned from the fieldwork that tracts sometimes contained several discrete neighborhoods; nonetheless, we thought it likely that adolescents would exhibit different levels of performance across the three types of neighborhoods.

In fact, the only strong and consistent difference was that youth residing in advantaged neighborhoods were much more likely to engage in prosocial activities. Youth in these neighborhoods had consistently higher levels of participation in after-school sports, church, and recreational groups. This finding is wholly consistent with other research showing that the presence of institutional resources is much greater in better-off communities. Less-pronounced and consistent differences emerged on some of the subscales of the other measures; however, no differences appeared on the global measures of success.

As might be expected, youth in the better-off neighborhoods were more likely to be in advanced classes and less likely to be in remedial programs. They were less likely to have been held back a grade in school. Parents reported that their children had better grades, but youth did not confirm these reports. No differences appeared in school misbehavior and problems. According to the subscales, the overall difference was in the expected direction (favoring children living in more favorable circumstances); the association between residence and school performance, however, was not statistically significant.

The measure of problem behavior revealed that, if anything, youth in the better-off neighborhoods were exhibiting more problem behavior. These findings may seem anomalous, but they are not inconsistent with previous research on delinquency and acting-out during early adolescence (Elliott, Huizinga, and Menard 1989). This literature fails to find any strong association between problem behavior in early adolescents of the type that we are measuring and the affluence of communities.

Neither the global indicators nor the subscales for mental health revealed any consistent association with neighborhood characteristics. Overall, then, quality of neighborhood is not strongly linked to measures of success in our sample of younger adolescents. This finding is completely out of line with public perceptions that behavioral problems among young adolescents are much more prevalent in disadvantaged communities. Is this a peculiarity of our sample or a more general finding? We revisit this question in the concluding section and later chapters.

CONFIGURATIONS OF SUCCESS

A tension underlies our analysis here and in subsequent chapters between our desire to examine discrete variables amenable to statistical techniques and our interest in preserving a sense of youths as individuals living in real families and neighborhoods. It is unsatisfying and not entirely informative to use measures of central tendency that describe average differences or even distributions across groups, as if girls typically acted one way and boys another, or as if children living in desirable neighborhoods had a similar pattern of success compared to those growing up in communities with fewer resources.

Of course, we cannot treat the cases in our study as five hundred individuals, describing each one in detail and leaving it up to the reader to form impressions of which ones were alike or different and why these patterns of similarity and difference occur. We have adopted an intermediate strategy that allows a measure of individuation among our adolescents and yet provides a way of summarizing commonalities with properties that can still be subjected to statistical analysis. This procedure, called cluster analysis, divides the youth into groups that share similar profiles of behavior. It is almost as if we were sorting our youth into peer groups based on common behaviors as the youth themselves sometimes do, informally typing their high school classmates "nerds," "jocks," or "burnouts" (Eckert 1989; Kinney 1993).

Using our five domains of success, we were able to sort the sample into four main clusters comprising youth with very similar profiles of performance. Using less colorful terms than ones employed by the students themselves, we have labeled these groups (1) academically competent, (2) organizationally involved, (3) at-risk, and (4) delinquent.

The *academically competent* cluster is the second-largest group (30 percent) and is characterized by well-above-average levels of psychological and academic competence as reported both by adolescents and parents. These youth are low on problem behavior but also on involvement in extracurricular and community activities (the exception being church involvement). In our qualitative interviews, eight (of thirty-five) teens fell into the academically competent cluster (see appendix table A.3.1 for a brief summary of the adolescents in the qualitative study). Robert James was one of these. An African-American living with his parents, brother, and sister in a neighborhood with below-average resources, Robert and his parents rate his mental health quite positively, and he is not at all involved in problem behaviors. His involvement in activities, primarily positive, are centered around his Jehovah's Witness church, in which the entire family is actively involved. Almost all Robert's friends attend the church, and their joint activities are encouraged and supported by parents in the church. Quite comfortable in his neighborhood, Robert knows most of the youth nearby, although he does not consider them his friends. He also knows how to avoid trouble on the street through his use of body language and words.

Christine Lang is another academically competent youth from our study. She lives with her parents and younger brother in Kensington, an entirely white, high-resource neighborhood. At the time of our survey, she was doing well in her local parish school, although she was not involved in many prosocial activities. Although Christine goes to a Catholic school and attends mass weekly (and thus has mostly Catholic friends), her religious involvement was not as consciously felt as Robert's. In this respect, she is typical of many European-American Catholics, who were enmeshed in a Catholic culture based on social and institutional ties as much as personal beliefs.

Like Robert, Christine is comfortable in her neighborhood, but there is a qualitative difference in their neighborhood climates. Robert lives in a neighborhood in which drugs and violence are epidemic, whereas Christine's neighborhood has very little violence, and drug use is limited to specific locations.

The *organizationally involved* cluster of youth, which includes 17 percent of the survey sample and ten out of thirty-five of the qualitative sample, scored lower than the academically competent youth, but not significantly so, on the psychological and academic competence measures. The involved youth are characterized by a high level of social activities and a low level of problem behavior. They are generally doing well at home and at school, but what distinguishes them from their peers is their high level of engagement in extracurricular activities and community programs. On all four of the subscales that make up the global measure of positive activities (involvement in *sports* at school and in the community, involvement in programs sponsored by *religious organizations*, and the parent's and youth's separate reports of involvement in other *community organizations* like the Y or Scouts), the adolescents in the involved cluster had high scores (see figure 3.4).

We wondered if there was a different distribution of social activities for the boys as compared with the girls in the involved cluster. We found, not surprisingly, that the boys in the cluster were significantly more engaged in sports activities and the girls more in religious ones.

Lakisha Wilkenson, whom we introduced in chapter 1 was an involved youth. Her most positive characteristics at the time of the survey were her high level of involvement in positive activities and her very high self-confidence and sense of self-efficacy. During the eighth grade she was president of her class at her Catholic school and was actively involved in Girl Scouts. In high school, she has been very involved in the Future Business Leaders of America. She also works part-time at a job she takes quite seriously. Like other socially involved youth, Lakisha scored very low on problem behavior. She lives near Robert James, and Lakisha's discomfort with her neighborhood is high: she has been robbed in broad daylight near her home.

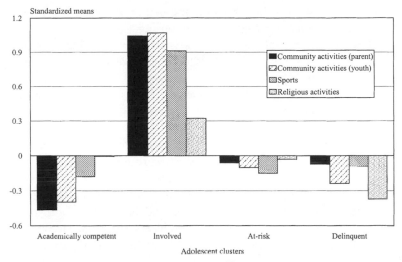

Figure 3.4 Youth Activity Involvement by Cluster Groups

Greg Ellis also exemplifies the involved group. A European-American living in a white neighborhood with relatively low resources, Greg lives with his parents and two sisters in the same house in which his mother was born. Like Lakisha (although not necessarily like other socially involved youth), Greg was an indifferent student in his parish elementary school in 1991. However, he was very involved in sports teams in an adjacent neighborhood with more community resources. As he entered high school, his sports participation dropped somewhat, and he became more involved in paid work and school activities, including developing an interest in TV production at his high school. Greg's family is unique in the qualitative sample: although he lives in one neighborhood, almost all his socializing occurs in an adjacent, and much safer, neighborhood.

These four youth—Robert, Christine, Lakisha, and Greg—reside in somewhat different worlds within the city of Philadelphia. Differing by gender, race, family income, family structure, type of high school, and neighborhood, all four, like approximately half of our survey sample, are doing relatively well using our four measures of success. But what of the other 50 percent of the teens, those who are not quite as successful? What are some of them like?

The *at-risk* group provides a contrast to the academically competent and the socially involved adolescents, and is also the largest group in our adolescent sample (48 percent). We have labeled them so because they were tottering on the brink of serious problems in school, at home, or in their communities. The at-risk teens are low on adjustment, self-competence, and activity involvement, and higher on problem behavior, though they are not yet conspicuously in serious trouble.

JJ Newman was one of eleven at-risk youth in our qualitative study. At the time of our survey, JJ had very low self-efficacy and poor mental health. His academic performance was relatively poor; he engaged in a moderate level of problem behaviors such as fighting with other children and assaulting teachers, and he was uninvolved in school or community activities.

Unlike JJ, Shawanda Jones lives in a high-resource African-American community. But like JJ, Shawanda's grades were mediocre to poor; she had been suspended from school several times, and she exhibited poor mental health. Although she lived in a neighborhood that appeared to have relatively high resources, Shawanda and her mother both complained about the neighborhood and the problems Shawanda faced in the local school, from which she had dropped out in the tenth grade. According to Shawanda,

> I didn't like [school] mostly because of the children that bust on you. Made jokes about you that weren't funny to me and um, the guns and the violence and stuff. There was always some kind of fight every day, and I just couldn't deal with that. And people picking on you and stuff, and I'm not a fighter.

JJ and Shawanda characterize at-risk teens who appear to lack the economic resources, parental guidance, and social resources that could help them become more successful. Another of the youth in our field study, Paul Pulaski, did not face these disadvantages, yet he was equally uninvolved in community activities and displayed a relatively high level of problem behaviors such as smoking cigarettes, drinking alcohol, and hanging out with delinquent friends. Involvement in risky behavior is neither an inevitable consequence of living in a poor community nor automatically avoided by having the advantages of a stable neighborhood.

To qualify for being in the *delinquent* cluster, youth had to be below average on every positive dimension as well as have a high level of problem behavior. The mean score of the delinquent group was three standard deviations below the overall average. Only twenty-three youth (5 percent of the sample) and five qualitative cases met this abysmal standard.

Jessor and Jessor (1977) proposed a "problem-behavior theory," in which adolescent behavior could be characterized on a single dimension ranging from behaviors such as substance abuse and delinquency, which would be regarded as socially undesirable, to those that would be rated more positively, such as church-going and academic success. Our cluster of delinquents is at the negative pole of this dimension.[7] Problem behavior scores were generally low in this sample of youths, who at eleven to fourteen years of age were just beginning to enter the developmental phase of increased delinquency, but this small cluster was responsible for most of these negative activities.

Mark Sanders, a European-American, living in a neighborhood with moderate resources, was one of our delinquent youth. Mark differs from JJ primarily in the extent of his involvement in problem behaviors. He actually scored better than JJ on our other indicators of adolescent outcomes: he managed to do well in school when he put in the effort, expressed confidence in himself, and appeared to have good mental health. But he stood out among all those interviewed in engaging in a wide range of problematic behaviors, including drinking excessively, participating in gang activities, stealing, and getting into violent fights.

Demographic Differences and Configurations of Success

When we compared the *internal* structure, that is, the pattern of associations making up these clusters for different gender and racial subgroups, they were nearly identical. The properties of these groups do not depend on gender, age, or ethnic differences. Apparently, the underlying components that link behaviors together work similarly for girls and boys as well as for blacks and whites.

The similarity of structure within the clusters does not tell us whether the types distribute evenly across the demographic groups that we have been considering in this chapter. Figure 3.5 provides the answer. Females, regardless of race, are overrepresented among the academically competent, and males are somewhat more likely to be in the involved and delinquent subgroups. Racial differences were modest across the clusters.

When we examined the distribution of age within and across groups, the only difference we found was that, as noted earlier, adolescents in the delinquent group were older on average than adolescents in the other clusters. Otherwise, there was a fairly even distribution of age across clusters. The age differences described above are likely to be reflected in the composition of one's peers. We also examined the nature of peer associations as reported by the youth in the four different clusters. Predictably, they differ markedly: academically competent and socially involved youth reported that their peers were similarly engaged in positive activities, but at-risk and delinquent youth associated with peers engaged in similar problem behaviors. The youth in the study were embedded in social worlds that reinforced their activities, frequently supporting but sometimes undermining the influence of parents and teachers.

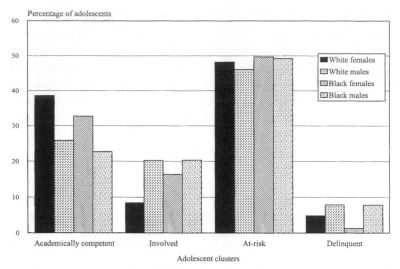

Figure 3.5 Categories of Youth by Race and Gender

Neighborhoods and Configurations of Success

We observed earlier that the distribution of youth performing well was not strongly linked to characteristics of neighborhoods. This was true for the separate domains of success, but possibly the configurations of success may be more sensitive to discerning differences.

Predictably, more involved youth reside in the more advantaged neighborhoods. The availability of community resources and social opportunities in these areas appears to facilitate involvement of youth in activities and success in other aspects of development.

In other respects, the results hardly match popular impressions. Competent youth are underrepresented in the better neighborhoods, and their negative counterparts, delinquent youth, are slightly overrepresented in communities that are more organized and socially coherent. These findings are as perplexing as they are surprising. Given the modest strength of the associations, we are inclined to believe that they may be due to chance. Possibly, too, our sampling procedure, relying as it did on phone screening, may have led us to select those youth in poorer neighborhoods who may have been performing better than average. However we interpret these results, the link between neighborhood quality and how youth are faring in early adolescence is relatively modest in our sample. It remains to be seen whether this is due to the ways in which families are functioning in particular neighborhoods or because it is too early to notice incipient differences that will become more visible in time.

The purpose of this chapter has been to acquaint the reader with the dimensions of successful development that will be applied in later chapters. Merely describing how youth are doing in the domains of academic performance, social involvement, mental health, and problem behavior is revealing, especially in the extent of variability within the sample. Comparing these youth to their counterparts in prior research provides the general impression that on most counts, the participants are about par for the course. The majority seem to be well adjusted in school, express positive self-evaluations, and are similarly described by parents. Only a small minority are in serious trouble on any of the measures.

When the domains are examined simultaneously, a slightly less rosy picture emerges, if only because it is difficult for all in the sample to be above average. Beyond this, however, a substantial minority of our sample youth are having problems in school, often a warning sign of more severe difficulties to come. A small minority are engaged in moderately high levels of delinquency and substance abuse or are encountering mental health problems. All told, about half of the sample were considered to be at risk, and 5 percent were classified as delinquent.

Predictably, these broad clusters were age-related, with a higher proportion of youth experiencing adjustment behavioral problems as they approached their mid-teens. Girls were academically more proficient, while boys were somewhat more socially involved, largely because of their sports activities. The delinquent cluster, though small, was dominated by males.

The most surprising finding in this chapter was the generally weak link between neighborhood characteristics and youth performance. In one respect, the findings followed the expected form: adolescents in the more organized neighborhoods were much more likely to be in the socially involved cluster. However, we did not find that the academically proficient youth predominated in the better-off neighborhoods and the delinquent youth in the disadvantaged communities. If anything, our findings pointed in the opposite direction.

The lack of association could be an artifact of the sampling procedure or the kinds of measures that we used. No doubt, had we used test scores, we would have discovered greater variability by community. It is also possible, then, that in many of the white, working-class communities, many families have moved out to better neighborhoods to advance their children's prospects, leaving behind a greater share of families with children who are underachieving. Keep in mind, of course, that our sample excludes the wealthy areas of the city and the suburbs as well as some of the worst sections of Philadelphia. Still, a broad range of communities is represented. Even if we acknowledge this possibility, the findings suggest that, at least at this age, successful performance is not neighborhood-linked. We are inclined to take seriously the fact that youth, at this age, at least, are performing better in poor neighborhoods than is publicly perceived. The next several chapters delve more deeply into the sources of successful adjustment both within and across neighborhoods.

Four

How Parents Manage Risk and Opportunity

With the assistance of
SARAH E. LORD, W. TODD BARTKO, AND KAREN WALKER

You have to know what to protect them against, what to tell them, give them different signs to look out for [when you live in a neighborhood like this]. When they want to go outside it's just, you, know, [if] it's like crowded or like something that's going [on]. You know, sometimes, you can just feel it. You know they have to come in, they have to stay in the house. They wouldn't go to the store. And if you see like groups of boys out there and stuff like that, you know, my husband or myself will go. It's safer for one of us to go as opposed to Robert.
　　—Michelle, mother of Robert James

But she's, she's getting older and I gotta keeping on learning just to, to let go and have confidence in her. It's hard letting go, and I think once they get past a certain age I'll be able to act a lot better than what I know now.
　　—Beverly, mother of Christine Lang

As these quotations illustrate, being the parent of an adolescent involves walking a fine line between just the right amount of control and too little or too much control. Maintaining a balance depends on the relationship that has been forged previously between parent and child. It's a lot easier if a store of trust has been built up and the adolescent is already on a successful track. This chapter describes the role the caregivers in this study currently play in managing their adolescent children's lives. Already we have gotten some impression of the families from demographic data, but now we will become a little more acquainted with the parents as we examine their child-rearing practices. Retaining our special interest in neighborhood differences, we will pay particular attention to whether parenting practices and family management strategies vary by features of the neighborhood.

Our perspective on family management was outlined in chapter 1, and here we reemphasize two key points from that discussion. First, family management can occur in two different spheres: within the home and out of the home. Traditionally, psychological research has stressed the day-to-day, dyadic interactions between parents and children in the home. Much of this interaction involves managing children's behavior. We refer to this type of management as family process. Out-of-home management focuses on regulating the interaction between one's child and the larger community and neighborhood, as well as peer groups, and school. Managing in this second sphere includes some aspects of family process, namely, monitoring and control; it also includes activities that do not necessarily involve direct interaction between parent and child.

Second, our attention to *family management* adds an important dimension to the traditional family process perspective precisely because of its explicit focus on understanding the meaning of what parents are trying to do, particularly with regard to their child's stage of development and the specific features of households and neighborhood settings. "Appropriate" parenting depends on the risks and opportunities in the broader community in which the family resides, the age and competence level of the child, and the goals, values, and resources of the parents. How much parents "should" monitor their children's behavior, and how much autonomy "should" be granted to a child, depends on the family's social context, on the parents' goals, and on the child's maturity (as demonstrated in past behaviors).

This ecological and developmental perspective is especially important in interpreting group differences in the prevalence of any particular parenting behavior or practice. A growing number of studies compare the parenting styles of families from different ethnic groups and socioeconomic classes (e.g., Steinberg et al. 1991, 1992). Often these studies ask the question, "Who does more of X?" without probing in greater detail why that might be true. In many of these studies, a particular group is then labeled as more or less authoritarian or authoritative in their parenting style, with little regard to the meaning of that behavior in the context in which the family is living. From an ecological perspective, labeling either a specific type or amount of monitoring as representing a particular parenting style can be misleading (e.g., Baumrind's [1989] authoritarian or authoritative parenting). For instance, Michelle James occasionally restricted her children to the home when trouble was brewing on the streets outside. And she was careful to advise them of the corners they should avoid. In the context of neighborhood violence and drug activity, her restrictions seemed eminently appropriate, even though they might be called authoritarian by some standards. Consistent with this point of view, Eccles and her colleagues argue that the "developmental fit" between the socialization practices and the subjective, psychological needs of the child is the critical ingredient for assessing the relation between socialization practices and child outcomes rather than the specific amount or mode of the practice being studied (Eccles et al. 1993).

PROMOTIVE STRATEGIES

The first two sections of this chapter focus on two types of family management strategies: *promotive* strategies that foster children's talents and opportunities and *preventive* strategies that reduce children's exposure to various types of dangerous circumstances. In the first instance, parents are investing in developing skills and competencies, usually by exposing their children to structured learning situations. In the second instance, parents are generally constraining their children to avoid costly behaviors or exposure to very risky situations. Subsequent sections discuss management strategies that may accomplish both aims at once. We also assess the extent to which family management strategies and behaviors differ across different types of neighborhoods. Our specific measures of family management are summarized at appropriate points throughout this chapter.

Explicit Attempts to Influence Activity Involvement and Skill Acquisition

ACTIVITY INVOLVEMENT. To assess parents' direct role in shaping their adolescents' activities and organizational participation, we first asked parents whether anyone in their family participated in each of a series of organized activities, such as religious activities, school or community recreational and athletic programs, civil rights groups, and community-watch programs. If the parent responded yes, she was asked who participated. Each time the parent indicated that the youth was a participant, the parent was asked who was responsible for involving the youth in this activity (the parent, the youth, another person, or both the youth and the parent). The youth answered a similar set of questions. Responses to these questions are summarized in table 4.1.

Most of our adolescents (65 percent according to the parents' reports and 59 percent according to the adolescents' self-reports) are involved in one or more organized, after-school activities. The most common youth

Table 4.1
Youth Activity Involvement, Parent Reports

Activity	Percent involved	Percent with youth initiation	Percent with caretaker initiation
After-school recreation	27.6	94.8	31.1
Summer program	40.1	67.9	38.2
Small youth clubs/Scouts	9.8	91.7	18.8
Community athletics	12.5	100.0	57.4
Tutoring	2.9	57.1	64.3
Y or boys'/girls' clubs	14.9	98.6	45.2
School athletics	11.9	94.8	5.2
Volunteer programs	5.7	3.6	3.6
Religious activities	11.7	0.0	100.0
Community activities	27.0	73.5	34.8

activities were after-school and summer recreational/sports activities (27 percent–40 percent participated in such activities), and community activities (27 percent), and both community-based clubs like Scouts and center-based activities at places like the Y and Boys' and Girls' Clubs (15 percent).

As one might expect for this age group, both parents and adolescents indicated that the adolescents themselves were primarily responsible for their involvement in various forms of recreational activities (57 percent–98 percent depending on reporter and activity type). Parents claimed most responsibility for helping their adolescent become involved in organized summer recreation (38 percent), scouting and other youth clubs (18 percent–45 percent), tutoring (64 percent), and religious activities (100 percent). Similarly, although the majority of youth (57 percent) claimed responsibility for their participation in tutoring programs, a substantial minority gave their parents credit for involving them in other kinds of programs. Twenty to twenty-five percent also gave their parents some credit for their own involvement in religious and volunteer service activities. Thus, how parents manage their children's organizational involvement varies across specific activity domains: the adolescents were most responsible for their involvement in recreational activities, while their parents were more active in connecting them to educational, spiritual, and health-promoting activity settings.

We saw this pattern repeatedly in the qualitative case studies. Some mothers worked hard to get their children to attend church services and to be involved in church social activities. Joanne Collins, whose daughter

Trisha was a good student and an athlete at a public vocational high school, drove her and her siblings to meetings and functions several times a week. Joanne also saved money so that her children could attend a church camp for a week each summer despite the family's difficult economic situation. This pattern of connecting children to spiritual activities was common among a sizable minority of the families in our study. Speaking for many of these parents, Joanne said,

> I went to church and I still do. I always will. But that's what made the difference with my kids. I thought, "If you don't expose them to it, no one [will]." You can't force someone to believe. Not anyone. But if you don't expose it to them. I thought, "That's my duty. I should take them, you know."

In contrast, although many parents, Joanne among them, expressed pride in their children's athletic or other recreational activities, they did not see themselves as responsible for connecting their children to those activities. Indeed, they sometimes saw such activities as interfering with their adolescents' educational or spiritual progress. One mother insisted that her son stop playing high school football when his grades fell. Another mother discouraged (although she did not forbid) her extremely active daughter's participation in sports even as she encouraged the girl's involvement in academically and religiously oriented activities. And Michelle James forbade Robert from going out for the high school football team, explaining,

> Now, it's nothing wrong with sports or anything like that, but the reason why, um, we wouldn't let him join the team was because of its association, that was the main thing, and competitive spirit it's win at all costs. And that's not good, that's why there are a lot of injuries, get him out, get him down, whatever. And that's not good, they've taken the fun out of sports. And as far as the association, the language, and you know, the things like that.

SKILLS.　In order to elicit more specific promotive strategies, parents were asked whether their child had any special talents, skills, or interests and what they had done in the last year to help the child improve in this area. Almost all (85 percent) of the parents provided a specific skill or interest: 35 percent mentioned sports, 25 percent music, 13 percent an academic subject, 13 percent art, and 7 percent dancing. The most frequently mentioned strategies involved either verbal encouragement at

Table 4.2
Parents' Promotion of Children's Talents and Skills: Percentage of Parents
Giving Each Qualitative Measure

Category	Percent
Nothing	5.0
Talked to child	.7
Told child talent was important	.7
Told child talent could help	.2
Encouraged child	58.0
Found out about program	21.6
Signed up for program	1.5
Gave lesson to child	68.2
Took child to programs	14.5
Transferred child to better school/special school	.7
Coached/worked with child at home	5.2

home or out-of-home instruction (see table 4.2). Relatively few parents reported working directly with their children themselves.

These open-ended questions were followed by a series of structured items asking the parents how frequently in the last six months they had used each of the specific promotive management strategies to assist their children in further developing the particular interest or skill mentioned. The results for the individual items are summarized in table 4.3. Consistent with the results from the open-ended questions, verbal encouragement was the most frequently used strategy. Large numbers of parents also reported making their children practice at home. The results were more mixed for enrolling children in programs outside the home; although a slight majority of parents employed this strategy at least some of the time, a sizable minority never did. Again, few parents participated in the activity with their children on a regular basis, while one-third indicated that they rarely did the activity with their children.

We asked the adolescents a parallel series of open-ended questions, beginning with the general question, "Do you have any interests, skills, or something you do well like music, art, drama, or athletics or some other ability?" If the youth responded yes (which 83 percent did), we asked whether their parents had done anything to help them get better at this activity. Only 40 percent of the youth indicated that their parents had provided any assistance. Of this group, 48 percent indicated that their parents had helped them by either coaching or working with them at home. Another 28 percent said their parents had enrolled them in an out-of-home organized program, and 23 percent said their parents had helped by giving them encouragement. Thus, although they gave their parents some credit for actively helping them improve their skills at home, the

Table 4.3
Parents' Promotion of Children's Talents: Percentage Giving Each Quantitative Response

Response	Percent giving response		
	Often	Sometimes	Almost never
Point out how it will help in the future	56.5	14.5	29.0
Point out how it helped a relative get ahead	13.2	69.0	17.8
Discuss how to get better at it	38.5	39.0	23.0
Point out what will happen if child doesn't get better at this talent	10.6	32.8	56.6
Found out about programs that could help child get better	29.2	48.3	22.5
Signed child up for classes and programs	23.8	51.1	25.1
Took child to program	48.3	26.8	24.9
Arranged for someone else to take child to program	10.1	45.2	44.6
Made sure child practiced at home	22.1	45.7	32.3
Did activity with child	16.7	47.6	35.7
Praised child for doing well in the activity	95.7	3.9	0.43
Praised child in front of others for having the skill or working hard to get better	77.9	21.2	0.9

adolescents reported relatively low levels of parent involvement in this type of proactive management.

Involvement in Shared Activities

Closely related to our notion of promotive management strategies is the extent to which parents spend time with their children doing a variety of activities, such as going to movies, shopping, or working on homework together. Many studies have documented the importance of this type of involvement in children's lives, particularly with regard to school achievement, internal locus of control, behavior regulation, and mental health (e.g., Comer and Haynes 1991; Eccles, Wigfield, and Schiefele 1998; Grolnick and Ryan 1989). To assess this type of involvement, we asked parents how often they did several different things together with their adolescent on a series of activities, using a 5-point Likert scale anchored at the extremes (1 = almost never, and 5 = almost always).[1] The most frequent shared activities included talking about what's going on at school ($M = 3.96$), doing homework together ($M = 3.24$), going shopping together ($M = 3.81$), and working together on something around the house ($M = 3.40$). These responses indicate a moderately high level of daily involvement in their children's lives. There was also substantial variation, with some parents responding "almost always" to all activities but others reporting "almost never" to the majority of activities.

Support of Autonomy/Negotiation/Democratic Decision Making

The closest constructs in traditional parenting research to our notion of promotive family management are those linked to the amount of support provided for children's involvement in family decision making and autonomy. This aspect of family process is especially critical during adolescence, given the centrality of developing a sense of self (Eccles et al. 1993; Erikson 1963). In order to adapt to and negotiate the opportunities and pressures for independence, adolescents need not only support for their autonomy from their families but the right kinds of support. Parents must provide sufficient monitoring and control (to help their adolescents resist the abundant temptations to engage in risky behavior) as well as opportunities for their adolescents to learn and practice autonomous decision making. Playing this role well requires a continual renegotiation of the authority structure within the family as the adolescent becomes more and more competent at self-management.

Under the best of circumstances, this renegotiation process involves increasing mutuality between parents and their adolescents in problem-solving and decision-making situations. In such families, adolescents are likely to believe that their parents respect their opinions and trust them to be involved in important decisions. This respect and trust, in turn, should foster the adolescent's developing sense of independence, personal competence, and efficacy in her or his expanding roles in the world (e.g., Epstein and McPartland 1977; Grolnick and Ryan 1989; Leahy 1981). At the same time, these parents also need to provide sufficient structure and control to prevent their adolescents from making serious mistakes that could have long-term negative consequences.

Eccles and her colleagues (Eccles et al. 1991; Eccles et al. 1993) have related the notion of increased opportunity for decision making in adolescence to person-environment-fit theory. Drawing from this theory, they proposed that when provisions for autonomy are not made for the adolescent, adjustment will be adversely affected. Empirical research supports this hypothesis: Eccles and colleagues have found both a longitudinal increase in adolescents' desire for participation in decision making (Eccles et al. 1993; Flanagan 1990; Yee 1987) and a positive association between adolescent's participation in decision making and their intrinsic motivation and positive self-esteem (Flanagan 1989; Yee and Flanagan 1985).

Several measures of developmentally appropriate levels of support for autonomy and joint decision making were devised to explore these propositions. These measures were specifically selected to capture the provision of opportunity for joint decision making, conflict over behaviors on which adolescents think they should have some decision-making autonomy, and the collaborative and respectful nature of joint decision making.

Involvement in decision making represented mothers' perceptions of the degree of control versus autonomy they provided for their adolescent in decision-making situations.[2] Mothers were asked, for example, "How often do you ask your child what he/she thinks before deciding on family matters that involve him/her?" and "How often do you ask your child what he/she thinks before making decisions that affect him/her?" The *Conflict over behavior* scale measured a mother's sense of the degree to which she and her child disagreed about the adolescent's personal behaviors.[3] *Constructive versus destructive problem-solving* measured the extent to which parents and children use constructive and respectful versus destructive and highly conflictual strategies in joint problem-solving scenarios.[4] With regard to other research, the responses on all three scales, on the average, were appropriate for families with early adolescent children. The mean responses for the decision-making scale, for instance, indicated that these parents involve their early adolescent children in this type of decision making slightly more than half of the time. Similarly, as one would expect with early adolescent children, these parents also reported low to moderate levels of conflict over behavior (Smetana 1988).

PREVENTIVE MANAGEMENT STRATEGIES

In an ideal world all parents would be concerned about fostering their children's talents and providing opportunities to exercise and enhance them. Unfortunately, many have more pressing concerns related to their own precarious circumstances or the imminent dangers facing their children. To capture these concerns, parents were asked about the kinds of things they worried might happen to their adolescents and about their strategies for preventing these outcomes. A cluster of four types of related worries emerged with great frequency: drugs and alcohol were mentioned by 27 percent of the parents; various forms of crime and violence, including rape, by 25 percent; general physical safety by 18 percent; and negative peer influences by 19 percent.

The parents were then asked what they were doing to safeguard their children against these hazards. Their responses are summarized in table 4.4 (each parent can be represented more than once in these percentages). As was true for the promotive strategies, these parents, by and large, relied on within-home preventive strategies such as talking with the child

Table 4.4

Parents' Protective Strategies: Percentage of Parents Giving Each Qualitative Measure as Either First or Second Response

Category	Percent
Talk to child or encourage child to do better	45.9
Provide a positive role model	0.7
Spend time with child	7.8
Keep child busy	3.1
Monitor child's homework	0.2
Teach child to use good judgment	43.5
Enforce rules	22.0
Send to church	1.3
Provide transportation to get child to good programs	8.2
Restrict child's activities	2.0
Take child out of situation	0.4
Ground child	0.2
Attempt to sever child's friendships	6.4
Contact other parents to keep lookout for child	0.4
Speak to child's teachers	0.4
Complain to appropriate authorities	0.2

Table 4.5

Parents' Protective Strategies: Percent Giving Each Qualitative Response

Response	Percent giving response		
	Often	Sometimes	Almost never
Point out how dangers have destroyed lives of others	47.9	26.4	19.5
Get child involved in good activities in neighborhood	46.6	32.6	14.6
Punish child for doing things that lead to problems	15.1	29.7	49.0
Keep home as much as possible	47.0	37.0	11.0
Make sure you know the friends the child is with	76.0	15.0	2.0
Keep child away from danger	61.8	11.6	20.2

(46 percent), teaching the child to use good judgment (43 percent), and enforcing rules (22 percent). A minority also reported restricting their children's activities by either keeping them at home as much as possible (2 percent) or by keeping them busy at home (3 percent).

This open-ended question was followed by series of structured items asking the parents how frequently they had tried each of a series of preventive strategies in the last six months to keep their children from getting involved in the kinds of activities that worried them. The results for the individual items are summarized in table 4.5. Consistent with the results of the open-ended responses, the most frequently reported strategies entailed talking with the children. Parents also reported very high rates of monitoring and protective strategies, such as making sure they knew which friends their adolescents were with and shielding their children from dangers. In keeping with the ethnographic evidence reported by Furstenberg (1993), a large proportion (47 percent) also reported trying to keep their adolescent at home as much as possible either most or some of the time—a proportion much larger than is evident from the parents' open-ended responses.

The adolescents were asked similar questions; for example, we asked what they thought their parents were most worried might happen to them. Thirty percent reported drugs and alcohol; 23 percent reported school problems and/or academic failure; 11 percent indicated crime and violence; 9 percent reported concerns about their physical safety; and 4 percent indicated negative peer influence.

Both the similarities and the differences between the adolescents' and the parents' responses are interesting. The adolescents were much more likely than their parents to report that their parents were particularly worried about school-related problems; they were also less likely than their parents to report that their parents were very worried about negative peer influences. Clearly, adolescents are quite aware of their parents' concerns about the importance of schoolwork and about the dangers of drugs and alcohol. They appear to be much less sensitive to their parents' concerns about peer pressure, perhaps because they do not think they are influenced by their peers as much as adults think they are.

The adolescents were then asked what their parents were doing to deter them from these types of outcomes. Like their parents, the youth reported that talking with them (33 percent), teaching them to use good judgment (16 percent), and enforcing rules (19 percent) were the most frequently used strategies (provided as first or second responses). Between 5 percent and 8 percent (for each item) also reported that their parent kept them at home, monitored their homework, or spoke with school personnel.

Both parents and adolescents were also asked more specific questions about restrictive prevention strategies linked to mobility and friendship networks, curfews, and both after-school and evening supervision. These questions were coded to capture the extent to which the parents used highly restrictive strategies. In general, these families reported being actively and consistently engaged in monitoring and restricting their adolescents' whereabouts and in providing high levels of supervision. Most (82 percent) parents reported that they knew most or all of their adolescents' friends; 64 percent indicated that they had told their adolescents to avoid hanging around with specific other adolescents; and 62 percent felt that their adolescents had cooperated with this restriction.

The same pattern recurs in adolescents' responses to similar questions. Somewhat fewer (47 percent versus 64 percent) indicated that there were kids they weren't supposed to hang out with. Although 22 percent claimed they argued with their parents about this restriction, 70 percent of the total sample indicated that they would either stop seeing, or reduce the amount of time they spent with, particular friends if their parents objected to these friends.

Both parents and adolescents were then asked if there were particular places the adolescents weren't allowed to go. Seventy-nine percent of the parents and 67 percent of the youth replied positively. Although 41 percent of the youth indicated that they would argue with their parents about such a restriction, 79 percent said they would comply if their parents insisted. Along similar lines, we asked the parents where their adolescents went after school; 50 percent indicated that they came home to a supervised situation, and another 20 percent that they went to some other supervised situation like a relative's house or an after-school organized program; only 28 percent said that their adolescents passed their afternoons unsupervised. Consistent with this picture, 65 percent of the adolescents reported that they were expected to come right home after school. Finally, we asked both parents and adolescents about curfew rules. Over 84 percent of the parents and the adolescents reported that they had curfew rules on both school and nonschool nights that were enforced most or all of the time.

Further evidence of this relatively high level of control and monitoring emerges from our qualitative follow-up interviews. For example, one summer, when the neighborhood was overrun with gangs of teens who were fighting with one another and committing acts of vandalism, Trisha Collins's mother, Joanne, and her neighbors tried repeatedly to get the police to take care of the situation. When this didn't work, Joanne resorted to an active but very individualized management strategy, insisting that her daughter come home before dark and that her son come in the house whenever the gangs were roaming around. Thus, although Joanne had tried to use neighborhood resources to help monitor her children's behavior, she resorted to a much more restrictive pattern when these attempts failed. In addition, she actively managed her children's friendship networks. Summarizing a particular situation involving her younger daughter and some girls she did not want her daughter to get too close to, Joanne recounted,

They would try to have a friendship with Jeannette and I wouldn't say nothing to the girls, but I knew, I've seen these girls walking, they're from her soccer team. And um, I told her, "You can have a casual relationships in the soccer, but you will not have these girls as friends, going out with them, because I've seen them up and down the streets a couple of them, where their language was awful."

Marcia Lawrence's mother also used a variety of preventive strategies with her children. Despite their very good relationship, Patty was very worried that Marcia might associate with the wrong kinds of kids. She was also quite worried about guns, about her daughter's starting to have sex, and about AIDS. Marcia did not let her children play in the front of the house, and discouraged them from hanging out at the corner with other neighborhood children. Finally, she imposed and enforced very strict family rules about a wide variety of behaviors and activities, ranging from monitoring phone use to setting curfews and limitations on where the children could socialize.

Discipline Effectiveness and Consistency

Closely related to the preventive strategies discussed above are the more traditional, in-home family processes related to disciplinary effectiveness and consistency of rules within the home. The importance of consistent discipline for successful development is well documented (e.g., Baumrind 1989; Grolnick and Ryan 1989; Patterson and Stouthammer-Loeber 1984) Furthermore, the provision of both a consistent set of rules and effective discipline may be particularly important for adolescents, given their increased involvement with peers, the opportunities for out-of-home activities, the new-found roles and expectations, and the identity issues and physical changes that accompany this developmental period. These changes can be overwhelming and render adolescents vulnerable to socioemotional and behavioral difficulties. Home environments that do not provide consistent guidelines for action or do not follow through on rule infractions ultimately make it more difficult for the adolescent to acquire a sense of personal control and an ability to navigate in the world beyond the household (Grolnick and Ryan 1989). Such helplessness can lead one to distrust others as well as oneself, and can result in more general psychological distress and anxiety. To gain a sense of control over seemingly uncontrollable circumstances, adolescents may also turn to involvement in dangerous or illicit behaviors, testing external limits or seeking their own internal limits.

Our interview included several measures of these types of discipline effectiveness and consistency. Our *monitoring* scale reflected the degree to which parents were aware of their adolescents' activities when they were not with the child. *Discipline effectiveness* measured how effective the parents felt they were in disciplining their adolescents.[5] *Discipline consistency* measured how consistent parents felt they were in disciplining their adolescents.[6]

In general, the average responses of the primary caregivers to these quantitative measures indicated a relatively high frequency of the developmentally appropriate levels of monitoring and effective discipline practices. Of course, parents may overestimate these capacities, but our field data suggests that most possess a reasonable degree of self-awareness.

Summary

According to both their own reports and the reports of their early adolescent children, the parents in this study actively engaged in promotive and preventive family management strategies. The levels on all of our measures fall within a developmentally appropriate range, although some of the parents exercised a high degree of control, perhaps in response to the dangers in their neighborhoods. It seems, then, that these parents overall are managing their early adolescents quite well at this point in their children's lives. These findings parallel the account of the adolescents' behavior provided in the previous chapter. Later we will report the extent to which family management strategies and practices vary across different types of neighborhoods and whether these strategies are linked to patterns of success among the youth.

OTHER FORMS OF FAMILY MANAGEMENT

Interestingly, our notion of family management did not necessarily correspond with the way parents understood their task of managing their children. In our view, parents manage their children's experiences through a wide variety of behaviors and practices, including the daily organization of activities, the celebration of various special occasions like holidays, involvement in their children's daily activities, and involvement in many types of organizations and institutions. Although our conceptualization purposefully included this wide range of practices, behaviors, and institutional affiliations, parents frequently failed to report many of these kinds of behaviors in response to our explicit family management questions. Parents who take their children to church regularly, for example, are clearly managing their experiences. Yet few of our parents mentioned church attendance as one of their management strategies. Why don't more parents refer to church attendance in these terms? Data from other qualitative interviews, which probed deeply into parents' motivations in a way the survey did not, indicate that most parents, such as Joanne Collins, viewed church attendance as both an important promotive and preventive strategy. However, many also took church attendance for granted because it was so much a part of their family tradition that it did not seem worth mentioning as a conscious personal strategy.

Daily Routines

Much of what we consider family management probably occurs informally through the daily structure and organization of family life. When we say that an organization is well managed, we mean that the organization runs smoothly and in a predictable manner. Family management probably operates in a similar way. Parents may have the greatest impact on children's development through the daily routines that guide the family's activities on a regular basis and through the general level of chaos versus organization in the family's life (Eccles, Wigfield, and Schiefele 1998; Whiting and Edwards 1988). Because these practices are such a regular and ingrained part of family life, however, it is unlikely that either parents or adolescents would mention them spontaneously in response to our open-ended questions about family management practices. Instead, we tried to capture this aspect of family management through a series of questions about the regularity of events in the family's lives—events such as where one sleeps, when one eats, and when one does homework.

First, we asked both parents and adolescents how often a number of things had changed in their family in the last year. Seventy percent of the adolescents and 72 percent of the parents indicated no change in the composition of their household. Eighty-nine percent of the youth and 90 percent of the parents reported that there had been no change in address in the last year. Finally, 86 percent of both adolescents and parents reported that there had been no change in where the adolescent slept in the last year. Overall, these families had been living in stable circumstances over the previous twelve months. Again, it is important to remember that we may have undercounted the more-mobile, least-stable families by relying on telephone screening to obtain our sample.

We next asked about the regularity of various daily activities. These results are summarized in table 4.6. Again, the majority of the families appear to follow very regular daily schedules. The greatest variability occurs regarding when dinner is eaten and both when and where home-

Table 4.6

Regularity of Activities: Percentage of Parents or Adolescents Reporting Each Category

| | Parent report | | |
| | | Percent giving response | |
Activity	Same time	Usually same time	Different time
Do homework	39.6	50.5	9.7
Eat dinner	26.6	47.1	26.2
Go to bed	41.1	52.7	6.2
Be home on school night	44.1	18.6	6.4

| | Adolescent report | | |
| | | Percent giving response | |
	Almost always	Sometimes	Hardly ever
Regular place to do homework	60.1	22.7	16.7
Regular chores	47.9	38.6	13.0
Regular time to get up	90.5	7.5	1.9

work is done. But even for these two categories, 70 percent or more of the families reported that their schedules were regular most of the time.

Finally, we asked both the parents and the youth whether someone regularly made sure that certain events, like preparation of breakfast and dinner and checking adolescents' homework, happened, and who that person was. These results are summarized in table 4.7. Although the parents reported somewhat greater regularity for these activities and greater personal responsibility for the activity, both parents and adolescents reported relatively high levels of regularity. Getting breakfast and having homework checked are the two activities that occur with somewhat less consistency across the week; but even these occurred with great regularity in the majority of the families.

We saw several examples of just this type of management in our follow-up qualitative interviews. Robert's family operates on specific and consistent daily schedules built around church attendance and other family activities and responsibilities. Dinner is served at the same time most days and is a family affair. All of the children have regular, daily chores and a regular time to do their homework before they go out on their own after school. And all of the children must be home by dark and cannot go out on weekday evenings at all.

Much like Robert's family, Marcia's two-parent family is very well

Table 4.7

Monitoring of Daily Routines: Percentage of Parents or Adolescents Reporting
Each Category

| | Percent giving response | | | |
| | Almost | | | |
Activity	every day	Never	Caregiver	Youth
Parent report				
Child got breakfast	66.2	1.2	63.7	30.9
Child got dinner	90.4	0	62.3	9.2
Child got to school on time	91.2	0	68.9	28.4
Homework checked	50.6	11.1	14.0	18.5
Adolescent report				
Child got breakfast	83.7	2.1	65.6	30.9
Child got dinner	83.7	2.1	81.8	15.3
Child got to school on time	82.9	4.4	68.6	31.1
Homework checked	53.3	15.7	79.7	17.3

organized. Marcia is the oldest of four children and attends a parochial school. Religion is a very central part of this family's life. Patty, Marcia's mother, runs a tight ship. The family eats together every day and does organized activities together at least once a week. There is a regular schedule for daily events like waking up, getting to school, mealtime, and homework time.

Other parents were less able to maintain consistent routines. Jeannette, Mark Sanders' mother, is an example of a parent who has had a great deal of difficulty structuring family life. A single mother who supports her daughter and two sons from her wages as a grocery store cashier, Jeannette has been ineffective at monitoring her sons' comings and goings and has been unable to keep them attending school regularly. When Mark was seventeen and in his sophomore year of high school for the third time, Jeanette reported that he was skipping school at least one day per week. She explained that she would try to wake him up in the morning, and he would say he was getting up but then would stay in bed. Eventually Jeanette would leave to take her younger son to school and Mark would stay at home and sleep. Jeanette said, "I tried to like explain to the kids more about why, you know, they shouldn't do the things they do and stuff like that and just try to explain to, you know, but with teenagers it's like, they got their minds set."

While Jeanette clearly felt a need for consistency and structure in her family's daily life, her own irregular work schedule and Mark's ongoing resistance prevented her from effectively maintaining a regular routine within the family.

Parents' Involvement in Organized Institutions

We have already reported on one type of involvement in institutions, namely, childrens' participation in a variety of organized activities. We include parental involvement in a variety of community-based organized activities as another indicator of family management. Modeling community involvement is an important way of managing children's social worlds. Parents who are actively engaged in community-based organizations or in other organized activities can have a positive influence on their children's development in several different ways. Role modeling is one such mechanism. We suspect that by engaging in these activities, parents are demonstrating an approach to both problem solving and citizenship that can inculcate a positive sense of efficacy in their children.

Organizational involvement among parents may also help adolescents acquire social capital. Participation in organizations increases the family's social networks; adolescents can then draw on these social networks for assistance in finding a job, getting into a desired post–high school training program or college, and negotiating a second chance if they end up in serious trouble.

Finally, participating in organizations may also increase the likelihood that adolescents will be involved in positive after-school organized activities—activities that will increase their own social capital as well as providing them with safe and productive ways to spend their time and to develop the skills and attitudes associated with a successful transition from adolescence to adulthood.

As a group, the parents in this study were much less likely to be involved in organized, community-based activities than their adolescents. The highest proportion of parents were involved in community organizations such as neighborhood councils (28 percent), community watch programs (37 percent), local politics (13 percent) and local health service programs (14 percent). Twenty-two percent claimed to be leaders of community activities; about half of these indicated that they were leaders in their church and half indicated that they were leaders in the local school parent organizations. We also asked specifically about involvement in school. Only 8 percent indicated that they helped at school one or more times during the preceding year, but 79 percent indicated that they had attended a school meeting, with 40 percent attending at least three times.

Such community involvement was common among several of the families participating in our qualitative follow-up. Patty, Marcia's mother, sings in a choir, is a leader in the parish school parent-teacher organization, is involved in other church activities, works part-time, and has a wide social support network in her community. Patty is a particularly interesting case, because her own mother rarely was involved in activities outside of the home. Patty describes her mother as having been socially withdrawn, a veritable "hermit." This important family story had major implications for both Patty and her daughter. Like her mother, Marcia is also highly involved in activities at both church and school. Patty takes great pride in her daughter's leadership abilities and obviously encourages such activity both directly and through the family story regarding the need to avoid becoming a "hermit" like Marcia's grandmother.

Involvement in Religious Organizations

Parents' and youths' involvement in religious activities is another important type of family management, although, as we noted earlier, few parents specifically mentioned attending church as one of the strategies they used to promote positive values. Questions about participation in organized religious activities revealed that religion plays an important part in the lives of many of the families, particularly among black families. We have already reported that more than half of the youth reported attending religious activities on a regular basis. When asked how often they attended church, 52 percent of the youth reported that they attended church at least once a week; another 19 percent attended church 1–3 times per month; only 12 percent indicated that they never attended church. Finally, when asked how important religion was to their daily lives, 81 percent of the youth said that religion was either very or somewhat important to them (on a 4-point scale). Parents reported similar patterns: 30 percent indicated that they attended church at least once a week; another 19 percent attended church 1–3 times per month; and only 20 percent indicated that they never attended church. And when asked how important religion was to their daily lives, 67 percent indicated that it was very or somewhat important (again on a 4-point scale).

The role of religion in some of our families is even more evident in the qualitative interviews. Robert James and his family, for example, attend religious services three days each week at their Jehovah's Witness church. In addition, the family's entire social life centers around people who attend their church. Michelle, Robert's mother, clearly sees church involvement as a way of structuring both their children's time and friendship networks. As she told us,

All of his friends are Jehovah's Witnesses, and that helps because that's the same interest. We know what they're doing, what they're involved in, everything, that is a protection [from] different things that they can get involved in outside. That's why we're really conscious of bad association. Um, but they have parties and go to games and um, trips, and, you know, really everything.

Religion is equally prominent in Marcia's family. Both parents are extremely active in the church. Marcia's father is a Eucharistic Minister in their local parish, where Marcia's mother sits on the Parish Development Committee and the Pastoral Council. Her mother is also on the board of the parish grade school's Home and School Committee, and until the birth of her youngest child, she frequently volunteered her time at the school. All three of the children go to parochial schools and are involved in their local Catholic Youth Organizations (CYO). Marcia's mother is a moderator for the younger children's CYO, and Marcia is heavily involved in the high school CYO. She goes to leadership workshops through her CYO and does community service work. In many ways, their values and family life are structured around their involvement with the Catholic church. In turn, their involvement in so many church-related activities makes it easier for the parents to monitor Marcia's activities and friendship networks. Marcia's mother explains,

> Yeah, we're very involved [in our parish]. If we stay involved and the kids stay involved, it keeps everything. It keeps them busy and it keeps them from getting in gangs and things like that. I think if parents [are] involved then the kids will be involved.

Their religious orientation also provides the backdrop against which "strict" parenting practices become meaningful and tolerable to Marcia.

Selection of Adolescents' Schools

Many families in this study reported that they would like to relocate to better neighborhoods. This is among the most powerful family management strategies, but it is also difficult to implement without adequate economic resources; consequently, it is not possible for most families in inner-city Philadelphia. Instead, many parents have chosen to send their children to private or, more often, parochial schools. Twenty-three percent of them were sending their adolescents to parochial schools; another 4 percent were sending them to some other form of private school; and 6 percent had enrolled them in one of the several public magnet schools in Philadelphia. The adolescents in the remaining 66 percent of our families were attending regular public schools.

More than our other indicators of family management, the use of this strategy was closely tied to social class and ethnicity. Sending one's children to private schools was much more common among families with higher income. It was also more common among two-parent families and among families with higher education. Finally, it was more common among white families, even when family income and marital status effects were taken into account. Thus, unlike religion and involvement in other social institutions, this strategy seems to be linked to both the economic and cultural aspects of social class and being white. Interestingly, this is true even though involvement in religious organizations per se, and spirituality more generally, is more common among the black families. Probably this difference reflects jointly the prevalence of Catholic schools in Philadelphia and the greater involvement of white ethnics in Catholicism. Although the benefits of being educated in parochial schools may be real, religious-affiliated primary education is much less available to non-Catholics, especially those with limited means.

OVERVIEW OF FAMILY MANAGEMENT RESULTS

Family management strategies both within and outside the home are diverse. The various practices that we have discussed present a picture of fairly high levels of family management in some domains and relatively lower levels in others. Given the ages of the youth in this study, the parents are predictably less actively involved in managing their children's exposure to positive recreational settings. When this kind of management does occur, it seems to be motivated more by parents' desire for supervision than interest in skills training (i.e., parents were more involved in getting their children enrolled in organized summer programs than in school-based athletic programs and clubs).

We suspect that the families in our study might have provided somewhat different accounts of their management strategies had they resided in the nearby suburbs of Philadelphia. Annette Lareau (1989a) describes a picture quite different from the one revealed in our interviews of parents actively managing their children's free time with a host of after-school activities aimed at cultivating the children's social and cognitive skills. Lareau's observations are also reinforced by Joan Wynn's Chicago study of families living in both a poor urban and a wealthy suburban community (Wynn et al. 1988). The dearth of resources in the poor community led most families to rely on in-home strategies; privileged families could find many alternatives in the community for their children.

Possibly, too, parents may be doing more than they indicated in the interviews, underreporting preventive strategies that were being employed to protect their children or promote their opportunities. From the results of the prior ethnographic study of family management in neighborhoods very similar to those included here, we had expected that the semistructured questions in the survey would elicit from more parents a detailed description of their preventive management strategies. Two factors are probably responsible for this scarcity. First, the interview format may have inhibited parents' responses. Most of the questions required simple responses on preset scales. Answering a series of such questions could have left parents primed to give short, quick answers. Second, as noted earlier, much of what parents do as prevention is part and parcel of regular family routines; thus, these strategies may not come to mind when they are asked what they are doing to prevent bad things from happening to their children. Both these explanations are given some support by the parents' responses to the closed-ended questions about the same issues and by the much richer descriptions we obtained when we reinterviewed a subset of our parents and adolescents using qualitative and in-depth conversations.

Much higher levels of management are evident in responses to these more direct questions regarding specific family management practices. This is especially true for indicators of daily routines and religious activities. Despite the adversity present in many of their neighborhoods, the majority of these parents reported reasonably high levels of active family management practices. Perhaps these reports are biased in a positive direction: respondents are anxious to present their parenting in the best possible light. Three additional pieces of evidence, however, suggest that, while such a bias is undoubtedly present in the parents' reports, it does not account for our results. First, although the correlational relations were modest, we found consistent evidence of both convergent and discriminate validity across the various measures of family management. Second, as mentioned in chapter 2, parents confirmed much of what they had told us in a follow-up qualitative interview several years after these data were collected. Finally, some families reported being highly disorganized: between 10 and 20 percent of those in our sample reported quite chaotic life situations when asked about daily routines (see tables 4.6 and 4.7).

NEIGHBORHOOD INFLUENCES

Having described a range of family management strategies, we can now return to the question of whether parents use different family management strategies in different types of neighborhoods. Early adolescence is a particularly salient time to investigate neighborhood effects on family management practices. As children mature from childhood into adulthood in this society, they pass through a period when they are no longer children but are not yet clearly able to assume full responsibility for their own behavior. Parents must provide increasing opportunities for their early adolescent children to practice making responsible decisions about their own behaviors while at the same time protecting them from dangers and temptations that could mortgage their futures. This process is likely to be much easier in a neighborhood that has accessible programs for youth and relatively few dangers and problematic, distracting opportunities.

The Philadelphia study was specifically designed to explore the link between neighborhood characteristics and parenting. As a first step toward addressing this issue, we looked at the variations in family management strategies across the three global types of neighborhoods referred to in chapter 3 (i.e., the bottom and top 20 percent and the middle 60 percent of the neighborhoods, based on resident reports of resources, opportunities, and social support). Contrary to our expectations, we found only a few strong associations between the neighborhood typology and parenting strategies. Although variation in parenting within each of the three types of neighborhoods is substantial, mean-level differences between neighborhoods are modest, suggesting that parenting is more influenced by proximal factors like parental mental health and family income than by the more distal characteristics associated with neighborhood setting. The significant ($p \leq .05$) effects are summarized in the next sections.

Promotive Strategies

Did the promotive strategies vary by neighborhood type? Not as much as we had anticipated. Neighborhood variations in school-based activity programs like after-school and summer recreation programs were not found; however, a pattern of modest differences did emerge for the level of involvement in community-based activities like community-based athletic teams or clubs, community-sponsored dances, trips, and other outing-type programs, and community-organized centers like the YMCA or YWCA. According to the parents, adolescents living in high-resource neighborhoods had independently joined more of these kinds of activities than adolescents living in either the medium- or low-resource neighborhoods. These results mirror neighborhood differences in both the availability of community-based activity settings and the ease of accessing these resources in nearby neighborhoods. They also may reflect the parents' confidence in the safety of their neighborhoods.

Few neighborhood differences in specific parental strategies used to promote skill acquisition appeared; the few that did were consistent with the neighborhood differences in activity involvement just reported. More specifically, no neighborhood variations appeared in parents' reports of their daily involvement with their children in such activities as the amount of time spent together focused on schoolwork and school-related discussions. The only major neighborhood patterns occurred in parents' use of out-of-home resources versus in-home strategies: parents in the better neighborhoods were more likely than parents in the low-resource neighborhoods to take their adolescents to, and enroll them in, organized programs. In contrast, parents in the low-resource neighborhoods were more likely than parents in the high-resource neighborhoods to use in-home verbal strategies, such as pointing out what would happen if the adolescents didn't develop their talents.

Preventive Strategies

A somewhat different picture emerged for the preventive strategies. As one might expect, given the greater level of dangers in the low-resource neighborhoods, parents in these neighborhoods reported higher rates of preventive strategy use. For example, parents in the low-resource neighborhoods were more likely than parents in the other two types of neighborhoods to report using the following strategies as ways to prevent bad things from happening to their children: keeping their children home as much as possible, keeping them away from the dangers as much as possible, talking to them about the dangers as much as possible, and getting them involved in prosocial activities outside their neighborhood as much as possible. In contrast, and consistent with the differences reported for promotive strategy use, the parents in the high-resource neighborhoods were more likely to report getting their child involved in positive activities within their neighborhood as a protective measure.

Comparable variations occur in other types of restrictive practices. Parents in the high-resource neighborhoods were more likely than parents in lower-resource neighborhoods to send their adolescents to a store alone at night (42 percent versus 30 percent) and to let them walk home alone from school (61 percent versus 50 percent). In contrast, parents in the low-resource neighborhoods were slightly more likely than parents in the medium- and high-resource neighborhoods to indicate that there were places in their neighborhood that they would not let their adolescents go ($p \leq .10$).

These neighborhood variations in preventive strategies are consistent with the parents' reports of both their worries for their children and their desire to move. Strong neighborhood differences emerged in the replies of parents to a question regarding their concerns about specific neighborhood dangers. Across all neighborhoods, 45 percent of the parents indicated that they were worried about specific dangers. Although drug use was the most common response in all neighborhoods (given by 58 percent of those who responded), the distribution of this response varied dramatically by neighborhood type: 77 percent of the parents in the low-resource neighborhoods gave this response compared to 62 percent of the parents in the medium-resource neighborhoods and 37 percent of the parents in the high-resource neighborhoods. Similarly, when asked whether they would like to move and why, parents living in the low-resource neighborhoods were particularly likely to reply positively, giving one or more of the following reasons: to get away from drugs (32 percent); to get away from people being killed, injured, or threatened (13 percent); and to get away from gangs (12 percent). Many of these parents also indicated that they wanted to move in order to improve the quality of life for their families and to find better schools for their children. Unfortunately, according to their own reports, 62 percent of the parents who wanted to move were financially unable to do so (see also Cook et al. 1992).

The prevalence of these types of restrictive practices among families living in low-resource and high-risk neighborhoods was even more pronounced in our qualitative interviews. One mother living in a dangerous neighborhood reported that she did not allow her academically competent son to take public transportation for fear he might meet trouble. Instead she made sure that someone was available to drive him to school, church, and social activities. Other parents gave their children specific advice about how to behave on dangerous streets, or forbade their children to go to certain playgrounds.

A similar neighborhood difference was evident in the parents' responses to our questions regarding sex education. Because emerging sexuality is one important characteristic of adolescent development that is of great concern to many parents, and because other studies have suggested that the onset of sexual behavior is likely to vary by neighborhood (Hogan and Kitagawa 1985), we ask parents whether they had talked to their adolescents about several aspects of sex, including how to decide whether to have sex or not, methods of birth control, where to obtain birth control, and how to avoid getting AIDS or STDs. Figure 4.1 summarizes by neighborhood type the percentage of parents who said yes to each of these questions. Neighborhood type made a near-significant or significant difference for all questions except the AIDS/STD question. In each case, parents in the low-resource neighborhoods were more likely to have talked to their adolescents about these issues than parents in the high-resource neighborhoods.

The importance of this issue and its tie to neighborhood context was also evident in the qualitative interviews. Consider, for example, the differences between Lakisha's and Christine's mothers' reports of their involvement in their daughters' sex education. Lakisha lives in one of

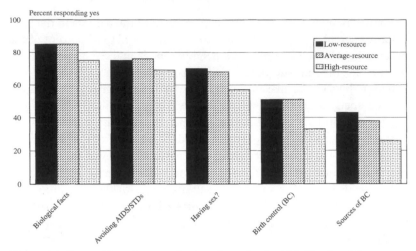

Figure 4.1 Parent-Teen Communication about Sex by Neighborhood Type

our most-distressed neighborhoods; Christine lives in one of our better neighborhoods.

Alicia, Lakisha's mother, claimed that she knew when her daughter was first becoming sexually active. She conveyed the following sequence of events:

> We need to have a family meeting. We had a family meeting and I said, "Are you having sex?" "Oh, Mom!" You know, like I'm embarrassing her. "Baby sis, I mean, young lady, there's ladies here, you know. It's nothing that goes on that we can't discuss." So I made a appointment, we went to teen clinic, we talked to a social worker. The social worker asked her what did she wanna do in life. And she [said], "Architect, you know, I want to do this, I wanna build planes," and things like that. They told me that I didn't really need to be there. So I said I was just comin' cause I wanted to know that we approve of any kind of birth control that might wanna do. So my middle daughter had got the Nora Plant [sic] right after [the birth of her daughter]. And that seem to be working pretty fine, so um, Lakisha went and got it and she's had it now for almost going on three years.

In contrast, Marcia's mother has done little to help her daughter think about sex, birth control, and sexually transmitted diseases. The family lives in one of the better neighborhoods, a neighborhood very close to the one Patty, Marcia's mother, grew up in. Patty, an extremely energetic and intelligent woman, regrets that she did not get a college education because she became pregnant with Marcia while still in high school. Her parents made her finish school and insisted that Marcia's father get a job before they would allow Patty to marry him. Consequently, Marcia was born out of wedlock. Patty is now very worried about the possibility that Marcia will start having sex. She expressed concern about the fact that she had not discussed these issues with her daughter in any depth, opting instead for simply discouraging her from having sex before she marries. She also indicated that she was quite confused about how she should approach the topic now that the threat of AIDS is a real risk. Although she thinks she would have helped to get her daughters on the pill ten years ago so that they wouldn't become pregnant, she does not know what to do in the face of today's risks.

WITHIN-HOME PREVENTIVE STRATEGIES. In sum, we observed some differences in preventive management strategies across neighborhood types; most were relatively modest, and there continued to be considerable overlap in parents' strategies even when they lived in very different kinds of neighborhoods. Our qualitative data revealed why the overlap was so substantial. Popular stereotypes about cities portray them as anomic and brutal places, and we found that even parents living in the high-resource neighborhoods responded to this image of the city by restricting their adolescents' freedom. As one mother living in one of the safer neighborhoods put it,

> Like a lot of times she doesn't believe that anything can happen to her in this neighborhood. She feels it's the safest neighborhood anywhere. That scares me because I tell her, "No, it's everywhere. It's in this neighborhood too. You might not hear about it as often, but it's here."

Following the same pattern that we observed in the use of promotive strategies, few significant neighborhood trends emerged in the within-household monitoring and disciplining strategies that parents were using. No differences occurred either in rules regarding curfews or in parents' reports of whether they would know if their adolescents were home on time or not. Similarly, there was no variability by neighborhood type in where the adolescents went after school and whether they were supervised by adults when they arrived there.

In addition, we found no evidence of neighborhood variations on measures of discipline consistency, with a single exception: parents in better neighborhoods appeared somewhat lax in their discipline enforcement, perhaps because they were less concerned with neighborhood dangers and thought that they could afford to allow their adolescents greater lati-

tude. As we noted earlier, parents and adolescents in our study have begun to renegotiate their relationship. This process usually involves some
awkward maneuvers on the part of both parties. This initial awkwardness
can play itself out in what looks like inconsistent discipline practices. If
children in better neighborhoods seek greater autonomy at earlier ages,
they could elicit more inconsistent discipline practices from their parents
during this early adolescent period.

In addition, effective parents in more dangerous neighborhoods are
undoubtedly aware of the need to be particularly consistent in their discipline practices due to the adolescents' increased risk of encountering serious dangers outside the household. Michelle, Robert's mother, for instance, recognizes the need to increase the flexibility of her discipline
practices now that her son is getting older; at the same time, she is extremely cognizant of the dangers present in her neighborhood. Consequently, she feels she cannot afford to risk being too flexible. When we
first interviewed her, she insisted that Robert be in the house by dark
each evening, and she continued to maintain clear and consistent structure in the rules and daily routines within the family. When reinterviewed later in the year, she had loosened up the curfew rules some
and had given Robert a bigger voice in decision making, but was still
quite concerned about the dangers in their neighborhood and among the
peer networks in which Robert might get involved.

In sum, then, we found little evidence of neighborhood effects on the
within-household types of monitoring and controlling strategies that
parents use. The major neighborhood effects are linked to controlling the
freedom of early adolescents outside the household. But even this practice is not uniform. Within each type of neighborhood, wide variation
was evident, signifying a high amount of discretion from household to
household in the same geographic area. Marcia's family, for example,
used very controlling and restrictive strategies, even though they lived
in one of our better neighborhoods. Both Robert and Marcia expressed
some disappointment in their parents' continuing high level of control
and restrictions. But there was a strong positive relationship between
these young adolescents and their parents, and their parents' restrictiveness was understood to be part of a set of practices linked in each
family to religious values and norms. Both Robert and Marcia indicated
that they respected their parents' efforts to protect and guide them.

These examples illustrate the wide range of factors that we must take
into account in order to understand the connections between neighborhoods, resources, family management strategies, social capital, and successful adolescent development. Effective parenting relies on management strategies that make developmental good sense within the complex

contexts in which the families dwell and within the distinctive family cultures that have developed over many years. In other words, the family practices are shaped by a myriad of local conditions, many of which are even more local than neighborhood milieus.

Other Family Management Strategies

DAILY ROUTINES.   We also assessed the regularity of the parents' and adolescents' daily schedules: getting up in the morning, mealtimes, doing homework, and going to bed. As one might expect, families in the low-resource neighborhoods reported more irregularity in their time schedules than families in the better neighborhoods. However, most families in all three types of neighborhoods reported relatively high levels of regularity (the means ranged from 1.05 to 2.00 on a 3-point scale, with 1 = same time every day, and 2 = same time about half of the time). Families living in the low-resource neighborhoods experienced slightly more changes in such family characteristics as the house the family lives in, the place the child sleeps, and the child's school than families living in the high-resource neighborhoods. However, it should be noted that the absolute number of these kinds of changes in the previous twelve months is low in all three neighborhood types (1.09 versus 1.26).

INSTITUTIONAL INVOLVEMENTS.   The only significant neighborhood differences relating to institutional involvement occurred on our school-related measures. Parents in the best neighborhoods reported participating in activities at their adolescents' school much more often (M = 6 times) than parents in either of the other two neighborhood types (M = 2.0; see also Lareau 1989b). Families in the better neighborhoods were also much more likely to have enrolled their children in private schools, particularly parochial ones. Fifty-three percent of the children living in the high-resource neighborhoods, compared to only 14 percent of the children living in the lowest-resource neighborhoods and 20 percent of the children in the medium-resource neighborhoods, attended private schools. This difference in private school enrollment is the largest neighborhood difference we found and accounts, in part, for the neighborhood differences in school involvement by parents. Private schools provide more opportunities for, and have higher expectations regarding, parent participation at the school (Bryk, Lee, and Holland 1993).

Given the close connection between sending one's child to a private school and other social-class characteristics such as income, parent education, and two-parent marital status, this difference reflects the power of family economic resources coupled with family beliefs regarding the differential payoff of attending private versus public schools. The decision to put one's child in a private school also varied by race, even in the most economically advantaged neighborhoods: white parents were much more likely to have placed their children in private schools in all three types of neighborhoods. Black families appear to be less likely to use this family management strategy even when they have the economic resources to do so. Instead, black families rely more on other social institutions such as the church for help in raising their children, and the level of these kinds of institutional involvements did not differ across these three types of neighborhoods.

Attending private school is also closely related to successful academic outcomes among the adolescents living in our worst neighborhoods. Although a substantial portion of the most successful adolescents in all three neighborhood types attended private, religious-affiliated schools, this was particularly true for adolescents living in the low-resource neighborhoods. For example, Greg Ellis, who lives in a very bad section of a predominantly white neighborhood, attends Catholic high school. His mother, Linda, indicated that it was very important to her and her husband to send all of their children to Catholic schools despite the fact that doing so prevents them from moving out of their distressed neighborhood and is forcing them into debt.

It is instructive to contrast the neighborhood difference found for parent participation at school with the absence of neighborhood differences on parent-adolescent interactions on homework. Why is there a neighborhood difference on involvement at school when there is no neighborhood difference on involvement in school-related activities at home? This may reflect the race difference in neighborhood membership. A similar finding has emerged in other studies. For example, in another study of adolescent development being conducted by Eccles and Sameroff, also in conjunction with the MacArthur Research Network on Successful Adolescent Development in High-Risk Settings, African-American working- and middle-class parents were more likely to focus their school-related interactions with their adolescents on activities at home than on various activities at the school. The white middle-class parents showed the opposite pattern: high rates of participation at school coupled with somewhat less direct, school-related interaction with their adolescents at home. In an earlier study, Clark (1983) also found that black parents of high-achieving youth differed from black parents of low-achieving youth primarily in the level of their involvement in their children's schoolwork at home.

These results suggest that it is primarily white, middle-class parents who define their role in their children's education in terms of participation at school (Lareau 1989b). Other groups of "involved" parents appear to see their role more in terms of working with the children at home to support learning. This difference may reflect different cultural understandings of the "proper" role of parents as guardians of their children's success in school as well as parents own schooling experience. Some parents, for instance, may view the school and its personnel warily, either because of racial or social-class discrimination or because of their own unsuccessful experiences at school while they were growing up. These parents will be less likely to join traditional parent-school organizations, feeling more comfortable with expressing their commitment to their children's education in a home setting. Unfortunately, teachers may misinterpret this lack of involvement at school as a lack of parental interest in their children's education.

Alternatively, the neighborhood difference could reflect the lack of receptivity of schools in poorer neighborhoods to parent involvement. Staff at these schools may believe that parents either do not want to be involved or do not have the skills necessary to be involved (Epstein 1990). The "horror stories" related by some parents during their longer interviews lend support for both of these interpretations. Mark Sanders' mother's experience in trying to intervene on her son's behalf is a case in point. When Mark was failing the tenth grade, Mrs. Sanders went to school to try to request assistance for him. She spoke to the dean of men, who, she claims, not only did not provide any sympathy or helpful suggestions, but seemed eager to write Mark off, telling her to sign her son out of school and get him a job. She never went back to the school again, even though she continued to pursue other avenues of outside help—for example, seeking psychological counseling for herself and her younger son when he began to get into trouble with the law. Negative experiences like the one Mrs. Sanders relates can effectively undermine any collaborative efforts that schools and families may make on behalf of a troubled teen.

This chapter has provided a descriptive overview of the management strategies and parenting practices used by the families in this study. Most families appear to be functioning at least moderately well, using parenting practices appropriate to the ages of their children. Nonetheless, a wide range exists in parenting practices and family management strategies that is largely independent of neighborhood quality. We found no evidence of greater family dysfunction in high-risk neighborhoods. Neighborhood variations that we found are consistent with ones that emerged in the earlier ethnographic study: greater circumspection and restrictiveness in the areas with high dangers and low resources. Neighborhood differences were much more likely to occur in out-of-household family management strategies than in family process measures relating to within-household parenting practices.

As might be expected, families in the low-resource neighborhoods were more focused on preventing bad things from happening to their children than families in high-resource neighborhoods. Those living in the better neighborhoods were more involved in community-based promotive activities. Moreover, the children themselves were more likely to have sought out such activities independently than were adolescents living in the low-resource neighborhoods, reflecting the greater autonomy granted to adolescents in these communities, largely because of the presence of co-socializing institutions.

More objective dangers are present in the low-resource neighborhoods, and competent parenting in these neighborhoods requires greater attention to them. Similarly, since fewer community-based resources are available to adolescents in these areas, competent parents are more hesitant about allowing their children the autonomy to pursue activities on their own. They keep a tighter reign on their children, relying on preventive strategies.

One might assume from these findings that the parents in the low-resource neighborhoods were more "authoritarian" in their parenting practices (and some researchers have reached this conclusion). We think such a characterization is overly simplistic and decontextualized. Competent parenting requires parents to adapt their strategies to the community they live in, to the values that the family holds, and to the age of their child. The literature that links an "authoritative" parenting style to positive outcomes has focused largely on families living in reasonably good neighborhood settings. And the designation of what constitutes "authoritative" versus "authoritarian" parenting is often made on the strength of a few indicators broken into categories based on the sample being studied. Yet these studies often read as though there is some absolute standard for classifying families into these categories. We believe one must adopt a contextual and developmental perspective on what constitutes competent parenting. This view leaves us reluctant to attach labels—such as authoritarian, authoritative, or permissive—to specific patterns of parenting. We prefer instead to focus on what constitutes competent parenting within the particular community where the family lives.

Marcia's family highlights the fact that adopting a simplified view of Baumrind's (1989) classification system, even in white, middle-class families, is problematic. Although this family might appear authoritarian in terms of the restrictions placed on Marcia's autonomy, the family is functioning very well, and its restrictive practices take on a more benign character in view of the family's value system and the close and very positive emotional relationships among the family members.

Although some of the predicted associations between neighborhood characteristics and family management strategies were significant, by and large the distribution of parenting strategies was quite similar across the neighborhoods of different qualities. There were many more variations in parenting practices within a neighborhood than between neighborhoods. As discussed in chapter 3, a similar pattern characterizes the distribution of our adolescent outcome measures. These patterns suggest that both parenting and adolescent outcomes are linked more strongly to proximal forces such as individual differences and family-level processes, than to more distal forces, such as neighborhood contextual characteristics. In the next two chapters, we explore this hypothesis, first by assessing the extent to which variations in parenting practices are related to successful adolescent development, and then by gauging the degree to which parenting processes are influenced by the parents' psychological characteristics and by family-level organizational characteristics.

However, neither of these sets of analyses addresses the more fundamental question underlying this study: namely, does the very nature of "effective" parenting depend on the characteristics of the neighborhood in which the family lives? Thus far, the findings suggest that parents in all types of neighborhoods are doing what experts would consider to be good parenting. In addition, at this point in their lives, most adolescents in all types of neighborhoods are developing along what experts would consider to be "successful" pathways. And, as we will learn in the next chapter, variations in parenting practices are linked to variations in adolescent outcomes in the manner one would expect.

As adolescents get older, however, they spend increasingly less time at home and increasingly more time in their neighborhoods. They are likely to be more exposed over time to both the assets and the dangers of their larger community. To the extent that this is true, they should be affected by these neighborhood conditions. This shift in influence will complicate the role of parenting. Parenting practices that would be more than adequate to ensure successful development in safe and resource-rich neighborhoods may be insufficient to protect adolescent development in higher-risk neighborhoods. Parents may need to exert exceptional control and efficacy in these neighborhoods to protect their adolescents from the dangers and risks in their communities.

Parenting Matters

With the assistance of
SARAH E. LORD

Being able to bend and not [saying], "All right, this is the rule, you know, this is how things have to be." Because circumstances dictate certain behaviors. What kinds of rules would you bend? Okay, even with his bedtime. Um, his bedtime is 10, especially during school hours, school week, but there are times when, um, like football season, Monday night football. Now every Monday he can't stay up, but if it's a big game that he feels is a big game or if it's his favorite team, then I'll let him stay up a little while longer. I think you have to be flexible because life is flexible you know.
—Michelle James

I got him to the tenth (grade). I mean, I went through so much getting him to the tenth. I mean, I raised sand. I got on the ball, I kept on his toes, and he passed.
—Tina Newman

I tried and talked to him and I do the best I can . . . but I just don't know how to get it through.
—Lisa Sanders

We learned in the previous chapter that parents use diverse strategies to realize their goals. As the quotations above indicate, some are quite specific and strategic. They may, for example, be involved in organizations that benefit the local schools or support extracurricular programs. They may be helping their children stay out of trouble by participating with them in joint activities sponsored through church or civic groups. Most, however, rely on in-home strategies, insisting that their children stay inside the house and off the streets, reminding their children to do their homework, and requiring them to help out at home. A number of these parents are also following the conventional path of emotional support, consistent discipline, and sponsored independence.

The question to be explored in this chapter is whether and how these parenting efforts matter. Responses to open-ended interviews reveal some mothers despair at their lack of effectiveness. Mark's mother, for example, feels that she has lost the battle and has no idea how to regain control of behavior and the respect due a parent. Other parents, like Michelle, are more confident about their actions as parents and believe that they are still able to influence the course of their young adolescents' lives. But even in the family experience of these more effective parents, one detects the hard struggle to be effective amid the adversities of street life and gang violence.

Our data highlight the subtle differences among parenting practices in a complex system of social relationships. Within the family, parenting practices reflect the parents' goals for their children as well as the history of parent-child interactions and parents' personal dispositions toward the exercise of control (Maccoby and Martin 1983). Over time, parent and child develop a style of interacting with each other. The nature and quality of this style varies greatly across families in ways that relate systematically to successful and unsuccessful outcomes in children's behavior.

Under optimal conditions, parents and children develop a trusting attitude and a warm emotional bond from the beginning of their relationship. In such families, parents provide clear and consistent messages about expectations and rules. The children, in turn, are motivated to follow them because they are closely attached to their parents. Such parents are also likely to provide ample opportunities for children to develop skills necessary for success in important arenas outside the family (e.g., school, community, and the labor market). As children mature in expected ways, parents gradually allow them to engage in more self-management, at the same time making sure that they are protected from community dangers and risks.

It may be difficult to identify exactly what the parents of this type are doing to maintain discipline and positive behavior in their children, particularly once they enter adolescence. A successful parent-child system may need very few rules when children have incorporated parental norms as their own code of behavior. Similarly, parents are unlikely to carry out explicit family management when their young adolescent children are already well integrated into protective and promotive institutions outside the family. In such families, one would expect to see high levels of direct management only in response to emergencies.

Parenting is a developmental process: it is formulated over time amid a system of changing relationships. We must keep this complexity in mind as we explore the impact of parenting practices on adolescent behavior. The complexity of this interactive system is captured well in our qualitative interviews but, for various reasons, is less adequately represented in our quantitative analyses. This is so in part because we have data at only one point in time, making it impossible to determine the causal order of effects (if one can even speak in a causal framework when it comes to describing family interaction). Longitudinal data would probably not fully rectify this problem, because the nature of the interactive processes themselves are bidirectional and often quite subtle. Survey measures provide only a snapshot of a complex process that can take a variety of equally positive forms in different families. Consequently, we should not expect strong effects from the use of traditional regression analyses.

With these limitations in mind, we still think it is useful to make use of cross-sectional data as a means of identifying potentially important influences on the course of adolescent development, understanding full well that we must take great care in interpreting the results. We make use of traditional regression analysis to show the relative predictive power of the parenting measures for each domain of successful development, taking account of a family's ethnicity and the children's age and gender because these demographic factors are associated with parenting processes and children's behaviors. We supplement the regression analysis with a more person-centered approach to gain a broad overview of how parenting practices are linked to general patterns of success. We begin our analyses by providing some descriptions of what we learned from our case studies, as a way to present the daunting challenge of teasing out the potential sources of parental "influences" in a statistical analysis.

PROFILES OF ADOLESCENT COMPETENCE BY FAMILY MANAGEMENT STRATEGIES

Four profiles of adolescent competence were derived in chapter 3 from our measures of successful adolescent development: academically competent youth, socially involved youth, at-risk youth, and delinquent youth. Using case records based on intensive interviews, we first identify youth who represent each adolescent type and then compare them on family influences. This is followed by a quantitative analysis of family effects—modeling family processes and management strategies. To make our discussion of the qualitative data more focused, we return to the youth introduced in chapter 3. These adolescents, eight in all, exemplify the kinds of variations that we observed in our case studies.

Academically Competent Adolescents

Several of the families we interviewed had adolescents in the academically competent group; our examples are Robert James and Christine Lang. Robert's parents are confident of their parenting ability and appear to have worked out a reasonable balance between the control they exercise and the support they provide for his autonomy. In turn, Robert acknowledges that although his parents continue to place many restrictions on his behaviors, they are also granting him increasing latitude to make his own decisions now that he is older. He also endorses the values that guide his parents' restrictions.

As we have said, Robert's family is also intensively involved in a religious organization, and he attends activities at his church several nights each week along with most of his friends. Thus, his parents have managed to influence their son's peer associations through participation in a religious community. In light of this supportive and affectionate family context, it is not surprising to find that Robert is not involved in either problematic behavior patterns or peer groups.

> My Dad he's busy so we hook up time especially on the weekends and stuff. And you know, go out, play sports cause he's athletic and too and stuff as a kid and stuff. And see, we're alike, so ah, I play basketball a lot. We play chess, he taught me how to play chess. Sometime he bring out the chess board and we'll just play, see how far I be playing some of the games. They say I look just like him. A lot, a lot of friends. I guess, personality, ah, our facial expressions, I guess. And we're just about the same person almost, real, real close.

We should emphasize, however, that Robert's family (although not Robert's outcomes) was atypical of many families in our study in two important ways. They were the only Jehovah's Witnesses in our qualitative follow-up, and the community they belonged to, through their church participation, was truly remarkable. The family's social world revolved almost completely around their church membership. Also, Michelle James and her husband were extremely gifted parents, who balanced a high degree of restrictiveness with exceptional sensitivity to their children's developmental needs. The James's experience shows us one way, albeit a rare one in our sample of urban families, by which successful adolescence can be nurtured within a family.

Christine Lang, another academic achiever, belonged to a family more typical of our study participants. Like many European-Americans in the study, Christine comes from a two-parent household of modest resources. The family is Catholic, and Christine attended a Catholic high school for girls. Beverly, Christine's mother, did not exhibit the same level of parenting skill that Michelle James did. She and her husband tended to yield little control to their daughter. Whereas Michelle James was willing to be flexible about household rules as her children matured, Beverly Lang adhered to strict rules. Christine was forbidden to go out on week nights until she was in the middle of her junior year of high school, when she managed to negotiate one social evening a week.

In some important respects, however, these two families used similar strategies in managing their children's lives. Both families relied on church communities to provide structure and social support—with an important difference: The Langs' Catholic community was geographically based; the parish church was within two blocks of the family home, and until Christine went to high school, her friends had been drawn from the neighborhood and parish. The Jameses constructed a functional community that was spread throughout a larger area of the city. The Jameses' strategies were much more self-conscious than the Langs'. Michelle James spoke easily about her hopes that the church and its teachings would provide some "protection" from the dangers of the street, whereas Beverly Lang did not articulate such hopes.

Socially Involved Adolescents

Lakisha Wilkenson's family is much poorer than Robert's or Christine's, and her parents are divorced. Her father is an alcoholic, and her mother has been responsible for most of the parenting. Alicia is less confident of her parenting and disciplinary effectiveness than Michelle, and her disciplinary practices are not as consistent as those reported by Robert's family. Nonetheless, Lakisha's emotional relationship with her mother remains strong, and the disciplinary practices and support for autonomy are still within the competent range.

What distinguishes Lakisha's family is its heavy use of institutional resources. Alicia readily discusses her involvement in a variety of institutional settings as her children have grown, describing how she has changed her involvements over the years to reflect the age and needs of her children. Active in religious organizations when her children were young, she switched the focus of involvement to neighborhood organizations and then to the schools as they got older. Both Lakisha and Alicia also discuss the active role Alicia has played in helping Lakisha solve important life dilemmas, ranging from a dispute at work to obtaining adequate birth control counseling. Her efforts to get Lakisha involved in constructive activities may well have contributed to Lakisha's success in other areas of her life and development.

Greg Ellis's parents, Linda and John, have a parenting style that differs from Alicia Wilkenson's. Whereas Alicia's institutional involvement tends to change with her children's development, Linda and John Ellis have been members of a particular Catholic parish for many years. Within that community, John Ellis is a long-time softball coach, and Linda has maintained an active social life with other parishioners. The family, however, does not live within the parish proper but in a deteriorating adjacent community. Linda, who has expressed great concern for her children's safety in the neighborhood, encourages them to participate as much as possible in activities within the parish. In fact, Greg reports that *all* his friends live in the parish. Although Linda would like to move out of her current neighborhood to the community where her family spends time and feels comfortable, she and her husband are economically unable to do so. Linda reported that she and her husband decided to send their three children to Catholic schools, beginning with the parochial grade school, even though their decision has meant that they cannot always pay their bills, let alone save the money necessary to finance residential relocation.

At-Risk Adolescents

JJ Newman exemplifies our third profile on at-risk youth. He lives in one of the worst neighborhoods with a single mother who works part-time in the evenings as a barmaid. The family is quite poor. The parenting practices of his mother, Tina, are characterized by contradictory styles. On the one hand, by her own admission, she has lost control over his behavior. Tina's demanding work schedule has limited her ability to monitor JJ's activities after school and in the evenings, and thus she has been unable to provide much structure for him. When he violates her rules, she alternates between withdrawal and excessive restriction backed by emotional outbursts; she reports that neither strategy has worked very well since JJ became sixteen.

On the other hand, Tina describes having gone to great lengths to help her son pass the tenth grade. Her efforts involved both external and internal management strategies, ranging from going to the school as his advocate several times to pleading with him repeatedly. When he began to fail again in the eleventh grade, she tried to repeat this success. Again, she approached school authorities and she urged him to do his schoolwork. This time she made little progress, and JJ ultimately failed the eleventh grade. Thus, even though Tina's discipline effectiveness is quite low, she persisted in trying to help her son make it through high school.

Like Tina Newman, Ruth Jones, Shawanda's mother, is a single parent living on public assistance. The family lives in an African-American neighborhood that has average resources. Like Tina, Ruth's aspirations for her daughter are high, but her resources for helping her daughter are limited. She is a diabetic in ill-health, and is currently raising a two-year-old granddaughter—the child of her oldest daughter who had recently died. Ruth reported that she would have liked to have the money to send Shawanda to a Christian school; Shawanda experienced a lot of peer problems in the public high school she attended. Ruth also declared that she had become exasperated by Shawanda's troubles. Relating her advice to Shawanda after an English teacher called to inform Ruth that Shawanda was not doing her work, she said,

> I told her that it's not doing her no good, you know, not to do her work and not to go to school. I told her that she's getting close to graduation and she should try to keep up with her schoolwork. She wants to drop out and go to Job Corps.

Later, however, Ruth reported that she was not "opposed to her dropping out and going to get her GED in the Job Corps." And when she was asked what, if anything, had changed between the way she parented Shawanda and the way she had parented Shawanda's older sisters, Ruth replied,

> Shawanda has more freedom, my other children, they didn't stay out quite as late as Shawanda. How did she come to have more freedom? I guess because I'm older and sicklier and I don't chastise her as much as I guess I should.

In sum, Ruth's management strategies focused on exhortations to do better, and she was frequently inconsistent in responding to her daughter's problems.

Paul Pulaski was the third at-risk teen we introduced in chapter 3. He and his family lived in a high-resource, European-American neighborhood. Like Tina and Ruth, Paul's mother Katja expressed considerable frustration at her child's behavior. She too, attempted to restrict his whereabouts and complained bitterly about his friends. Katja worked extremely long hours, as did her husband, which made it difficult for them to supervise Paul's behavior, particularly after school.

Delinquent Adolescents

Mark Sanders fit into our fourth and most problematic profile of adolescent behavior. He lives with his widowed mother, Lisa, who works a full-time job to support the family and two younger siblings. Lisa is socially isolated and depressed, and has very little confidence in her parenting ability. She reports never having felt like an effective parent and regrets letting things get out of hand when the children were young:

> Yeah, with the boys I found myself, you know when they were younger and all, I always used to just give in to them and give them whatever. But then as they got older, that's when I started to realize I shouldn't have been doing that. And that's when a lot of our problems started.

Despite sporadic efforts to discipline Mark and to seek help from counselors, Lisa clearly has very little control over Mark. If he comes in after curfew, for example, she reports that she yells at him but that he just brushes it off. "I feel that he's just comin' here to goof around and, and when he does come he don't do his work and stuff like that. I tried and talked to him, and I do the best I can but I just don't know how to get it through." Mark is not doing very well on several of our measures of successful development. He dropped out of school, after failing the tenth grade twice; he drinks a lot of alcohol several times a week; and he was involved in very high levels of delinquent behavior at the time of our first interview.

These cases provide insights into the complexity of raising a teenager in inner-city Philadelphia. Clearly, parent behavior differs across these cases in ways that are consistent with the current development of their children, which points to a link between parenting quality and adolescent development. The stories also illustrate the bidirectional nature of parent-child interaction. The successful families have set up a dynamic that works well and involves both the parents and the children in a mutually supportive system. The less-successful families are caught in a negative interaction cycle that serves no one well. But how typical are these differences? To address this question, we examined whether parenting practices corresponded to different patterns of success among the youth in the larger sample surveyed in 1991.

As we have noted throughout, our measures of family process and management were designed with a family management perspective on parenting behaviors. This perspective enlarges the traditional focus on mother-child interaction, drawing on the role of parents and children in formal and informal social settings and institutions. More specifically, we developed indicators of both the quality of everyday interactions between parents and children and the ways in which these parents try to manage their children's interactions with the school and the community.[1] Like other family studies, ours includes measures of the two most widely acknowledged dimensions of parenting: control and emotional support

(Maccoby and Martin 1983). Parental control is measured by discipline effectiveness and support for autonomy.

Before assessing the effects of parenting and family management on adolescent outcomes, we combined the former into higher-order constructs, using factor analysis and theoretical considerations. Five summary measures of parenting resulted:[2] (1) *support for autonomy,* (2) *positive family climate,* (3) *discipline effectiveness,* (4) *investment,* and (5) *restrictiveness.* The last two measure family management within and outside of the household. The first two index more traditional aspects of family process and socialization. Discipline effectiveness reflects the traditional models of socialization *and* family management. Support for autonomy measures how parents regulate the balance between overcontrol and undercontrol of their children.

We also created summary measures of other family management strategies, such as *economic adjustments* that parents make because of their own relation to the external world.[3] Although these management practices are not directly aimed at managing children's connections with the outside world, they do affect their experiences both at home and in the outside world (Elder and Caspi 1988).

Another set of family management measures captures the informal connections parents have with social resources, networks, and institutions outside of the family, including participation in religious and other formal, community-based institutions *(institutional connections),* and connections to social networks that provide access to resources, positive role models, and job opportunities *(positive social networks).*[4] As noted in chapter 4, few parents included these connections and activities in their descriptions of family management strategies. However, these behaviors and institutional resources constitute one of the primary ways in which parents influence their children's connections to positive institutions and opportunities beyond the family and its immediate neighborhood.

A clear pattern, consistent with the qualitative data, differentiates the successful and less-successful groups, as shown in figures 5.1 and 5.2. Leaving "positive networks" and economic adjustment out of the analysis, we find that support of autonomy, discipline effectiveness, and positive family climate are significantly more prominent in the *academically competent* and *socially involved* groups than in the *at-risk* and *delinquent* groups. These traditional dimensions of parenting practices do a good job of differentiating positive from negative developmental outcomes.

Dimensions of parenting also differentiate the two problematic groups from one another. The delinquent youth are living in families that look less functional on most of these indicators than the at-risk youth (all except "family climate"). These findings are consistent with the work of

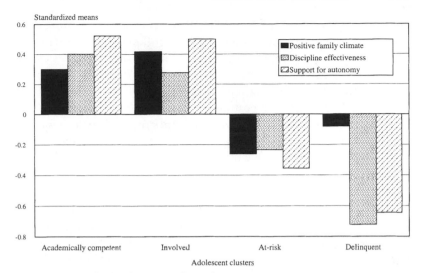

Figure 5.1 Standardized Means of Family Processes

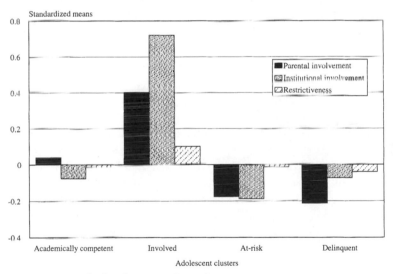

Figure 5.2 Standardized Means of Family Processes

Patterson, DeBaryshe, and Ramsey (1989), especially for the effective-ness of discipline. Delinquent youth, like Mark, are clearly living in situ-ations that lack either good communication patterns or effective disci-pline relationships with adults. In addition, the parents of these youth are not engaged in constructive efforts to involve their adolescents in appropriate developmental settings or circumstances. Although certainly functioning less well than the families of the two positive profiles of youth, the families of at-risk youth like JJ are less likely to report positive interactions with their adolescents, but they still make efforts to involve them in growth-promoting contexts. Presumably, the parents of at-risk families are engaged in unrewarding encounters arising from negative sanctions that they are exercising to bring their children into line.

Because "involvement in positive activities" is the primary adolescent outcome that distinguishes the two successful groups of adolescents, it is not surprising that parental investment and institutional involvement (as management strategies) differ most strikingly between them. These results suggest that the primary benefit adolescents derive from having highly involved parents is the opportunity to become highly involved themselves. Several investigators have stressed the importance of being involved in positive activities and organizations for subsequent adolescent development, especially as a protective factor against problem behavior and as a path into work and educational opportunities during the transition to adulthood (Carnegie Corporation 1992; Eccles and Barber in press; Holland and Andre 1987; Larson 1994; Otto and Alwin 1977). Involvement may be especially important for adolescents growing up in high-risk neighborhoods, where exposure to dangerous activities can be both prevalent and highly salient. To date, however, very little actual research has established the protective power of involvement in constructive activities.

In summary, the qualitative interviews and the profile-group analyses suggest that both face-to-face parenting practices and strategies of managing the world outside the households make a difference in adolescent development. Furthermore, the behavioral profiles indicate that specific practices may be differentially related to particular modes of successful development. Out-of-home strategies may be especially relevant for activity involvement because they link families with social institutions. In contrast, the more traditional measures of parenting practices, such as discipline effectiveness and warmth, seem to have particular relevance for the prevention of problem behaviors and delinquency. To explore these possibilities, we turn to regression analyses in prediction models.

PREDICTING ADOLESCENT SUCCESS AND PROBLEM BEHAVIOR

Regression analysis is a statistical procedure that can simultaneously compare the influence of a number of family factors on adolescent behaviors. When we compare the size of the betas in table 5.1 two conclusions are apparent. Parental behavior clearly makes a difference in adolescent success and problem behavior, as the profile groups attest. But the influ-

Table 5.1

Adolescent Competence and Problem Behavior by Family Processes and Management Strategies: Regression Coefficients in Standard Form and Zero-Order Correlation Coefficient

| | Adolescent competence and problem behavior | | | | | | | | | |
| | Activity involvement | | Academic competence | | Psychological adjustment[a] | | Self-competence[b] | | Problem behavior | |
Predictor	Beta	r	Beta	r	Beta	r	Beta	r	Beta	r
Family processes										
Positive family climate	.06	.15*	-.05	.13*	.15***	.43***	.04	.16*	.00	-.11*
Discipline effectiveness	.01	.05	.04	.15*	.19***	.43***	.09*	.19**	-.22***	-.27***
Support for autonomy	-.04	.07	.26***	.30***	.46***	.52***	.19***	.24***	-.08	-.18**
Management strategies										
Institutional connections	.42***	.48***	.17***	.17**	.06	.16*	-.10*	-.03	-.04	-.09
Social networks	.09**	.24**	.10**	.10	.05	.11*	.03	.01	.01	-.06
Economic adjustments	.02	.03	.09**	.10	-.01	-.05	.01	.05	-.08*	-.12*
Parental investment	.10**	.28**	-.01	.12*	-.03	.18**	.05	.08	.04	-.08
Restrictiveness	-.09**	-.04	.04	.04	-.03	.01	-.01	.01	-.07	-.10*
Controls										
Race (black = 1)	.00	.04	-.13***	.10	-.01	-.03	-.01	.01	.06	.09
Puerto Rican (PR = 1; other = 0)	-.02	.09	-.05	.04	-.01	.03	.00	-.01	.08*	-.02
Child's age	.02	-.06	-.01	-.02	.06	.03	.00	.00	.30***	.32***
Child's gender (male = 1)	.11***	.14ᵃ	-.17***	-.14ᵃ	-.03	-.01	-.06	-.06	.16***	.17***
F-Model	14.75***		8.47***		29.80***		3.54***		10.41***	
Adjusted R^2	.27		.18		.44		.08		.21	

a. Parent report

b. Adolescent report

$*p \leq .10; **p \leq .05; ***p \leq .01$

ence process is not the same across behavioral outcomes. Rather, *different* types of parental behavior seem to matter for different developmental outcomes; that is, parents appear to make a difference in their children's success, but they do so in different ways, depending on the domain of behavior examined.

Table 5.1 presents the results of ordinary least-square regression analyses of family effects. Each model, involving measures of family process and management strategies, is focused on an index of successful adolescent development, from activity involvement to problem behavior. We always control for the effects of caregiver's race/ethnicity (black versus white, and Puerto Rican versus other), adolescent age, and gender. The relative influence of types of parent behavior on particular outcomes is most readily identified by focusing our attention on the two types of family influences: family processes and management strategies. This contrast points out the strength of the association between each of the outcomes and traditional modes of parenting (family processes) as well as some of the management strategies that are less often referred to in the child development literature, ranging from institutional connections to parent restrictiveness.

Family Process

Consistent with findings from the profile groups, traditional measures of parenting relate most strongly to our measures of psychological adjustment, self-competence, and involvement in problem behavior.[5] However, even for these outcomes, different aspects of parenting seem particularly relevant. For example, a high incidence of problem behaviors is most strongly associated with ineffective discipline. We say "associated" because we cannot necessarily conclude that ineffective discipline precedes the occurrence of problem behavior. Healthy psychological development is linked primarily to developmentally appropriate support for joint decision making and autonomy. Again, the association is likely to be bidirectional.

SUPPORT FOR AUTONOMY AND SUCCESSFUL ADOLESCENT DEVELOPMENT. Support of autonomy is the parenting practice most strongly associated with successful psychological development. Once more, the causal direction of this association is hard to determine. Indeed, compelling theoretical reasons exist for suspecting that both directions of influence occur. For example, it is quite likely that parents are more willing to provide great support for autonomy if they believe their children are especially mature and psychologically healthy. Evidence from other studies also suggests a positive correlation between parental support for increased autonomy and children's behavior in the form of enhanced psychological development, intrinsic motivation, and positive self-esteem (e.g., Eccles et al. 1991; Epstein and McPartland 1977; Grolnick and Ryan 1989; Lord, Eccles, and McCarthy 1994). No doubt parents both respond to the increasing maturity of adolescents and foster further development by providing age-appropriate opportunities for children to participate in family decision making and to take greater responsibility for their own behavior.

Consistent with results from other research, support for autonomy is also a strong predictor of academic achievement. Several studies, for instance, have noted a positive association between the extent of adolescent participation in decision making and classroom performance, grades, and standardized achievement scores (e.g., Eccles et al. 1991, 1993; Grolnick and Ryan 1989; Lord, Eccles, and McCarthy 1994). This association is also quite likely to reflect a reciprocal relationship: parents use academic performance to judge their children's maturity, and support of autonomy has been shown to foster independent mastery and self-regulation (see Grolnick and Ryan 1989), which are in turn linked to better academic performance. Having a say in decisions that affect them directly, such as choice of clothing, family vacations, or summer employment, provides the adolescent with a chance to practice cognitive skills, which can facilitate academic gains at school.

As the next section makes clear, parents should continue to exercise control over their adolescents' behavior, but their control must be age-appropriate and should not undermine their children's growing autonomy. Recognizing the importance of appropriate control, both Ryan (1992), and Barber, Olson, and Shagle (1994) have distinguished between two types: psychological and behavioral. They stressed the negative consequences of excessive psychological control on the mental health of young people. Lack of support for autonomy at this age would be an example of excessive psychological control because it undermines self-confidence and prevents adolescents from getting the practice they need to develop decision-making and coping skills.

Behavioral control, particularly control over adolescents' interactions with the outside world, can have either positive or negative consequences, depending on the meaning of the restrictions within the larger family context. Given the neighborhoods in which many of the families in this study live and the age of the children, we expect a continuing need for high levels of extra-familial behavioral control. Most families in this study, as we learned in the last chapter, regularly engage in high levels of monitoring and restriction. The positive association of the discipline effectiveness scale, which includes monitoring, with psychological adjustment demonstrates the need for both appropriate psychological autonomy and high levels of behavioral control to assure successful development.[6]

The developmental benefits of strong support for autonomy *and* behavioral control are evident in the families of both Robert and Marcia. The parents of both adolescents exercise very tight control over their activities in the outside world. Both children were enrolled in special schools: Robert was attending a business-oriented high school, and Marcia has attended a parochial school. Their parents enforce strict rules regarding curfew and geographic mobility. But the parents' behavioral restrictions make good sense in terms of the neighborhoods in which they live and the centrality of religion in the families. The adolescents also acknowledge these justifications as part of their acceptance of parental rules and decisions. Equally important, however, is the parents' provision of support for autonomy and respect for their children's maturity at home. Robert's mother particularly emphasized the importance of knowing which rules to bend and which rules to enforce strictly. From an outsider's perspective, the parents might seem too controlling, given their children's age, and in fact both adolescents predictably expressed some discontent with their parents' continuing restrictions on their freedom outside the home.

What seems critical is that the "optimal level" of both types of control is critical for successful parenting of adolescents. Young people should feel that their parents respect and appreciate their growing maturity, and they in turn should respect their parents' judgment regarding rules intended to protect them from dangers in their external world. Roberta Simmons and Dale Blyth referred to this optimal level as a "zone of safety," in which individuality can be explored without excessive long-term risk (Simmons and Blyth 1987). Similarly, Eccles and her colleagues (1993) have argued that optimal adolescent development occurs only when there is a good fit between the provision for autonomy in the family (and at school) and the amount of autonomy the adolescents think is appropriate. This perspective leads to the prediction that both too much and too little parental control are likely to produce less-than-optimal development. In a recent and as yet unpublished focus group study of adolescents, Marta Tienda found support for this view in the explanations given by youth for teen pregnancy. They felt that some girls get pregnant partly as a rebellion against what they believe to be overcontrolling parents, while other girls get pregnant because their parents are too lax.

DISCIPLINE EFFECTIVENESS AND PROBLEM BEHAVIOR. Consistent with the predictions of developmental scientists, lack of discipline effectiveness is highly predictive of problem behavior. This result also illustrates an exchange of bidirectional influences. The subscales making up this construct are very similar to the family interaction patterns that Patterson (1992) and his colleagues describe as lacking in the coercive cycle of discipline that is common in the homes of adolescents with severe behavior problems. They include the following: how effective parents think they are in disciplining their children, how consistent they are in enforcing their disciplinary actions, and their degree of reluctance to enforce discipline out of fear of reprisal from their children.

Ineffective parents are frequently inconsistent in their discipline practices, and when they try to implement discipline, they often resort to harsh, coercive strategies that can involve violence. As aggressive children become adolescents, they respond to these coercive encounters with extreme anger, often culminating in violence. This pattern of interaction represented by the association between ineffective discipline and problem behavior is evident in the relationship between Mark and his mother.

Family Management Strategies

Unlike traditional parenting behaviors, out-of-home management strategies, particularly those linked to institutional connections, are strongly related to both academic achievement and involvement in constructive social activities (see table 5.1). In contrast, neither social network ties nor economic adjustments are related to patterns in successful behavior at this stage in the adolescents' lives.

INSTITUTIONAL CONNECTIONS. Parental involvement in organized activities can be thought of as a form of social capital. It strongly predicts youth involvement in similar types of activities. No doubt, parents' social capital can be drawn on by children who are, so to speak, automatically linked to constructive activities and organizations by virtue of their parents' connections.

Parents who participate in organizations also have children who are performing better academically. This finding has been suggested by Coleman and Hoffer's (1987) work on the impact of parochial schooling and by work documenting the importance of parent involvement at school for children's academic achievement (e.g., Comer and Haynes 1991; Eccles and Harold 1993; Epstein 1990). Our finding is consistent with this research, but "institutional connections" in our work includes involvement with institutions other than school. Parental involvement in these other institutions probably influences children's academic competence through exposure to role models, family access to social networks, and values socialization.

Assuming that parents often take their children with them when they go to church or community-based centers, the children get the opportunity to observe and work with other adults who are actively involved in positive, out-of-home activities. Many of these types of institutions have their own educational functions, particularly with regard to socializing positive values. Additionally, participating in these institutions provides both parents and children with a wide social network that can give access to positive opportunities or assistance in time of need. Finally, the fact that parents are actively involved in out-of-home institutional organizations provides an opportunity for children to see their parents in a favorable light outside the household. Many children come to admire and model their parents' accomplishments.

We have encountered examples of these benefits in the families of Robert, Greg, and Christine, where the church played a key role in organizing family life. Lakisha illustrates the advantage of other types of institutional connections and family social capital. Lakisha's mother, Alicia, uses institutions in socializing her children, but, unlike parents who rely heavily on one institution (the church) closely tied to their core values, Alicia aligns her institutional connections with the developmental needs of her children. Not surprisingly, Lakisha, like Robert and Christine, has also been very involved in community and school activities. She was president of her eighth-grade class at school. In high school, she has shifted her extracurricular energies to activities more directly related to her career goals, including doing a summer internship through the entrepreneurial programs at her school. When the children were young, Alicia made a point of going to church with her children so that they could attend a Catholic elementary school. As they got older, she worked with a neighborhood organization to have street lights put up in their neighborhood, and played an active role in her children's schools. She is less involved at school now that Lakisha is in high school, but she made a point of contacting Lakisha's employer when a problem arose at work in order to be an advocate for her daughter, making it clear what kind of family Lakisha is from.

PARENTAL INVESTMENT.   Parental investment is related most strongly to youth's involvement in social activities. This index includes measures of both proactive and preventive family management, as well as family activities and daily routines. Apparently, these management strategies have their primary payoff in the extent to which children themselves become actively involved in organized activities and institutional settings outside school.

These management practices also yield the largest variation between neighborhoods. As one might expect, both adolescents and parents in the better neighborhoods have more institutional connections. Substantial variation exists within neighborhoods: while parents are more likely to become involved in organizations in better neighborhoods, many do not, and some parents in the least-advantaged communities are able to make institutional connections. But there is also substantial variation within neighborhood contexts. In chapter 7, we examine whether these connections operate differently in resource-rich neighborhoods—where they come more or less with the territory—than in resource-deprived neighborhoods, where they must be more actively pursued.

RESTRICTIVENESS.   We were surprised at the minimal association of parental restrictiveness and aspects of successful adolescent development. The importance of this family strategy for successful development in high-risk settings has been stressed in several ethnographic studies of inner-city youth (Jarrett 1992; Spencer and Dornbusch 1990). In this study, restrictiveness is only negatively related to high activity involvement. We found no evidence of a protective function of restrictiveness for any aspect of successful adolescent development.

However, restrictiveness does vary among neighborhoods. It is concentrated in poor residential areas with high rates of violence and crime. It seems likely that restrictiveness serves different functions and has different applications for parent-adolescent relations across neighborhoods. For example, restrictiveness may reflect a distrustful and authoritarian relationship between parents and their adolescents living in safe and resource-rich neighborhoods in contrast to its protective function in dangerous neighborhoods.

Before taking a closer look at these neighborhood differences, we must first become acquainted with household-level sources of variation that may possibly account for some of the variation at the neighborhood level. For example, some inner-city families were supported by incomes above $35,000, while others are living in dire poverty. Moreover, households varied as well in structure and organization. Finally, parents possess different cultural and psychological resources for coping with the multiple demands of work and family life. Chapter 6 examines how these household-level resources are linked to family process and management strategies and, in turn, to adolescent success, moving us one step closer to our ultimate goal of linking neighborhoods, parenting practices, and patterns of adolescent success.

Family Influences and Adolescents' Lives

With the assistance of
MONIKA ARDELT

I talk with the kids. They're people, so I treat them like people. My kids are not disrespectful.
—Michelle James, speaking of neighborhood kids

As prior chapters have shown, parents and their children differ far more within particular neighborhoods than they do between areas. It seems that, strictly from their place of residence, we cannot learn much about the success and failure of the urban youth in our sample. Indeed, even in the worst neighborhoods of this study, a significant number of black and white youth manage to succeed. Is this success due largely to the qualities of individual parents and their children?

Specifically, what influences distinguish youth who live in the same neighborhood, only a few blocks away from one another, such as Lakisha Wilkenson and JJ Newman? Though both have been raised by single mothers, Lakisha is on her way to college, with good grades and savings from part-time employment, and she has avoided unwanted pregnancy by using birth control. JJ, on the other hand, eventually dropped out of high school and fathered a child. What, if anything, did Lakisha's family do to help make this difference? Were there other significant influences, such as a supportive teacher or adult friend? This chapter explores such questions.

Family interaction processes and management strategies in this study distinguish adolescents at-risk from successful youth (chapter 5), who are defined as academically competent and socially involved. Such influences include nurturant family interaction, guided self-direction, effective discipline, and family strategies ranging from the placement of children in developmental activities to involvement in community social affairs and responsibilities. These strategies may also establish "functional" communities that are not bounded by a family's neighborhood, but instead link children through activities to people with shared values, norms, and understandings.

This chapter adds another dimension to the impact of parenting by considering multiple domains of parental and household resources as a potential pathway from family influences to adolescent competence (see model in chapter 2). First, we assess the links between socioeconomic and demographic factors, the psychological resources of parents, and the dimensions of adolescent success and problem behavior. Included among the socioeconomic and demographic factors, are family income, the education of parents, welfare dependency, household size, race, single-parent status, marital discord, the ages of parent and child, and the child's gender.

Three psychological resources have special relevance to parenting: (1) personal efficacy or beliefs of mastery as a parent; (2) personal resourcefulness, understood as the ability to bounce back from disappointments; and (3) the absence of mental health problems, such as depressed feelings, exhaustion, and anxiety. Socioeconomic hardship may diminish the personal efficacy of parents and thus undermine nurturant parenting (Elder et al. 1995; McLoyd 1990). In addition, each level of education tends to increase feelings of personal efficacy and resourcefulness (Bandura 1995; Eccles et al. 1997), which in turn may enhance parental encouragement of self-direction

Our objective is to identify "chains of influence" that bear upon the success and troubles of young adolescents in our Philadelphia neighborhoods and then to specify circumstances under which they vary. For example, parental support for the child's autonomy may turn out to be less potent in developing academic competence in low-income households or in communities with inadequate schools because the child is unable to take positive advantage of the autonomy granted. Perhaps, too, lack of income may erode a parent's capacity to stay on top of things, because that creates so many more problems to juggle.

To identify potential links, we ask several questions. First, are socioeconomic conditions among families and youth associated with the psychological resources of parents? For example, are welfare-dependent parents less apt than better-situated parents to recover from setbacks? As we have said before, because our analysis is confined to cross-sectional data, we must not think of this connection as a causal one. Second, we ask about the relationship of parental social and psychological resources to family dynamics and youth outcomes. This we do sequentially, first examining the role of social and economic conditions in influencing parenting behaviors, and then examining the extent to which these effects are accounted for by parents' psychological resources.

MEASURING SOCIAL INFLUENCES AND PERSONAL RESOURCES

Three sets of factors influence the self-appraisal of parents: their social and economic conditions, family composition and structure, and the parents' age as well as the age and gender of the children. The first category of socioeconomic conditions includes total family income, welfare receipt at the time of the interview, educational level of the parent or caregiver, race, and household size.[1] Factors directly relevant to the second category of family structure include single-parent household and a weak versus strong marital bond.[2] Single-parent status may result from the breakup of a marriage or it may result from procreation outside marriage, each of which could have different implications for the parents' well-being and competence. The third category tells us something about the life stage of parent and child. The behavioral differences between boys and girls could also be relevant to the conditions under which parents feel competent or effective.

The parents' psychological competencies or resources were measured by use of a number of separate scales designed to tap coping capacities:[3] the efficacy of parents, their personal resourcefulness, and their lack of mental health problems. Parental efficacy indicates the extent to which parents and caregivers believe that they are making a difference in the lives of their children, both directly and indirectly, for example, by changing the environment of the school or community. The other two scales are broader in scope in that they tap the general psychological functioning of the main caregiver. As one might expect, resourceful parents—those confident of their ability to recover from setbacks—also tend to describe themselves as making a constructive difference in their child's life ($r = .27$). Parents who score high on these scales typically report few mental problems (an average r of .32). In other words the separate measures of psychological resources are modestly interrelated.

The correlation coefficients linking each social and demographic factor to the three measures of parental resources are reported in appendix table A.6.1. The major story from this analysis is surprising, for it highlights the relative independence of socioeconomic resources and the psychological competencies and mental health of the parents. Parents who feel efficacious, resourceful, and generally on top of things are more or less evenly distributed among high- and low-income households, and among households receiving welfare and those that are not. African-American parents score just about as high as white parents. The only noteworthy correlation between education and resourcefulness (beta $= -.17$, $\leq.05$), is little more than a chance finding.

By comparison, single-parent households and discordant marriages are substantially related to parental psychological well-being (compared with strong marriages). Parents feel even less resourceful, efficacious, and mentally healthy in troubled marriages than do single parents (beta co-efficients range from .09 to .24). One reason for this outcome is that these families offer less protection against external pressures and hardships than when relations are more harmonious. Earlier analysis of the black families in this study shows that parents in single-parent households and discordant marriages are most vulnerable to the adverse psychological effects of economic pressures (Elder et al. 1995), such as emotional depression and a sense of parental ineffectiveness.

Turning to the life stage of parent and child, it appears that older parents feel more resourceful and mentally healthy than younger parents. They seem to exhibit and experience the wisdom that comes with age. But this interpretation does not apply to their feelings of efficacy as parents. Other things being equal, younger parents are more inclined to view themselves as efficacious in the parenting role. Energy may be a factor here, and patience, especially among parents who believe that they must be involved in their children's world.

Consider Pamela, an unmarried mother of three children. She has worked part-time as a hairdresser and has a record of public assistance. Her eldest son, John, is a member of the study. He is socially involved in school and has a solid academic record as well. We classified him as *involved*.

To make sure that John had positive male models in his life, Pamela sought help from men in her church and encouraged him to join a male church group. She hoped that these experiences would help him become a better citizen in the community and a young man who would one day assume responsibility as a parent. Consistent with our portrait of the involved parent in family management strategies, Pamela has continually sought out resources that enrich the experiences of her children, from tutoring to summer employment. As she observed,

> I'm a strong individual, and I know that I have enough sense that whatever I can't get him or give him, I can get it from someone else—someone who can give it to him. Someone is always in his life who can give those things to him. I'm not ashamed to ask, or afraid to ask or too prideful to ask for it or whatever.

INFLUENCES ON FAMILY DYNAMICS

Three family interaction processes are especially relevant to the development of both academic and social competence (see chapter 5): the involvement of youth in family decision making and problem solving (support for autonomy), the consistency and effectiveness of discipline (discipline effectiveness), and the emotional tone of family relations (positive family climate). A fourth type of family process embodies cultural practices, including family traditions as well as parents' efforts to forge racial and ethnic identification. This latter set of measures proved statistically inconsequential for the outcomes and thus was excluded from this chapter's analysis.

Qualitative interviews suggested that our measure of family traditions did not reveal how traditions matter. Parents' interpretations of family traditions played a substantial role in whether and how they chose to rely on those traditions in bringing up their children. Thus, one parent who was forced to go to church every Sunday as a child decided that her children could choose whether to go. A second parent concluded that her religious upbringing had been valuable, and she required her children to attend church. Not only did the parents' use or abandonment of family traditions depend upon their interpretations of the usefulness or moral importance of those traditions, but their interpretations changed over time as they and their children faced new circumstances. Thus, although our survey data do not indicate that family traditions and cultural practices were significant, we do not dismiss their importance as an ingredient in predicting successful development. Indeed, we return to their potential effects in chapter 9.

Two family management strategies were especially relevant to successful development among adolescents in the study (see chapter 5): institutional connections, referring to the parent's involvement in religion, community organizations and activities, and school and service groups; and parental investment, which entails promotive and protective actions by parents, such as getting the child involved in outside programs and warning the child about dangers in the community. Placement in private schools is one example of a parental investment strategy, but we index this activity by itself because it constitutes a separate and unique strategy. A third family management practice, which proved less relevant to successful development, is restrictiveness—limiting freedom of movement by requiring children to stay in the house after school or go only to certain parts of the neighborhood. Other strategies were unrelated to successful or problematic behavior and were dropped from the analysis that follows.

The full set of regression coefficients and their respective correlations

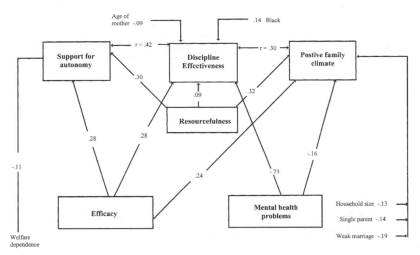

Figure 6.1 Types of Family Processes by Social and Psychological Factors: A Heuristic Model Based on Significant Regression Coefficients (Beta)

are presented in appendix table A.6.2. The first step of the analysis used multiple regression to estimate the effects of social and economic factors on each measure of parenting. Parents' psychological resources were added to the analysis in the next stage, although, as already noted, they did not add much to an explanation of socioeconomic effects, owing to their lack of association to parenting behaviors.

Three influence patterns emerged from the analysis, as shown in a set of heuristic models based only on statistically significant influences, direct and indirect. Figure 6.1 presents a model for our measures of support for autonomy, discipline effectiveness, and positive family climate; figure 6.2 presents a similar model for institutional connections, parental investment, and restrictiveness. All of the standardized coefficients reported in figures 6.1 and 6.2 were drawn from appendix tables A.6.1 and A.6.2.

First, support for autonomy and discipline effectiveness are linked primarily to the self-reported efficacy, resourcefulness, and mental health of parents or caregivers. Social resource and economic factors are of little consequence. Only welfare dependence lowered the prospects of parental support for the adolescent's autonomy. On the effectiveness of discipline, black parents tended to rank slightly higher than white parents.

Second, the family climate, as reported by the mother, varied by parental competence and family structure. Perhaps because of their resourcefulness in making a successful family, psychologically competent mothers are more likely to report congenial relations in the family when

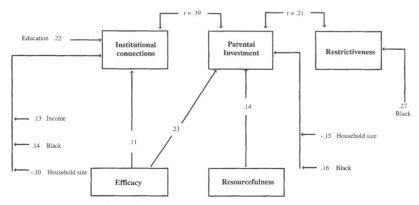

Figure 6.2 Types of Family Management Strategies by Social and Psychological Factors: A Heuristic Model Based on Significant Regression Coefficients (Beta)

compared with other women or caregivers. Compatible relations are less likely in large households, in families headed by a single parent, and in two-parent families with high levels of marital conflict.

Third, socioeconomic status and social influences made a larger contribution to family management strategies than the personal resources of parental self-efficacy and resourcefulness. Well-educated and higher-income parents were more apt to be connected to or engaged in community activities when compared with parents of lower status. However, parent involvement declines in large households. The larger the household, the more parents appear to shift their energies toward the family itself and away from community affairs.

Selective school placement belongs to the cluster of strategies that index parental investment, although we use it here as a separate measure, for both conceptual and measurement reasons. The selective placement of children emerged from our interviews as a particularly prominent strategy, one that comes as close as any of our measures to measuring the construction of a functional community. A logistic analysis revealed that using a selective school was far more common among families with a socioeconomic advantage.[4]

Black parents were generally more likely than whites to be involved in managing their children's world outside the household, but often lack the support available in many stable ethnic communities that benefit from both the presence of well-established Catholic institutions and largesse from political patronage. To protect and promote their children's development, African-Americans are frequently forced to look beyond their immediate communities, depend on sparsely funded public institutions, or rely on informal social networks. Lakisha Wilkenson's mother,

Alicia, illustrates this resourceful involvement in community roles and associations, an involvement largely intended to benefit her children.

A related explanation for the racial difference involves the greater dangers of black neighborhoods when compared with white residential areas, and the urgently felt need to do something about them. Black parents attributed more risks or dangers to their neighborhoods than did white parents in the Philadelphia sample (Elder et al. 1995). And black parents were far more likely to restrict their children's freedom (beta = .27); no other factor predicted the use of a restrictive management strategy. Some restrictions were enforced on a regular basis, such as forbidden places in the neighborhood and confinement to the house after school (see also Furstenberg 1993). But this strategy is also adjusted to the perceived danger, as in Michelle's household. Living in a high-risk neighborhood, she closely monitored her children's comings and goings in order to protect them from the danger "she could just feel at times."

As she put it, the "baddest kids" live just across the street, "the one that's involved with everything." But restrictiveness is a flexible strategy in her parenting efforts: "You have to be flexible because life is flexible, you know." Fortunately, Michelle's children have not had any trouble in the neighborhood. She attributes this to the way "we conduct ourselves. I talk with the kids. They're people, so I treat them like people. My kids aren't disrespectful." Michelle is known as a caring person in the neighborhood. Children living along the street frequently warn her when trouble is brewing.

DIMENSIONS OF SUCCESSFUL AND PROBLEMATIC BEHAVIOR

We have not yet established an empirical sequence that connects the resources of parents to the lives of adolescents through family interactive processes and management strategies. From the evidence at this point, the resources of parents have an influence on family dynamics and strategies, and the latter are linked to children's behavior (see chapter 5). We turn now to this sequence, beginning with the activity involvement of youth and taking up academic competence, psychological adjustment, and problem behavior. (The self-competence of youth, as reported by youth, does not figure prominently in this research, owing to its lack of association with social and economic factors.)

Social Ties and Involvement

Some households focus more on the interior life of family interactions, whereas others channel energies more toward the outer world and its social activities. Parents who were active in community life claimed more social and personal resources: they ranked higher on education and income, and felt more confident of their ability to make a positive difference in their children's lives. As reported in chapter 5, parents who are engaged in community affairs make a significant difference in their children's social involvement. Those who are active in the community had children who were likely also to be involved in school, church, and community affairs, experiences that are relevant to the development of achievement, social, and citizenship skills. A number of possible explanations could account for the similarity in social activity across the generations.

Engaged parents are likely to present themselves as attractive role models, as people who make things happen and are knowledgeable about the larger world. These parents are also involved in a broad network of relationships that open up social opportunities for their children. Parents of their children's friends may therefore be known to them, providing an unusual degree of shared priorities among adult influences. Access to community resources and opportunities is another factor that may account for the relationship. Involved parents are more likely to talk about community events and motivate such activity in the school experience of their children.

Thus we expect the socioeconomic and psychological resources of parents to influence the activity involvement of children primarily through the parents' own social involvement. We tested this two-step model by including all social factors, psychological resources, and family dynamics measures that made some difference in children's activity involvement (see appendix table A.6.3). Total family income and the education of the parent or caregiver emerged as the most important social determinants of children's activity. The higher the family status, the more socially active children are in organizations.

The second part of this analysis added the personal efficacy and resourcefulness of the parent as well as family strategies that make a difference—institutional connections, investment in the child, and restrictiveness. To assess their explanatory effect, we compare correlations and beta coefficients for specific variables and use path-analytic methods. As expected, family strategies largely account for the effect of parental education on children's involvement (see appendix table A.6.4). In a path analysis, over three-fourths of the effect of parents' education on children's activity is mediated by family strategies, especially the institutional connections of the mother or parent surrogate. These strategies also account for a third of the effect of income level. Both the efficacy and resourcefulness of parents are related to the activity involvement of children, and their effects are largely expressed in greater parental involvement. Placement in a selective school, however, made no difference in the child's level of social involvement.

For an overview of major lines of influence, we again develop a heuristic model based on significant effects pertaining to family management and child involvement. The model draws from prior analyses of the antecedents of family strategies (see appendix table A.6.2) and from the principal effects on child involvement (appendix tables A.6.3 and A.6.4). With few exceptions, and none of any note, social and psychological resources make a difference in the social involvement of children only through family strategies—institutional connections, parental investments, and restrictiveness. A good example is race. With income and education controlled, black parents still have more social ties than white parents, they are more invested in their children (both in the household and outside it), and they place more behavioral restrictions on them. These indirect linkages are the only important routes by which race makes a difference in the social activity of children.

The combined thrust of community involvement and specific investments in children becomes a powerful force in guiding development. Joanne, the mother of four children, typifies this approach to childrearing. Her philosophy is to be a living example of desired behavior, especially in relations with her children and in their world. She became a churchgoer for that reason. Deciding that her neighborhood should be free of gangs of young adolescents, she mobilized local families and tried to get the police to respond with preventive measures. Her eldest daughter, Trisha, a member of the group of involved students in this study, has emulated her mother's initiative, participating in school sports, religious youth activities, and a job during her school years.

Very similar to this family strategy are the practices of Linda, the mother of Beth, another involved student with a lengthy list of social accomplishments. Linda's strategy as a full-time mother was to get involved in activities that would be part of her daughter's world. She volunteered in the parish school library and became an advisor for the Catholic Youth Organization so that the high school students would have an adult who would help them organize activities; she also gave freely of her time to school affairs, in the classroom and out. Linda explained that these activities keep her informed of "what's going on in different situations" in the lives of her children. Low-income parents are less socially involved than parents with higher incomes, but social ties to the larger community are equally predictive of involved children in both high- and low-income groups. Thus the process of parental involvement generally reproduces parental inequalities regarding social activities in the child generation unless low-income parents are able to overcome the barriers to involvement. When this occurs, their children are no less connected to organizations.

The same pattern appears by family structure and race. In two-parent and in single-parent families, as in African-American and white households, social involvement extends across generations similarly. Surprisingly, children from single-parent households are no less involved than other children. If anything, they may be more involved when adjustments are made for socioeconomic status.[5]

Many years ago, Edward Sapir (1927) described socialization as the unintended patterning of behavior. By this he meant that a large part of a child's upbringing occurs through daily exposure to the way people live—their actions, beliefs, and values—rather than overt instruction. The impact of a parent's ties to the community on a child's social involvement seems to exemplify Sapir's astute observation. Parents who are involved in neighborhood watch associations, precinct politics, or a woman's service association are not directly involved in such activities for the purpose of instructing children in the virtues of social participation, but the lesson comes through nevertheless. They set a persuasive example for children that has real consequences for shaping their level of social involvement.

Academic Success and Failure

Inner-city children in Philadelphia are disadvantaged by many conditions, but these conditions cannot fully account for why many children succeed and others fail—at least in the middle years. For example, little more than a tenth of the variation in children's academic competence is explained by low family income, dependence on welfare assistance, parents who have not graduated from high school, and large family size. Moreover, neither race nor family structure adds much to the picture. When all of these social factors are considered, we still have most of the variation in children's academic competence to explain.

This is the puzzle that Clark (1983) addressed when he sought to understand why "poor black children succeed or fail." In a small sample of disadvantaged urban families, Clark found school achievement to be associated with many of the family processes observed in more advantaged homes, such as explanatory communication between parents and children, a decision-making arrangement in which children were involved in guided self-direction, standards of excellence and moral conduct coupled with consistent, fair discipline, and access to significant adult models.

Similarly, the Philadelphia youth who succeed in school are most likely to be involved in an open, supportive relationship with parents that encourages responsible autonomy, constructive problem solving, and the negotiation of disputes (see chapter 5). Also important are the institutional ties of parents in the community and the placement of a child in a selective school, a circumstance that occurs only rarely in low-income households. Finally, access to informal networks and parental investment in family strategies are also correlated with the academic success of Philadelphia youth, but do not appear to have an independent effect on this outcome. Rather, it seems that diverse community activity and advanced education involve parents in complex environments that enhance mental skills and growth (Coser 1991). In addition, the broader perspectives and informational resources generated by parents' civic roles establish a social bridge for children to the larger community that may contribute indirectly to academic achievement.

Parental investment and institutional connections include ways of establishing functional communities for children through parental involvement in church and school. A third of the parents reported that their children attended private or magnet schools. Not surprisingly, considering their more-stringent admission standards, children who attend selective schools score higher on academic competence than other youth. These schools tend to recruit more able students, but not all capable students attend such schools. What meaning should we attribute to this strategy of attending a selective school? Though higher grades may be needed to get in, this placement also represents an important family strategy, both protective and developmental. Attendance at such schools requires motivated and resourceful parents who believe in the advantage of demanding educational environments and to whom economic resources and social connections are available. Placement in a selective school has much in common with both parental investment and institutional connections. Surprisingly, this educational strategy adds only modestly to our ability to predict academically competent children. The explained variance increases from .21 to .24, perhaps because it is too soon to capture the full benefits of selective schooling.

Overall, the picture of academic success among the Philadelphia youth is summed up by three important results represented in figure 6.3, which shows the most significant pathways of influence to academic success. (The regression coefficients appear in appendix tables A.6.2, A.6.3, and A.6.5.) One of these pathways runs through support for autonomy, showing the critical role of parents and the constraints they face in bringing up children. Parents of successful children have a sense of efficacy as parents, a resourceful ability to bounce back from setbacks. Parents with these qualities were likely to be actively engaged in fostering academic success by granting autonomy to their children.

A second pathway links family management influences to academic

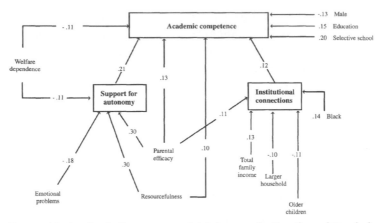

Figure 6.3 Academic Competence of Adolescents by Family and Psychological Influences: A Heuristic Model Based on Significant Regression Coefficients (Beta)

competence, including community social ties, enrollment in a selective school, and institutional connections. Demographic features of the household, including income, welfare dependence, education, race, and household size, are all related to the likelihood that these community ties will occur. Parents with more economic and social resources are generally more involved in the community, and in the process they become even more resourceful and empowered. Psychological competence is part of the picture, but it is not as important as social resources, which connect the child to the local community.

A third pathway involves the relatively modest link between socioeconomic disadvantage and school success. Academic troubles are not an assured outcome of a childhood of poverty or neighborhood disadvantage at this stage in the child's life. Moreover, social influences on academic achievement are similar for children in different income strata. Finally, consistent with the literature on gender roles and school achievement (Weston 1989), girls generally do better than boys in school, and this disparity tends to be greatest among low-income families.[6]

In theory, the socialization of academic achievement should be especially potent in family structures marked by strong partner relationships when compared with the single-parent household. Relationships of this kind tend to minimize the disruptive effect of economic hardship, support effective parenting, and encourage family ties to the community (Elder et al. 1992). To pursue this comparison, we examined children's academic competence as the dependent variable in single-parent and strong-marriage households among African-American families.[7] The influence process differs in predictable ways in these two types of households. Two-partner households tend to accentuate the positive influences of the parent's education and amplify the importance of institutional connections. Such households also diminish the adverse effect of economic pressures, although these differences are statistically not reliable. In contrast, the receipt of public aid has a negative effect on such achievement in single-parent households, and it is not offset by the stronger effects of institutional connections and education. Lacking the social resources of strong-partnership families, single-parent households are more dependent on in-home parenting practices such as the perceived effectiveness of parents and their support for the children's autonomy. The end result is that we account for a larger part of the variance of children's school success in two-partner than in single-parent households ($R^2 = .25$; $R^2 = .15$).

Overall, a substantial number of adolescents are successful in their academic work at school, more so than one would expect from knowledge of their background, defined by the education and personal efficacy of parents, support for autonomy, independence from public assistance, and household size. Can we find any clues to this achievement from other factors? As in the case of activity involvement, we identified children who were doing better than predicted (positive residuals above the median) and a group that was doing less well in relation to expectations based on their background (above the median on the negative residuals). The most distinctive theme of the achievers is their access to social resources. Youth who are doing better than expected are most likely to have the benefits of a supportive family environment. Likewise we also found that the presence of a caring adult outside the family seemed to boost the academic performance of youth. The successful youth reported higher levels of support from teachers and more support at school generally.

Psychological Adjustment

Popular views of inner-city children would have us believe that emotional distress and impairment are widespread, including such problems as depression, anxiety, anger, problems with mental concentration, and troubled relations with peers. We asked mothers' views on such matters because they see their children in situations that are largely divorced from the pressures of peers and personal ego involvement. Children are skilled in preserving their inner feelings amid peers, and in hard times they are known to protect both family and private feelings from the intrusiveness of school counselors and child-welfare personnel.

There are many reasons to rely upon mothers' reports on their children, as noted, but it is important to ask whether the same results would be obtained from reports by the adolescent or by the father. The mother scale tapped the absence of symptoms, while an adolescent report focused on positive resources, such as resourcefulness and resilience. The two measures are only modestly correlated ($r = -.30$), too unrelated to include in the same measure. However, the scales have similar correlates. As in the case of the parent's report, discipline effectiveness and autonomy support are the only predictors of the adolescent self-report, with beta coefficients of .11 and .18 respectively. The effects are much weaker than those for the maternal report, but the pattern is comparable overall.

As shown in chapter 5, psychologically adjusted adolescents tend to have parents who (1) establish a positive emotional climate in the home, (2) use discipline with consistency and fairness, and (3) encourage autonomy. These three processes are the only family influences that predict the emotional well-being of youth. Socioeconomic factors add nothing of significance to the picture. The sole parental correlates of children's mental health are psychological resources (efficacy, resourcefulness, lack of mental health problems—average $r = .39$) and the aforementioned family processes (average $r = .51$). The strength of the correlations undoubtedly reflects our dependence on the mother's report for all the variables. In a regression analysis, we find that over half of the effect of parental efficacy and resourcefulness on children's mental health is expressed through the parent's support for autonomy (see appendix table A.6.6).

It is reasonable to assume that parents who are able to support their children's autonomy acquire a sense of parental efficacy in doing so. The cross-sectional sample does not provide a measure of certainty as to the direction of causal influences. Nevertheless, parents who feel personally effective in child-rearing and resourceful are likely to bring up children in ways that enhance self-regard. They encourage children to be self-directed, responsible, and motivated. Not surprisingly, this is the same process that also fosters academic success in school among the children of this study.

In contrast to family processes, family management strategies are unrelated to psychological adjustment. Parental investment efforts (i.e., placing children in community activities) and the community ties or connections of parents do not protect children from emotional problems, whereas we have seen that they do enhance the likelihood of social and academic achievements. One might expect such achievements to strengthen self-confidence and resilience in the face of difficulties, but perhaps such traits in their children have not yet become apparent to the parents.

Socioeconomic conditions appear to make little difference in parental competence and childrearing practices, but they may nonetheless modify the effects of these characteristics. In particular, autonomy support is more predictive of the emotional health of children when income is above the sample average than among lower-income families (b [unstandardized regression coefficient] $= -.48$; b $= -.33$); but the difference is not statistically significant. Likewise, we find that autonomy support has greater significance for children's psychological well-being in strong marriages rather than in weak ones. The interaction effect is statistically significant (b $= -.16$, $p \leq .05$). When parents are mutually supportive, they are likely to present a more coordinated and influential strategy of parenting in the family. For example, marital conflict increases the likelihood of inconsistent actions on the part of parents. Youth with emotional problems are also likely to engage in antisocial conduct, a process suggesting the cumulative nature of disadvantage. Antisocial behaviors elicit negative reactions, which in turn produce emotional distress that fuels anger and social negativity. This leads us to consider the sources of problems among the families in our study.

Problem Behaviors

Only a small number of our Philadelphia adolescents engaged in problem behaviors of one kind or another. We focus mainly on those of an externalizing nature, such as legal offenses (e.g., hitting or threatening to hit a teacher), the abuse of drugs and alcohol, negative behaviors (e.g., belonging to a gang), and school delinquency.

Adolescents may use problem behavior to achieve their goals of social respect— a proactive strategy (Anderson 1990; Dance 1996). When aggressive responses are made to perceived threats, they exemplify a reactive pattern of behavior. Behavioral styles can, of course incorporate both proactive and reactive motivations. Family influences are also proactive and reactive. Even during the early months of life, the "difficult child" syndrome (irritability, temper outbursts, etc.) can play an important role in patterning a style of maternal response that evolves into a failed process of socialization.

Parents who combine inconsistent discipline with little, if any, monitoring and nurturant support markedly increase the risk of child aggression (Patterson, Capaldi, and Bank 1991). They also increase the prospects of indifferent parenting as the child acquires the physique and status of an inner-city teenager, whose life is affected ever more by the attractions of the street and neighborhood gangs. The reactive process may also take the form of severe restrictiveness as parents, desperate for an answer, try physical constraints, such as after-school "lock-ups" at home, to minimize the dangers of street life.

Problem behavior tends to peak during the adolescent years, and we find a similar age-trend among both African-American and white youth in our sample (see chapter 3). Again, this is a cross-sectional sample, so the trends should not be thought of as a developmental trajectory on the same children over time. Ineffective discipline and problem behavior covary in a system of reciprocal effects. Ineffective parents may well be fearful of their older problem-children and consequently employ inconsistent discipline and minimal supervision or monitoring.

In addition to ineffective discipline, a lack of parental efficacy is coupled with the problem behavior of offspring (beta $= -.27$; see appendix table A.6.3). Mothers are less likely to believe that they make a difference in their children's experiences and life chances—a lower sense of parental efficacy. Despite this account of failed socialization, the acting-out tendency of children is constrained to some extent by family structure. Harmonious two-partner families should provide greater support for the upbringing of children than conflicted or single-parent households. Among others, Frazier (1966, 265) has underscored the powerlessness of young single mothers. As one of the mothers put it, "I talk and talk and teach, and, when I have done all I know how to do, I can do no more. Children in these days are a heartbreak."

The presence of another adult in single-parent households has been linked in theory and analysis to greater control over children (Dornbusch and Wood 1989). We do not find this difference among single parents in the present study, but the key factor may be the quality of relations between adults in the household. Are they mutually supportive or often at odds over matters that concern the children?

To explore further the role of social control, we assessed the interplay of parental ineffectiveness and the child's problem behavior under two conditions: a relatively strong network of friends and relatives and a relatively weak one. In theory, the more embedded the family in a network of friends and kin, the weaker the association between a child's acting-out behavior and parent ineffectiveness. An index of informal networks (see chapter 5) was divided at the median to identify families in different conditions relative to social support. We focused on the older boys, who are most engaged in problem behavior. The central question is whether the problematic behaviors of parent and older boy covary to a similar degree across strong and weak networks.[8]

As expected, the covariation of problematic behavior across generations is greatest for the older boys in families that lacked network support when compared with youth in stronger networks (figure 6.4). The contrast between parent and son behavior is statistically significant between strong and weak networks. In a strong network, a single mother with such a boy might report the company of lots of close friends and people

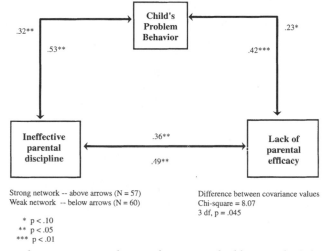

Figure 6.4 The Contingent Behavior of Parents and Older Boys by Informal Social Network

she could count on. Most likely, she regularly talked to neighbors and felt the area was safe.

When all findings are considered, structural features of family control clearly make a difference in the problem behavior of boys and its consequences. Larger households and harmonious two-partner families lower the risk of acting-out behavior. Supportive local networks of friends and relatives function in a similar manner.

One of the boys, originally classified in our delinquent category has followed a life trajectory that highlights the importance of a strong network of family and adult friends for inner-city parents. His mother is a widow on a very small budget. At the time of our 1990 survey, Jesse was fifteen years old and a sophomore in trouble at a local Catholic high school, with a reputation for street fights, marijuana use, and drinking. His close friends at the time were engaged in delinquent activity, including street fights and incidents that brought them into contact with local law officers.

During this difficult time, Jesse's mother sought out the help of his uncle, a policeman, and worked hard to nurture this relationship. She also turned to a close male friend and asked him to talk to her son. As she noted, "The boys need men, you know, a man to sit here and talk to them. I would say something to them—my brother or my friend and they'll talk to him on the sly like. They would talk, 'Well, man, what's up?' You know, things like that." Another important part of the picture is Jesse's strong desire to please his mother as well as a new girl friend who helped to "keep him off the street." In combination, these developments seemed to make a noticeable difference in his schoolwork and future. By his senior year, in 1998, Jesse was on the honor roll and held a steady job that led to a promotion as night manager. Thus it seems that single parents can sometimes offset the liabilities of limited resources inside the home with support beyond the household if it is there to be summoned.

The story of problem behavior among the early adolescents in this study has surprisingly little to do with low family income, unemployment, minimal education, and public assistance per se; rather, it shows how limited resources come into play when problems arise. With a full longitudinal record of their lives into adulthood, we might be able to detect a trajectory in which socioeconomic influences have progressively reinforced a dynamic of parental ineffectiveness that is not compensated for by resources deployed outside the home.

PROFILES OF ADOLESCENT BEHAVIOR

Our analysis of family influences has centered on individual dimensions of adolescent behavior taken one at a time, although we have drawn upon individual cases at various points to exemplify key developmental influences and processes. In order to bring our inquiry back to behavior profiles and life patterns, we turn to a comparison of the four cluster groups of youth.

As reported in chapter 5, the two profiles of success—the academically competent and the socially involved youth—are linked to parental child-rearing practices (support for autonomy, effective discipline, and a positive family climate), along with greater success in managing the external world—more developed social networks, greater institutional connections, and high levels of parental investment. The other two groups, at-risk and delinquent, rank below average on these aspects of socialization.[9] The four groups also differ in predictable ways on parent resources, personal efficacy, resourcefulness, and mental health or the absence of mental health problems. Competent and involved students have parents who are significantly more resourceful than the parents of at-risk and delinquent youth.[10]

In addition to these comparisons, we asked whether the social and psychological disadvantages of at-risk and delinquent youth were augmented by the perception that people were not willing to help them (see figure 6.5). Just as success fosters confidence in the achiever, adolescent troublemaking may foster distrust of adults, leading youth to devalue and perhaps reject assistance from adults. In the questionnaire, all adolescents

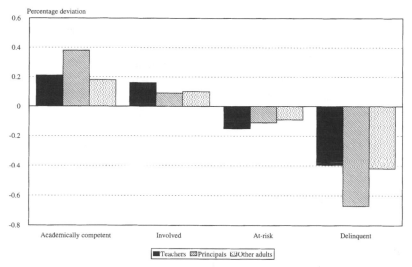

Figure 6.5 Adults Who Helped Adolescent Reported by Youth in Each Behavior
Type: Deviation from the Grand Mean

were asked whether they had received help from teachers, principals, and
other adults. The small number of delinquent youth rank far below average on the report of such help, while the prosocial adolescents score above
average in this area.[11] Clearly, disadvantages tend to accumulate, possibly
leading to more serious problems in later adolescence.

So far we have compared the behavior groups on each family influence, taken one at a time, even though the factors are often highly intercorrelated. For example, parents who describe themselves as efficacious
as parents also rank high on resourcefulness and mental health or the
lack of mental health problems. Each of these parent characteristics varies
across the four behavior groups, and yet they are unlikely to retain their
statistical significance in a multivariate analysis. To identify the most important sources of differentiation among the four behavior clusters, we
included four sets of influences in a multinomial logistic regression.[12]

Socioeconomic factors tend to affect adolescent behavior through family dynamics. Thus it is not surprising that low income and single-parent
status have little effect in this multivariate analysis once we take family
process into account. The results are similar for parental education, welfare dependence, and household size. Elements of family process carry
much of the weight in differentiating the behavioral clusters, followed by
parental efficacy and institutional connections. The promotive and preventive strategies of parent investment do not differentiate the groups as
much as the parent's social engagement or institutional connections.

The major contrast occurs between the two competent types and the at-risk and delinquent clusters. Consistently, both competent and involved youth rank higher on developmentally sensitive parenting when compared with the other two groups. They experience more effective discipline and greater support for autonomy, and their parents, predictably, feel more efficacious. Youth in the competent cluster rank high on both academic and social success, and their parents are highly involved in the community and in management of the external world. Both of these groups of more successful youth perceive greater parental support for autonomy: in this respect they differ sharply from both the at-risk and delinquent groups.

Choices, Constraints, and Turning Points

Children are influenced by the social circumstances in which they find themselves, but they and their families also make choices, no matter how constraining their world. Such choices provide access to certain transitions, options, and incentives that define life pathways, which in turn expose children to new opportunities and constraints. Thus some children in this study found their own way into extracurricular school activities, while others did not, but in both cases their choices hinged on the availability of an activity program. These activities, in turn, placed limitations on their freedom and ruled out competing and potentially corrupting options.

The empirical results of this chapter point to an unfolding story involving a series of subtle interactions between human agency and social structure. The limited opportunities faced by inner-city families have some effect on the level of success and problem behavior among youth in this study, especially when we take into account family interactive processes and management strategies that are in turn interconnected to the social environments of the families. But the differences are best portrayed as a "loose coupling" of social structure and youth behavior (Elder and O'Rand 1995). By this we mean that none of these processes, not even several together, are so powerfully related that they will determine the course of a child's development. Consider children in welfare households with relatively weak ties to the community. They did not do as well in school as children from more advantaged families, but a substantial number did succeed in school. The structural effect leaves room for other explanations, including children's self-directed motivation and choice, as well as parental support of autonomy.

Loose coupling between social structure and children's behavior appears in their activity involvement, problems of emotional health, and tendency to act out. Socially-involved children were likely to have educated parents who also participated in community activities and organizations, but this background does not adequately account for the activity level of children in the study. Likewise, parents who were depressed and lacked confidence in their ability as parents were likely to have children who felt depressed and inadequate, and much of this association occurred through failure to support the autonomy of their children.

As noted in prior chapters, a large number of the most able youth in this study are living and even flourishing in the very worst neighborhoods. How did they launch a positive trajectory in this setting while others remain mired in trouble and failure? How have they managed to prosper? In our ongoing interactions with some of the youth, we were impressed with how thin the line is for many youth between successful and thwarted development. Many youth are living in settings that provide few opportunities for engagement with encouraging adults outside the household. The abundance of adult influence—teachers, coaches, family friends, and professionals—available to many middle-class parents are less accessible to families with limited means in distressed communities. Thus, it may take more efficacious and skilled parents to foster success and establish the momentum of positive development that results in a process of cumulative advantage. These youth frequently stood on the precipice of making wrong moves and initiating a process of cumulative disadvantage.

In either of these cases, we see that development involves "cumulative and reciprocal mechanisms of behavioral continuity" (Caspi, Bem, and Elder 1989). Behavioral continuities are produced by social interactions that are sustained by a congenial social environment; that is, they evoke social responses to reinforce patterns of behavior. In cumulative continuity, family and individual dispositions support the choice of compatible environments for children, reinforcing and sustaining their actions. In contrast, problem youth tend to affiliate with other problem youth, and their interaction generally accentuates their behavior, producing over time a cascade of cumulative disadvantages.

Reciprocal continuity refers to a continuous interchange between person and environment in which action is formed by reaction and then by another cycle of action and reaction. The intemperate behavior of youth may initiate a cycle of parental anger and aggression, a widening gulf of irritation, and finally parental withdrawal, which reinforces the adolescent's initial aggression (Pepler and Rubin 1991). Thus the engagement in problem behavior is neither merely the inevitable product of involvement with negative peers or of family alienation, nor the result of an ongoing chain of minor decisions. Rather, it is interwoven with values and influences, along with the not-so-invisible hand of adults in the school. These influences, together with the emerging choices and values of adolescent subjects, serve to realign groups, so that they are consistent with personal as well as familial norms. (Cairns and Cairns 1994, 127)

After years of ineffectual parenting, Lisa, a single parent in the study, placed the blame on what she did after her marriage failed. As a mother of three young children, she followed the easy path at the time: "I always used to just give in to them and give them whatever they wanted. But then as they got older, that's when I started to realize I shouldn't have been doing that. And that's when a lot of our problems started." She has little or no control over Mark and Buddy, her two sons, and both have a history of antisocial incidents, including one arrest. In her words, "I tried and talked to them and I do the best I can but I just don't know how to get it through their heads."

Aggressive children generally expect others to be hostile, and thus behave in ways that elicit hostility, confirming their initial suspicions and reinforcing their behavior. Thus a self-fulfilling prophecy is set into motion.

If the dynamics of cumulative disadvantage evolve as stated, how is the cycle broken?[13] Change of environment is one possibility. Some Philadelphia parents sent their children to different schools and communities in order to break the undesirable influence of deviant friends. They constructed alternative "functional communities" for their children. One of the mothers quoted in this chapter decided to send her son to a suburban Catholic school in order to remove him from the intimidation tactics of local gangs. Strategies of family management can be thought of as efforts to establish more beneficial environments for children that, if need be, can "turn around their lives."

In general, African-American parents were more engaged in family management strategies that minimize danger and maximize opportunity than white parents, regardless of socioeconomic status. They were more inclined to protect their children from street influences by restricting their freedom, taking measures to confine them to the household after school and on weekends. They ranked higher on church and civic activities in the community and scored higher on family management strategies, such as placing children in constructive social activities. Black parents do not generally perceive the community to be as responsive to their needs as white parents, and were less willing than white parents to entrust their children to the community at large. Hence, they relied on more promotive and protective activities inside the household or selected activities outside the immediate community. An earlier study (Elder et al. 1995) found that black parents who felt efficacious in their roles were far more likely to be engaged in the specific strategies of family management than their white counterparts.

The explanation may well be related to ethnic differences in neighborhood support for effective parenting. Aggregate comparisons of neighborhoods suggest that there is less need for active management of children in high-resource white neighborhoods, owing to the presence of local collective support for parents. Under these conditions, even mothers who lack confidence in their parenting are able to count on neighborhood resources. In comparison, black parents are less able to depend on neighborhood help and resources because such programs are less available. In a previous analysis, Walker and Furstenberg (1994, 8) found that parents who live in neighborhoods where social cohesion is low and poverty is high must make sizable investments of personal energy and ingenuity to ensure a protective community for their children. Black parents are most likely to live in such areas. Consequently, African-American parents have to be more vigilant and proactive than their counterparts in white communities to ensure that positive experiences are available for their children.

These findings also have implications for the finding on family structure reported earlier in this chapter regarding the variables of single-parent household, conflicted marriage, or strong marriage. For the most part, we find no difference between black parents in single and conflicted two-parent households. The single parent household is far more common among African-American children than among white youth, but it stands out as an adverse family environment primarily among whites. Overall, family structure makes very little difference in the competence or mental health of both African-American and white children, though a strong marriage offers significant advantages on family climate and parental support in both racial groups.

Developmental advantages tend to beget more advantages, and behavioral disadvantages often give rise to more of the same. The temporal frame of this study is restricted to little more than a point within the life span, and it is necessary to take a longer view with questions about continuity and change. From the perspective of this study, boys' problem behaviors represent a plausible case of pathogenic continuity. A hostile, acting-out style of behavior may be sustained by the progressive accumulation of its consequences, whether as social rejection or as indifference, hostility, or social instability. The sequence brings to mind a subjective circle of causation in which failures, experienced and anticipated, make the child "hesitant to try. What to others are challenges appear to him as threats; he becomes preoccupied with defense of his small claims on life at the expense of energies to invest in coping" (Smith 1968, 277).

This account could apply to the past and future of inner-city youth, but in neither case is it complete without knowing how developmental trajectories are shaped by urban neighborhoods, their social structures, demography, and cultures. The loose coupling between family structures and children's options provides alternative pathways, and so also may particular neighborhoods, which vary in services, the availability of churches, stores, and schools, and perceptions of a shared culture. But do these variations matter? In the next chapter we address this question and in doing so add another level of analysis to the study.

How Do Neighborhoods Matter?

With the assistance of
JEONG-RAN-KIM, WING-SHING CHAN, RICHARD A.
SETTERSTEN, AND JULIEN O. TEITLER

The preceding chapter examined how parent and family characteristics are associated with family management practices and success in early adolescence. The most central discovery was that each family management practice is related to a unique set of parent and family attributes, as is each successful outcome. Thus, understanding how family composition and process relate to family management and adolescent success requires a complex contingency theory linking development to context. This same impression is reinforced by our qualitative interviews and is implicit in a central assumption of this book—that family management and adolescent success depend on neighborhood and institutional involvement as well as family circumstances. Previously we emphasized how a neighborhood's social and material resources might influence the types of family management found there and the level of success that local adolescents experience. Now we turn to a more nuanced exploration of how neighborhood resources are related to family management and adolescent success.

American communities differ considerably in the race and social class of families living within them (Massey and Denton 1993). How much they differ in some of the family attributes explored in earlier chapters and found to be important—attributes such as parental warmth, autonomy promotion, or discipline effectiveness—is not clear. Nor is it clear how much neighborhoods vary in social resources such as the availability and quality of local organizations; the size, dependability, and composition of social networks; and features of the neighborhood social climate such as the local level of social problems, social cohesion, and social control. Because existing literature provides few clues as to the amount of neighborhood variation to expect, our first purpose is simply to describe the level of neighborhood variation in terms of family process, social resources, family management and adolescent success. This analysis provides a more systematic assessment of the amount of neighborhood variation previewed in chapters 2 and 3.

To explain neighborhood effects, some scholars look primarily to details about the neighborhood's social composition, emphasizing in particular the percentage of local households that are poor and headed by someone from a minority group (Wilson 1987). Others prefer to focus on the local social processes and institutional resources, assuming that these mediate between a neighborhood's social composition and the behavior of the early adolescents living there (Furstenberg 1993; Sampson 1992). Both social composition and social process factors therefore need to be examined simultaneously to fulfill an aim of chapter 2—exploring how a neighborhood's poverty rate, racial composition, and level of social and institutional resources are related to family management and early adolescent success.

We can study neighborhood relationships through at least three processes. The first is through *summing up individual differences that happen to vary by neighborhood.* To understand this, imagine that poor parents tend to prefer restrictiveness as a family management style, and that such parents also congregate in some neighborhoods more than others. Given these assumptions, the neighborhood poverty rate will inevitably be related to a preference for restrictiveness as a family management strategy. According to this model, however, bringing a family that is better off into a poor neighborhood should not influence the newcomers' restrictiveness because restrictiveness results only from familial (and not neighborhood) poverty, and the incoming family is not poor. In the model that sums individual differences, neighborhoods affect children solely because neighborhoods differ in social composition.

Some social scientists are skeptical that summing up neighborhood-correlated individual differences represents a genuine neighborhood effect (e.g., Jencks and Mayer 1990). They believe that a neighborhood should be more than the sum of its parts and should show some *emergent properties* that account for community differences—properties such as unique local norms (Coleman 1988) or local ways of coordinating group behavior (Crane 1991). Imagine, for example, that having a high density of poor families in the neighborhood leads local residents to believe collectively that restrictiveness is the best way to deal with neighborhood problems. Given this local norm, any nonpoor family entering the neighborhood will be exposed to this shared understanding and may then adopt restrictiveness as a family management style, even though the family was previously disinclined to be restrictive. In this hypothetical example, the new arrivals are responding to a prevailing local norm about restricting adolescents' mobility. This collective response to dangerous local conditions is what functions as an emergent property.

One way to distinguish between explanations of neighborhood differences based on emergent properties or the summing of individual differences is to see whether a neighborhood difference in family management or adolescent success disappears when individual-level controls are introduced into the analysis. If neighborhoods continue to differ in this circumstance, this suggests that something other than neighborhood differences in social composition is accounting for the relationship between neighborhood and outcome. This "something" is, of course, an emergent property, perhaps some aspect of local culture, of social ties, or of institutional resources. Identifying the nature of this emergent property requires further investigation, however; it cannot be inferred solely from the failure of social composition variables to account for all of the outcome. Unfortunately, attributing a relationship to some emergent property or social composition depends on the validity of the statistical model used. If it does not include all the neighborhood compositional differences responsible for success, then unexamined social composition variables are likely to mimic the same pattern of results to which an emergent property is traditionally ascribed. Identifying emergent properties is not assumption-free.

A third type of neighborhood effect is more complex and reflects the possibility that family and neighborhood characteristics *jointly influence* how families manage children or how their children succeed. For example, socially isolated parents living in poor neighborhoods may fear that letting their children go out unsupervised will lead them to take part in undesirable activities on dangerous streets. Contrast such a family with two others. The first is similarly isolated, but lives in a less dangerous neighborhood. Parents living in such circumstances do not need to be as restrictive because the local streets are less perilous, and the adolescent activities occurring on them are more likely to be supervised. The second family resides in a neighborhood with strong links to other families and supportive institutions. Such parents can also afford to be less restrictive because they know that outside the home their child is likely to be with adults and peers whose behavior they consider appropriate. This suggests that family management might be the product of neighborhood and family circumstances *taken together,* implying a statistical interaction between the neighborhood and the family, in which the neighborhood level is represented by the fraction of local families who are poor, and the family level is represented by the quality of a family's social networks. In

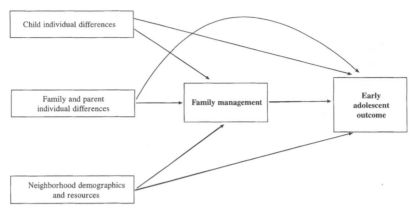

Figure 7.1 Heuristic Model of the Links among Family, Family Management, and Adolescent Success Indicators

this hypothetical example, family management depends on something like a chemical reaction between neighborhood and family conditions, or something more than the sum of the two.

This chapter considers whether any relationships between neighborhoods and family management practices or between neighborhoods and adolescent outcomes are due to neighborhood differences in social composition, to emergent properties that operate in certain kinds of neighborhoods, or the unique combination (statistical interaction) of neighborhood with family or individual characteristics. The analytic model we use to examine neighborhood relationships is necessarily more complex than prior models and is displayed in figure 7.1. A key assumption of the model (and of this book) is that use of a particular family management practice improves measures of adolescent success. But three other assumptions are also crucial.

The first is that the particular practices a family uses depend on a variety of influences, especially neighborhood demographic characteristics, neighborhood social and institutional resources, and individual family, parent, and child characteristics.

The second assumption is that neighborhoods can influence adolescent behavior directly without any causal mediation. Such direct neighborhood effects are common in the social science literature and have previously been attributed to the fraction of local residents who are poor and represent racial minorities (Crane 1991); to the quality of local institutions such as schools (Bryk, Lee, and Holland 1993) or recreation centers (McLaughlin, Irby, and Langman 1994); to the availability of informal social resources such as the strength of local norms about conventional behavior; and to the prevalence of social control in public settings (Elliott et al. 1996; Sampson 1992; Shaw and MacKay 1942).

The third assumption is that indirect causal paths exist from neighborhood attributes to student success. These arise because neighborhood characteristics lead to the use of certain family management practices that in turn affect adolescent outcomes. Indirect effects of neighborhoods are rarer in the social science literature. Yet parents—as we have seen in many of the case studies—select strategies for raising their children based on their understanding of what neighborhood circumstances require, what these circumstances permit, and what parental actions are likely to be effective. Granted that parents do select strategies in this way, then family management practices should mediate between neighborhood characteristics and adolescent success.

Relationships may be even more complex than this. Most neighborhoods are internally heterogeneous, and we should not assume that all the parents living in a particular community respond in the same way to the same circumstances. Parents have many alternative management strategies from which to choose, and some of them may not fit well with a particular family's repertoire of parenting. Moreover, some parents might already have tried a particular strategy and abandoned it in order to explore other tactics or to explore implementing several practices simultaneously. Other parents may be less able to respond creatively and develop alternative methods, and still others may not be much concerned with actively managing their children because they believe them to be on the right course. Family management practices reflect a complex accommodation that evolves over time between neighborhood conditions, the capacities of parents to read the local situation, and the child's response to past practices. Thus the model in figure 7.1 may not operate the same way for different types of parents and adolescents—a possibility we need to explore.

METHODOLOGICAL CAVEATS

Before presenting our results, we must mention again some of the methodological caveats discussed in chapter 2. First, we cannot discuss neighborhoods and human behavior without slipping into a language that is causal. But in this study behavior is measured at a single time-point, precluding unambiguous causal explanation.

Second, the neighborhood sampling design did not include the most or least affluent neighborhoods in Philadelphia, inevitably weakening the relationships we obtain, though probably not to a great extent.

Third, census tracts were used to operationalize neighborhoods and not block groups, zip codes, urban-planning neighborhoods, or expert reports about local neighborhood boundaries.[1] Because older cities were tracted fifty years ago, the geographic boundaries of many current tracts fail to reflect contemporary social boundaries.

Fourth, since there are only forty-five census tracts with a sufficient number of cases, our analyses can incorporate relatively few neighborhood-level predictors. Because of this restriction, we are compelled to construct higher-order composite measures out of many of the individual neighborhood measures.[2]

Fifth, to characterize a neighborhood by aggregating the neighborhood descriptions of families living within it requires specifying the minimal acceptable number of residents per tract. After pilot work with three, five, and fifteen residents, we decided that five provided the most stable data and the largest tract sample size. As a result, caregivers from tracts with fewer than five residents were not included in the neighborhood analyses, reducing the number of individual families from 489 to 436.[3]

Finally, the models we test examine each of the five family management strategies in isolation from the others, even statistically controlling for these others so as to identify what are likely to be the "pure" consequences of each strategy. Fortunately, the intercorrelations among the five were modest; the highest was .37, and most were under .20. Thus it does not seem that many parents combine strategies in systematic ways, though some undoubtedly do; nor does it seem that the control for other strategies makes much of a difference to the results presented for individual strategies. Nonetheless, future research should identify what happens when parents simultaneously implement different combinations of strategies, and the next two chapters present some intriguing results about what might happen when strategies are packaged together. When all the methodological limitations noted above are taken together, they suggest that this chapter should be seen as exploring the model in figure 7.1 rather than formally testing it.

HOW MUCH VARIATION IS AT THE NEIGHBORHOOD LEVEL?

The Resource Measures

The family management and adolescent outcome variables have been described in prior chapters. When aggregated at the tract level, these variables refer to the density of local families that are using a particular management strategy or whose children have attained certain outcome characteristics.

We have not yet introduced all the ways in which we measure resources at the neighborhood level. *Socioeconomic resources* were calculated from caregivers' self-reports about (1) the education level of the most educated adult in the household; (2) household income; and (3) household assets in terms of ownership of homes and cars, and access to capital through credit cards and bank accounts. A composite measure of global socioeconomic resources was also derived by standardizing and summing up the three separate measures above. When aggregated, it became an assessment of resources in each census tract.

The *availability and quality of local organizations* were assessed from caregiver reports about (1) the quality of teen programs; (2) the quality of schools; and (3) the availability of neighborhood organizations, which were subdivided into those that neighborhood residents rarely manage (like hospitals) and those that they often manage (like Scout groups). Respondents were free to define their neighborhood however they wanted, and again a composite was formed for each family; when aggregated, it refers to the organizations that characterize each neighborhood.

Family social networks were measured as to (1) the size of the networks; (2) the number of relatives and close friends in them; and (3) the extent to which residents thought they could count on members of their networks for material and emotional support. We also produced a composite measure and a neighborhood-level measure.

Neighborhood social climate was assessed in terms of the caregiver's (1) dislike of the neighborhood; (2) the extent of local social control; (3) the likelihood that local children could succeed, however success was defined; (4) the degree of consensus among parents about child-relevant matters; (5) the extent of social cohesion; and (6) the level of social problems stemming from crime, drugs, violence, and the like.

Family process is also a resource. This was measured in terms of family climate, autonomy, and discipline effectiveness. At the neighborhood level, the relevant measures refer to the density of local families in which members have a particular style of relating to each other. The assumption is that a neighborhood with a high percentage of families that have a good internal climate is a better neighborhood.

The final resources we consider are *caregiver psychological resources*, which have also been previously discussed. Understood at the tract level, they index the density of local residents with better mental health, a stronger sense of self-efficacy, and greater resourcefulness.

The Level of Neighborhood Variation

Table 7.1 presents the relevant intraclass correlation values (ICCs). An ICC is computed as the ratio of the amount of variation between units

Table 7.1

Intra-class correlations by census tract

Variable	ICC
Family socioeconomic resources	**.179**
Household education	.106
Household income	.198
Household assets	.134
Total welfare received	.084
Institutional resources	**.078**
Internally managed organizations	.119
Externally managed organizations	.047
Quality of teen programs	.063
Quality of schools	.050
Social network	**.162**
Informal network that one can count on	.113
Size of social network	.119
Number of relatives/friends in neighborhood	.107
Climate	**.242**
Negative affect	.122
Social control	.098
Possibility of children's success	.130
Normative consensus among neighbors	.033
Social cohesion	.127
Lack of neighborhood problems	.201
Family processes	**.010**
Positive family climate	.001
Autonomy	.018
Discipline effectiveness	.040
Caregiver's psychological resources	**.007**
Mental health	.051
Self-efficacy	.002
Resourcefulness	.001
Family management	**.102**
Institutional connections	.072
Parent investment	.038
Positive social network	.119
Parent restrictiveness	.132
Private schooling	.151
Success measures	**.020**
Emotional problems reported by parents	.004
Emotional problems reported by child	.000
Behavior problems	.044
Academic competence	.073
Activity involvement	.044

(i.e., census tracts) relative to the amount of variation within them, with the latter being the product of both genuine differences between individuals from the same neighborhoods and measurement error. An ICC value greater than .50 indicates that more of the variation is between neighborhoods than within; a lower value indicates the opposite.

The first important finding in table 7.1 is that no ICC value exceeds .25, whether for social resources, family management, or early adolescent success. All domains, then, show more variation within census tracts than between them.

However, the values in table 7.1 underestimate the true neighborhood variation. One reason for this is that they take no account of measurement error. When we use corrections for unreliability based on Raudenbush, Rowan, and Kang (1991), the ICC values increase by up to 25 percent, depending on the degree of unreliability. But this is from the low baselines in table 7.1, so none of the adjusted ICC values exceeded .30. A second reason for underestimation is that some restriction exists in the range of tracts. But this influence is also likely to be minor, because the range is still considerable—from tracts as low as 5 percent poor to a tract as high as 62 percent poor. A third reason for underestimation is that we use census tracts to index neighborhoods, and ICC values would inevitably increase if we used a neighborhood measure whose boundaries reflected more homogeneous social dynamics. Indeed, great physical changes have taken place in Philadelphia since these tracts were created—new roads and businesses have emerged to influence who lives where; most of the immigrant groups of a hundred years ago have now moved out of what were once ethnic enclaves; and the newer groups moving in have not always respected the social boundaries created by their predecessors. We therefore recalculated the ICC values in table 7.1, using official city-planning neighborhoods and census blocks instead of census tracts. But the resulting ICC values hardly differ from what they were when tracts were used. Unfortunately, no analyses are possible that are based on neighborhood boundaries drawn up by local housing experts from their knowledge of current social dynamics. Nonetheless, we are prepared to conclude that neighborhoods are highly variable internally—that, in Philadelphia at least, economic and social resources, family management practices, and adolescent behavior vary more within neighborhoods than between them.

The modest level of between-neighborhood variation was a surprise to us. But in hindsight we should note that many changes have occurred in the United States since, say, World War II that may make neighborhoods less relevant today than they were in the heyday of community studies in sociology (Coleman 1988). We now have many more roads and cars, wider-ranging urban public transportation systems, high schools with large catchment areas, employment practices that are citywide even for teens (Newman 1996), and family, school, and work networks that are often spread across a city and its suburbs. Psychic and physical mobility are salient attributes of American life, and the media present social worlds and personal possibilities to young people that they do not observe locally. Do such things make young people less and less dependent on their geographic neighborhoods? Is there more need today to study the spatially dispersed, community-like aggregates of family, friends, acquaintances, and professional support persons that families carve out for themselves without necessarily paying much attention to physical proximity to the home? Families are freer now to choose schools (public or private), peer groups, and work sites for reasons that have little to do with their neighborhoods, making even more relevant the dispersed sites and social networks in which many of the most important needs of Americans are met.

A second finding in table 7.1, foreshadowed in the descriptive findings presented in chapter 3, is that the neighborhoods vary only slightly, if at all, in academic competence, acting out, involvement in conventional activities, and mental health—the major outcomes used throughout this book. Of course, we must remember that the sample is composed of younger adolescents, ages 11 to 15. For many of these outcomes, ICC values increase with age (Elliott et al. 1996). Nonetheless, our finding about early teens is consistent with survey data showing that crime rates hardly differ by race and social class during early adolescence, but differ more strongly by late adolescence. Because race and class are important neighborhood attributes in the United States, the individual relationships between crime, race, class, and age imply that larger ICC values will inevitably result in an older representative adolescent sample. But even the late adolescent ICC values in the Denver study sample by Elliott et al. (1996) do not exceed .45, further supporting the contention that there is nearly always more variability within a city's census tracts than between them.

We should not conclude, though, that the neighborhood differences obtained in table 7.1 are trivial. Research on how schools and classrooms influence student performance traditionally constructs theories and empirical tests around ICC outcome values as low as .05—even lower in some cases (Bryk and Raudenbush 1992). Indeed, if we took .20 as the cutoff point for deciding what is worth explaining, we would probably have no literature at all on the determinants of school climate or even of school differences in achievement levels (Bryk and Thum 1989; Raudenbush, Rowan, and Kang 1991). Seen in this light, our ICC results are less surprising, but they should still be a source of discomfort to those theorists of neighborhoods who have lost sight (1) of how much communities vary internally and (2) of the possibility that superficially dissimilar settings may contain some families that are similar to one another in important ways. Neighborhoods are not monolithic.

A third finding in table 7.1 is that neighborhoods differ more on some attributes than others. Tract variation is just under .25 for the local social climate and is between .20 and .15 for the socioeconomic standing of neighbors and for the size and dependability of social networks. Only slightly smaller are the ICC values for two of the family management strategies—parent restrictiveness and sending a child to a private or selective public school. The other family management strategies are associated with values of about .10, while for indicators of the availability and quality of local institutions, the values fall to .05. Somewhat surprisingly perhaps, the ICC values are close to zero for neighborhood differences in the psychological attributes of caregivers (and children) and for family processes associated with warmth, support for autonomy, and discipline effectiveness.

Thus, while psychological factors and internal family processes vary between individuals, they do not appear to vary between neighborhoods. We doubt whether this conclusion would change much if, instead of self-report measures, clinical assessment techniques had been used to assess mental health, or if observation techniques had been used to measure family process. The other assessment techniques would have to be considerably more valid for the very low ICC values we obtained to increase by much. We are prepared to conclude, therefore, that neighborhoods hardly differ in the gross psychological health of their average resident or in how children are reared in the average family. This conclusion has considerable theoretical import because it suggests that no simple causal link can exist between neighborhoods and the traditional, in-home family management practices based on support for autonomy, discipline effectiveness, and family warmth.

The ICC values for management practices (average about .10) are higher than for traditional family process measures. The latter deal with processes that occur in the home and typically involve face-to-face interactions, which are thought to be a major part of parenting quality. In contrast, the family management constructs are meant to indicate how families react to the outside world, either through linking their children to resources or restricting their mobility if the world outside is dangerous. That family management varies more by neighborhoods than does family process provides an empirical indication that family management is different from family process and is more closely related to how families are situated in their local context.

Neighborhoods differ most in their social climate (particularly around the prevalence of social problems), in their economic and human capital sources, and in the size and quality of social networks. Neighborhood theorists emphasize these domains when they assign a central causal role to community disorganization and local resource levels. Their emphasis is thus well placed relative to the other potential causes examined here, though the amount of neighborhood variation in these processes might surprise them.

WHICH NEIGHBORHOOD VARIABLES PREDICT RESOURCE LEVELS?

Appendix table A.7.1 presents tract-level, bivariate correlations between census tracts variables, family management variables, and our neighborhood resource indicators based on the availability of institutions and organizations, attributes of social networks, and the quality of the local social climate. The relevant tract means and standard deviations are presented in appendix table A.7.2.

The correlations show strong clustering. The census demographic attributes cluster together so that a tract's poverty level is predictably associated with fewer college graduates, fewer whites, and more single-parent families. The neighborhood resource variables also tend to cluster together. Social climate is correlated .62 with organizations and .27 with social networks, while organizations and networks are correlated .43. Finally, the social demographic and resource variables cluster with the family management variables, so that the Philadelphia neighborhoods with more social resources also tend to be the places where more protective and promotive forms of family management occur. It seems, then, that children in economically advantaged communities in Philadelphia also enjoy many other benefits as well.

In regression analyses not reported here we found consistent evidence that poor neighborhoods with more minority residents have the fewest resources of all kinds. This suggests that such neighborhoods suffer a "double whammy"—the first from their poverty status and the second from their racial composition. However, we found no evidence of a statistical interaction between the two, implying that no qualitative transformation in resource levels takes place because a tract is both densely poor and predominantly minority. There is only an additive effect. Henceforth, therefore, we need not use the interaction of racial composition and poverty level as a separate predictor of family management. The two main effects will suffice.

These results also have a substantive implication. Living in a poor neighborhood is sometimes thought to engender active attempts by individual families or local groups to improve the local social climate and develop better institutions and networks (e.g., Stack 1974). If this occurs to any noteworthy degree, it will attenuate correlations among the neighborhood factors. But they were high here, suggesting that such local self-empowerment is relatively rare, although there may be some individual neighborhoods in Philadelphia where a low level of material and social resources has indeed galvanized family or community action. Nonetheless, the high level of resource clustering suggests the validity of those theories asserting that social and economic resources tend to cluster together within neighborhoods, more often undermining than enhancing individual and collective efficacy (Bandura 1995; Wilson 1987).

The positive correlations among social networks, organizational availability, and social climate suggest the possibility of constructing a general social resource measure that combines various features of a "good" neighborhood. We developed a global measure based on an equally weighted scale of neighborhood organizations, social networks, and social climate that we refer to as neighborhood social resources.[4] It may also be thought of as a measure of neighborhood-based social capital.

WHICH NEIGHBORHOOD FACTORS IDENTIFY FAMILY MANAGEMENT STRATEGIES?

We used only three aggregate measures to identify the determinants of the five family management strategies: the percent white, the percent poor, and the standardized neighborhood social resource composite. No individual-level predictors were used at this stage because the purpose was to describe how management practices vary by neighborhood. To determine the source of these relationships requires the simultaneous use of tract- and individual-level predictors. This analysis comes later.

The neighborhood-level analyses duplicate many of the individual-level findings reported in earlier chapters.

1. *Social networks are more positive* in tracts where poverty rates are lower and more minority residents live. They also tend to be higher where neighborhoods have more social resources, but this relationship does not quite reach statistical significance.

2. *The number of organizations* to which caregivers belong is higher

in tracts where poverty is lower, minorities are more prevalent, and social resources are more abundant.

3. *Investment in children* is greater in neighborhoods with more minorities, but it is not related to levels of poverty or social resources. (Remember that the ICC for investment was only .04, indicating little neighborhood variation to predict in the first place.)

4. *Restrictiveness* is greater where there are more minorities, but as with investment, it is not strongly related to either poverty or social resources, even though the ICC value for restrictiveness is relatively high (.13).

5. *Parochial, private, and magnet schools* are attended more by adolescents living in white neighborhoods and neighborhoods with more social resources, but attendance at such schools is not related to local poverty levels.

Note that four of the five family management strategies are more prevalent in predominantly minority neighborhoods than in white ones. Investment and restrictiveness require the most time and child-centered effort from parents and probably elicit frequent negative reactions from early adolescents, given that these practices occur within the home and that early adolescents increasingly desire autonomy and the freedom to be with their peers. In minority communities we also find a higher prevalence of those management practices that depend on creating quality links outside of the family home, through the greater use of both social networks and links to local institutions. It seems, then, that minority neighborhoods are where the most active family management occurs.

Even so, a difference exists between more and less advantaged minority communities. The more advantaged minority communities place relatively more emphasis on social networks and institutional connections, while the less affluent ones emphasize restrictiveness and investment. There is a certain poignancy to this social class difference. Residents of poorer minority tracts have less access to better-behaving and better-performing peers, role models, and extended social networks, and they may resort to restrictiveness and investment in order to deal with their more restricted local opportunity structure and with their greater exposure to local dangers. But in so doing they have to expend more onerous and sustained daily effort when compared with parents who principally rely on their social networks and institutional connections to cosocialize their children. Restrictiveness and investment may be the most practical options available to parents living in poor minority neighborhoods, but they may be options that many adolescents come to resent. We learned in earlier chapters that skilled parents are able to deal with this dilemma by gaining their children's confidence, but many parents have trouble gaining compliance from their children as they enter the adolescent years.

The level of management found in predominantly white neighborhoods is generally low: actual parental investment and restrictiveness are lowest of all in all-white tracts, and social networks and institutional connections are particularly low if predominantly white neighborhoods are also poor.

These results provide no support for the idea that parents in poorer white communities are especially sophisticated in managing their children's well-being because they feel physically beleaguered by local minorities whose behavioral predilections they fear will negatively influence their own children (Furstenberg and Hughes 1995). Instead, when they can afford to do so, it seems that white parents link their children to better schools in order to protect them and promote their positive development. In effect, they subcontract responsibility for their children's development to superior schools where their offspring are exposed to more conforming peers, to more attentive teachers and staff, and to more out-of-home supervision, both during school hours and probably also more often after them. Many urban whites see these schools as functional communities that counter some local negative influences and link children to a broader range of informal and formal supports than ordinary public schools allow.

ARE NEIGHBORHOOD DIFFERENCES IN FAMILY MANAGEMENT DUE TO INDIVIDUAL DIFFERENCES OR TO SOME EMERGENT PROPERTY?

Determining whether neighborhood differences in family management are due to individual differences or to some emergent property requires statistical models in which measures of individual differences are examined simultaneously with tract-level measures. The key issue is whether neighborhood differences are still related to family management once differences in social composition are (at least partially) accounted for. In the accompanying tables, the individual measures vary slightly from one model to another, depending on the pattern of relationships with family management practices discovered in previous chapters. We conducted analyses with the individual differences specified as fixed effects and the mean neighborhood effects specified as random. This permitted us to describe some of the ways in which family management differs for different kinds of people in different types of neighborhoods.

Appendix table A.7.3 shows that, of the nine tract differences in family management discussed earlier, two persist after using individual-level controls and three others are marginally significant. This suggests that neighborhood variation in individual differences accounts for most of the previously reported relationships between family management and a tract's racial composition, poverty status, and level of social resources. Thus the predominant evidence does not suggest that certain types of neighborhoods engender unique social or cultural norms that sustain a particular form of family management regardless of who lives in them. It is as if families import their management practices into neighborhoods rather than develop them in response to the social influences they find there.

However, some important exceptions arise to this general conclusion. One is that when individual-level controls are used—including an individual respondent's own race—the relationship between the tract's racial composition and use of restrictiveness decreases but remains large and statistically significant. This suggests that restrictive family management practices are promoted as a stronger social norm in predominantly minority neighborhoods. Why is this? It is not because only the white residents of predominantly minority neighborhoods are disposed to keep their children indoors. In a racially segregated society like that of the United States, the most segregated neighborhoods have so few whites that they cannot plausibly account for the strength of the observed relationship between restrictiveness and the percent minority. Perhaps the density of minority families functions as a social signal to all residents that their children will somehow be put at risk on the streets, whether because police are harsher in minority neighborhoods or because parents of all races and classes fear that their children will be adversely affected by any links—real or perceived—between race and lower-class street culture (Anderson 1990; Waters 1990). Whatever the explanation, it seems that in neighborhoods with more minorities, restrictiveness increases to well beyond what we would find based on a family's individual characteristics, including its race.

A second exception to the global finding that social composition accounts for most of the observed relationships between neighborhoods and family management is that social networks tend to be larger in census tracts with fewer poor residents, even after controls are instituted for income, education, and single-parent status. The implication here is that something about the social dynamics in more affluent urban settings helps to place families in more extensive and more resource-laden social networks. And we know that many benefits result from knowing more people, for through them one can also know the people they know (Granovetter 1973).

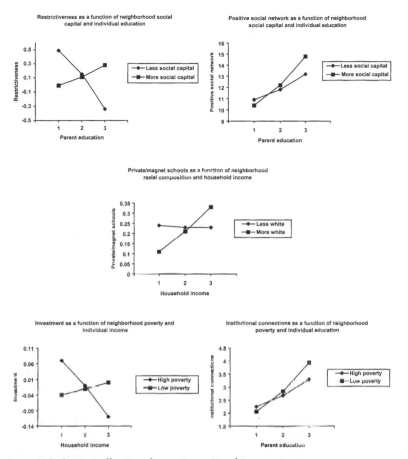

Figure 7.2 Statistically Significant Cross-Level Interactions:
Family Management

DO DIFFERENT TYPES OF FAMILIES PREFER DIFFERENT FAMILY MANAGEMENT STRATEGIES IN DIFFERENT KINDS OF NEIGHBORHOODS?

Whenever neighborhood factors were significantly or marginally related to a given family management strategy, we probed for statistical interactions between the neighborhood factor and individual family or child variables. The significant interactions are shown in appendix table A.7.3 and are graphed in figure 7.2.[5] The findings show the following.

1. In neighborhoods with less social capital (measured by the unweighted sum of networks, institutional resources, and social climate),

parents with the least education tend to be more restrictive about their child's use of space. In contrast, in more advantaged neighborhoods the better-educated parents tend to be more restrictive. The most restrictive parents of all are the least-educated ones living in the worst neighborhoods, and the least restrictive are the most educated ones living in the worst neighborhoods.

2. Although parents with more years of education tend to have more positive social networks overall, this relationship is more pronounced in neighborhoods with more social capital. This suggests that education has less of an effect for those who live in the most-advantaged settings and has less of an effect in the least-advantaged neighborhoods.

3. Parents with more years of education tend to have more institutional connections. But once again the slope is steeper in the most-advantaged neighborhoods, though this time advantage is explained by the neighborhood's low poverty rate rather than its level of social capital.

4. In minority neighborhoods the likelihood that a child goes to a selective school is not related to household income. But income is so related in white neighborhoods, for the more affluent white families are those most likely to send their children to better schools. Once again, we see that the family advantage variable (income) has a greater influence in the more advantaged settings where most whites live.

5. The final result was only marginally significant, but is presented because it bears a close conceptual resemblance to the first one presented above. In more advantaged neighborhoods, households with higher incomes tend to invest more in their children at home, whereas in high poverty neighborhoods, the least affluent do the most investing.

At first sight these complex relationships present a confusing picture. At the tract level, poverty is sometimes implicated as a causal variable, but at other times the level of social resources is implicated, or the tract's racial composition. At the individual level, the caregiver's education is sometimes implicated, but at other times household income is. Remember, however, that social resources, poverty rate, and minority rate are all correlated at the tract level, just as caregiver education and household income are at the individual level. If we recast the above findings in terms of *neighborhood advantage* (a lower poverty rate, more social resources, or fewer minority residents) and *family advantage* (more years of parent education or higher household income), then the complexity is reduced to two simple propositions that support many of the results presented in earlier chapters.

1. Institutional connections, positive social networks, and private/ magnet schools are most often used as management strategies when *both* the family *and* the setting are relatively more *advantaged*.

2. Parental investment and restrictiveness are most often used when both the *family* and *setting* are relatively *disadvantaged.*

Why is it that the least-advantaged parents in the worst neighborhoods do the most restricting and investing, and also tend to have the worst institutional connections, the worst social networks, and the weakest links to selective schools? One possibility is that the neighborhoods in which these residents live offer fewer opportunities for connecting to resource-laden institutions and social groups. Also, being personally less advantaged, these families may find it difficult to generate connections for themselves through their limited material resources, or they may lack whatever networking skills and opportunities higher social class promotes. The options most readily available to them therefore involve in-home strategies like restrictiveness and investment, and they cannot as easily rely on their environment to cosocialize their children with them—or even for them. They cannot count on the local setting to help their children learn and sustain the conventional values they themselves prefer (Cook and Curtin 1986). We can only speculate how well their in-home strategy works as adolescents grow older and want to spend more time with peers outside the home.

The present findings also show that the most advantaged parents living in the most advantaged settings enjoy the greatest number of institutional connections and the most positive social networks (especially if they are black), and that they also enjoy the highest rates of attending private or magnet schools (especially if they are white). But such parents do not invest as much in their children or restrict their movements any more than their less fortunate neighbors, perhaps because they get more support for their socialization goals both from formal institutions (including better schools) and informal social networks. Such parents are in a particularly good position to rely on their community and personal networks to cosocialize with and for them, reducing the need to make the special efforts other forms of management require. This finding replicates the results of our earlier ethnographic study and confirms much of the qualitative data collected following the survey (Furstenberg 1993; Walker and Furstenberg 1994).

Family management practices are less obvious when the relationship between family and neighborhood advantage is incongruous—that is, for worse-off families in better neighborhoods and for better-off families in worse neighborhoods. The least-advantaged parents living in the most advantaged settings are low in both institutional connections and social networks and are also among the least likely to send their children to selective schools. Yet they do not seem to be more restrictive and to invest more than their more advantaged counterparts in the same sorts of neighborhoods. Do the less advantaged parents living in advantaged neighborhoods feel socially uncomfortable using whatever resources are locally available to them? Or is it simply that they feel less able to afford access to institutions—including private schools—because of the membership fees or lifestyles associated with these institutions? In any event, their children may be in an especially precarious position.

Management preferences are also less clear for the relatively advantaged parents living in the worst neighborhoods. They do not restrict their children or invest in them as much as the less advantaged residents from the same kinds of neighborhoods, and they have fewer links to institutions and networks than their more affluent neighborhood peers. Have they given up the fight? Or does their philosophy of childrearing preclude too much control because they rely heavily on a child's self-directedness? Or do they choose their management strategies as a response to the fact that their children are faring better in school and elsewhere when compared with children from the least-advantaged families in the vicinity?

We do not yet know the answers to these intriguing explanatory questions.[6] Future research needs to replicate the relationships found here and probe the interpretations offered. We found it was easy to construct ex post facto explanations of the complex interactions involving neighborhood factors and individual-difference variables, and undoubtedly other interpretations could also be offered. Of course, offering them would only be worthwhile if the interactions discovered here are stable, which they may not be, considering the relatively small sample size in this study.

NEIGHBORHOODS AND EARLY ADOLESCENT SUCCESS

Neighborhood Variation in Success Indicators

Table 7.1 shows that for both the child's and parent's ratings of the child's emotional well-being, ICC values are close to zero. The ICC values for behavior problems and activity involvement are higher, but still quite modest: .044. The value for academic competence is highest, but still only .073.

These low values place a major constraint on the role neighborhoods can play in predicting adolescent success. If neighborhoods hardly vary in a variety of success indicators, then how can we hope to discover robust neighborhood predictors of such success? These ICC outcome values might well increase as young people enter late adolescence and early adulthood (Elliott et al. 1996), although we should note that the resource measures in table 7.1 are presumably less susceptible to variation in the development stage of individuals—and even these vary much more within census tracts than between them, at least as parents report on these resources. The modest ICC values for the early adolescent success outcomes suggest that simple, direct neighborhood influences on developmental outcomes are not likely to be large.

Which Neighborhood Characteristics Predict the Obtained Neighborhood Variation in Success?

Simple analyses limited to tract-level predictors revealed no reliable predictors of academic competence, behavioral problems, or either of the two mental health measures. Thus for four of the five success measures, the variation by tract is so small that it cannot be reliably predicted using the percent poor, the percent white, or the level of social capital in a neighborhood.

Only for participation in conventional activities is there predictable variation by tract. Analyses without individual-level controls reveal that such participation is reliably higher in tracts with less poverty, more social resources, and fewer whites. But when we introduce individual-level controls into the analysis in a fixed-effects design, none of the relationships between tract attributes and activity involvement remains statistically significant. When we allow the individual-level factors to include some random slopes, one of the earlier findings does remain. Neighborhoods high in social resources have residents who are reliably involved with more organizations. But this one result may well be due to chance, and anyway, it depends on a minor variation in model specification and so does not take much away from the three more general conclusions: (1) Neighborhood predictors of family management do not generally predict adolescent success; (2) however, tracts with less poverty and higher levels of social resources have higher rates of activity involvement; but (3) this relationship is more likely due to neighborhood differences in social composition than to any emergent social property at the neighborhood level.

Is Success Related to the Operation of Different Types of Family Management Strategies in Different Types of Neighborhoods?

The foregoing statistical models also included interactions between tract variables and family management strategies. These probe whether different management strategies have different "effects" on adolescent outcomes in different types of neighborhoods.[7]

Only two statistical interactions between family management and neighborhood factors are statistically significant, while two more are mar-

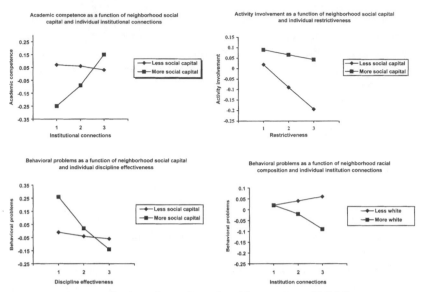

Figure 7.3 Statistically Significant Cross-Level Interactions: Child Outcome

ginally so. They are all noted in appendix table A.7.4 and are displayed in figure 7.3. One shows that institutional connections help increase reported academic competence, but only if the neighborhood has more social capital. A second shows that more effective discipline reduces behavioral problems, but once again only in neighborhoods with more social capital. A third shows that institutional connections reduce behavioral problems, but more so in neighborhoods that are predominantly white. What is striking about these three cases is that the family management strategy under analysis has the originally expected positive effects only in more advantaged settings; there is no evidence that family management variables are related to outcomes in the least-advantaged settings where trends are generally flatter. Note also that student outcomes are only more favorable in the more advantaged neighborhoods when the management variable under analysis is at higher levels. At lower ones, it is surprising that outcomes tend to be better in the less advantaged settings.

The fourth cross-level interaction arises because parents who restrict their children's activities have offspring who are involved in fewer growth-promoting activities outside of the home, especially when they live in neighborhoods with less social capital. The substantive implication of this is that the greater restrictiveness found in less advantaged neighborhoods may impede young people's chances to get involved with prosocial activities from which they could benefit. With restrictiveness there is obviously a point where good intentions prove harmful, both because of the tensions that arise between parents and autonomy-seeking youth and also because the young person, being cocooned at home, is exposed to fewer positive growth experiences. What the tipping point is for any child or population of children is not clear. But it is obvious, we believe, that at some point restrictiveness is counterproductive.

The results in figure 7.3 are not definitive, though. There is only one wave of outcome data; the causal ordering of variables is not always totally clear; and although we used many individual-level variables to deal with selection, we may have failed to choose the right variables. Also, there is undoubtedly some capitalization on chance, given the large number of possible interactions between the family management, neighborhood, and student outcome attributes. Nonetheless, it is intriguing to hypothesize that (1) family management strategies involving institutional connections and discipline effectiveness have larger positive effects in neighborhoods that are economically and socially more advantaged; and (2) restrictiveness has a particularly deleterious effect on young people's exposure to the outside world when neighborhoods are more economically disadvantaged. We believe that these hypotheses should be examined.

CONCLUSIONS

The Modest Intraclass Correlations

Within the limits imposed by the design of this study, the intraclass correlations in table 7.1 suggest that variation in social resources, family management practices, and early adolescent outcomes is considerably greater within neighborhoods than between them. This evidence conflicts with the belief of those who contend that neighborhood cultures play a dominant role in problem behavior, poor academic success, and other indicators of well- or ill-being.

One possible implication of this finding is that families may be less dependent on their physical neighborhood today than formerly and may, instead, be more prone to seek opportunities and resources outside their immediate communities. Does this mean that local geographical communities are now less important than the networks that families cobble together to meet their needs across a much broader area? Is this even true for urban ghettoes to a larger degree than Wilson (1987) specified? There may well be more social isolation there than in other neighborhoods, but still not as much as journalists portray when they describe families that have never been to a city's affluent downtown even though they live in close proximity to it (e.g., Kotlowitz 1991).

We need to be cautious, though. Even at an early age, local communities could be laying the groundwork for large neighborhood differences that will eventually emerge in later adolescence or early adulthood. Younger adolescents from poor neighborhoods have presumably already learned that opportunity structures are more restricted for them than for others, even though this study presents few indications that such knowledge has yet influenced their behavior or mental health. However, we did not assess some of the cognitive and affective forerunners of later behavior change, even though they may be crucial components of growth trajectories that vary by neighborhood but do not influence the success outcomes examined here until the young person is somewhat older.

Table 7.1 also shows that, in general, neighborhoods differ more in economic and social resources than in most of the practices families use for managing the external world. In turn, these family management practices vary more by neighborhood than do early adolescent outcomes, traditional measures of family process, or parents' psychological attributes. This pattern of results undermines the simple premise that neighborhood circumstances cause family management practices that then cause children's behavior. A more complex theory is called for, and we begin to sketch the broadest outlines of this theory, first by examining how neighborhood attributes relate to management practices and then by examining both the direct path from neighborhoods to success and the indirect path through family management.

From Neighborhoods to Family Management

The results indicate several patterned relationships between neighborhood characteristics and referred family management strategies from among the five we are examining. The most salient among these relationships are the following: (1) In predominantly white neighborhoods, private and selective public schools are used more than elsewhere; (2) in predominantly black neighborhoods with greater resources, we find the heaviest reliance on institutional connections and positive social networks, though restrictiveness and in-home investment are also higher than in mostly white neighborhoods; and (3) in black neighborhoods with the fewest resources, we find the heaviest dependence on restrictiveness and in-home investment.

When individual-difference variables are used in the analysis, we typically find that neighborhoods influence family management in complex rather than simple ways. Statistical interactions reveal that the more prosperous families from within predominantly white neighborhoods more often use private or more selective public schools; the most advantaged families in the most favored minority neighborhoods most often use institutional connections and positive social networks; and the least-advantaged families in the worst neighborhoods resort to restrictiveness and investment. Many of the links from neighborhoods to family management depend on the interplay between neighborhoods and family factors rather than on neighborhood, family, or personal attributes examined separately.

The neighborhood-level differences in family management that we discovered can generally be accounted for by individual-level variables. This suggests that most of the differences we observe at the tract level are created by neighborhood compositional characteristics resulting from neighborhoods' having unique mixes of different kinds of people. They do not result from some unique normative climate influencing all or most of the resident families. The major exception to this generalization involves restrictiveness, which increases as the percentage of minority neighborhood residents increases, even after individual-difference controls are used. "Something" about the nature of an increasingly non-white neighborhood amplifies parents' wariness about letting their children go outside the home, and this occurs regardless of the affluence level of a community, although it does tend to be slightly stronger in poorer settings. Our guess is that the racial composition of the neighborhood acts as a social signal about dangers on the street from a variety of sources, engendering local norms about the need to be restrictive, but we do not know this from the data examined. Nor do we know about the family costs of having to implement restrictiveness, which can obviously run counter to the developmental needs of adolescents for greater autonomy.

From Neighborhoods to Adolescent Success

This chapter has shown that neighborhoods hardly vary in the particular set of success indicators examined, and that the variation that exists cannot be predicted well. Some suggestive leads about a few contingent relationships arise, but these do not fit together into an easily interpretable pattern. The surprising implication is that the Philadelphia neighborhoods we sampled appear to have very little direct impact on the outcomes studied—at least in the form in which we measured them and at the early adolescent age at which we measured them.

Predictably, then, very little evidence indicates that neighborhood circumstances improve early adolescent success *because* of the management practices families use either in or outside the home. If such a causal sequence occurs, it is likely to be contingent on highly specific combinations of neighborhood factors, management practices, and individual adolescent outcomes. Indeed the exploratory analyses we presented suggest that the more institutional connections a family has, the better the child's school performance is and the more he or she succeeds in avoiding behavior problems. But this holds only in the more advantaged neighborhoods. In the less favored ones, institutional connections do not vary with either outcome. Discipline effectiveness is also associated with fewer behavioral problems, but once again only in the better neighborhoods and not the worse ones. And finally, restrictiveness seems to keep children away from positive experiences more in disorganized than organized neighborhoods. In all four cases, family management practices confer fewer positive benefits in the less advantaged settings.

If this last relationship could be replicated elsewhere, it would suggest one reason why we found main effects of neighborhood variables on family management but not on our measures of adolescent success. This last link is more contingent than we originally envisaged, and it may occur more strongly in better neighborhoods rather than in the worse settings where we had originally expected it to be. Since it is not clear why this should be so, the most judicious conclusion would seem to be that this chapter produced a much better understanding of the causal links between neighborhoods and family management practices than between management practices and early adolescent outcomes. With so little variation in the outcomes (see table 7.1) and only forty-five neighborhoods, the capacity to identify subtle relationships is inevitably limited in any analysis with so many neighborhood attributes; so many family, parent, and child characteristics; five separate family management practices; and five unique outcomes for adolescent success.

Adolescent Competence and the Effects of Cumulative Risk Factors

With the assistance of
W. TODD BARTKO, CYNTHIA HARPER, AND CHRISTOPHER C. WEISS

The findings presented in the last several chapters have shown how parents with differing amounts of resources employ strategies either deliberately or indirectly aimed at improving their children's prospects of success. We have paid particular attention to how families manage their children's environments to enhance their development. By and large, the statistical analyses leading to these results relied on a fairly conventional mode of exploring the links between the contexts, family management practices, and domains of success. That is, we have looked at each of these realms discretely, organizing the building blocks of the analysis variable by variable. This is standard practice in most developmental and sociological research.

Qualitative analysis generally eschews this approach of breaking down the world into discrete variables, preferring a more holistic and contextual perspective of analysis. We discuss this again in chapter 9. It is not our aim in this book to advocate one perspective over the other but rather to exploit the advantages of each and, whenever possible, to juxtapose the results gleaned when both modes of analysis are examined in concert. We have tried to work back and forth, attempting to verify one way of looking at the data by testing it against the findings produced by the other.

This chapter adopts a somewhat different approach to looking at the data than we have used in earlier chapters. It reiterates the multivariate statistical results presented in earlier chapters, but uses instead an aggregated or cumulative treatment of the information from the survey, making no attempt to tease out either the causal pathways of influence or the separate contributions of each measure. We employ what is frequently referred to as a risk-and-resiliency framework, a perspective that has emerged from epidemiological research aimed at identifying high-risk environments and the conditions that mitigate the dangers these environments pose. This approach has been particularly favored in the public health and clinical research that attempts to discover how children who grow up in extreme adversity manage to "beat the odds" of failure.

RISK AND RESILIENCY

Although differences in outcomes are frequently associated with single environmental risk factors, these differences rarely explain large proportions of outcome variance. To gain more predictive power, a number of researchers have begun to examine the effect of combinations of risk factors. Many years ago, Rutter (1979) argued that it was not any particular risk factor, but the *number* of risk factors in a child's background that led to psychiatric disorder. He showed that psychiatric risk for a sample of ten-year-olds rose from 2 percent in families with zero or one risk factor to 20 percent in families with four or more. The risk factors considered included severe marital distress, low socioeconomic status, large family size or overcrowding, paternal criminality, maternal psychiatric disorder, and admission of the child to foster care. More recently, Williams, Anderson, McGee, and Silva (1990) related behavioral disorders in eleven-year-olds to a cumulative disadvantage score based on number of residence and school changes, single parenthood, low socioeconomic status, marital separation, young motherhood, low maternal cognitive ability, poor family relations, marriage counseling, and maternal mental health symptoms. When outcomes were compared for groups with increasing levels of risk, only 7 percent of children with less than two disadvantages demonstrated behavior problems, whereas the rate was 40 percent for the children with eight or more disadvantages.

Sameroff and colleagues (Sameroff et al. 1987, 1993) examined the effect of multiple risk on intellectual as well as mental health outcomes of four-year-olds; they found that in families with fewer than two risk factors, no children had IQ scores below 85, while in high-risk families, 24 percent of four-year-old children had low IQ scores. An even more dramatic story played out in the long run: when the relation between cumulative risk and outcome was reexamined almost a decade later, the percent of youths with IQs below 85 had increased to 44 percent in the high-risk group, whereas it still remained at zero percent in the low-risk group.

What is important in these studies is the difference in predictive power when using single versus cumulative risk factors. The group of children in families with a single risk factor had lower intelligence and emotional health than the children in families without that risk factor, but the overlap in outcomes was significant. For example, although children with an emotionally disturbed mother did worse on average, many children with such mothers were doing quite well. But if the comparison was made between children with only a few risk factors and those with many risk factors, such as an emotionally disturbed mother, low income, no father in the house, many stressful life events, and no social support, then there was almost no overlap in outcome. Moreover, it did not seem to matter what the risk factors were, only how many there were. Families with any combination of the same number of risk factors had children who where doing equally well or equally poorly. Again, we must emphasize that counting the number of risk factors did nothing to describe the processes by which children in these families were achieving or failing, but it did indicate which children fell into each group. For the purposes of preventing negative outcomes, identifying such groups is a necessary initial step that can provide insights into the potential mechanisms that increase the odds of success or failure.

This chapter adopts a risk-and-resiliency perspective, but modifies it in some important ways. We examine the extent to which family management practices mitigate the cumulative risks created by unfavorable neighborhood conditions, demographic disadvantages, or parents' psychological liabilities. We make use of the multivariate analysis presented in previous chapters to identify the components of risk and resiliency. This analysis thus reiterates or summarizes what we have learned thus far, but it does more than just that: it offers a different way of testing whether family management practices actually do mitigate environmental risks by examining the set of "protective factors," in the form of parenting practices, that actually may buffer the child from these potential hazards. Following the scheme adopted in previous chapters, we combine these into two broad clusters that represent parental socialization techniques and strategies for managing the external world. Our objective is to determine whether and how much these family patterns offset the risks of coming from a disadvantaged neighborhood, a family with limited resources, or one in which the parents are not psychologically robust.

MEASURING RISK

The separate components that we use to measure risk and protection are the same that we introduced in earlier chapters and used in the multivari-

Table 8.1
Variables in analysis

Outcome measures

Academic competence
Activity involvement
Mental health problems (parent's report)
Behavioral problems

Family protective variables

Family management
    Institutional connections
    Social networks
    Parental investments in child
    Private/magnet schooling

Family processes
    Family climate
    Autonomy
    Discipline

Explanatory risk variables

Caregiver's resources
    Resourcefulness
    Self-efficacy
    Mental health

Demographic variables
    Age of child
    Gender of child
    Race
    Parent education
    Parent marital status
    Household income
    Welfare
    Number of children in household

Neighborhood variables
    Percent of families in poverty, 1990 census tract
    Institutional resources
    Climate

---

ate models presented in chapters 5–7 (see table 8.1). We need to explain how we grouped them together and our rationale for including or excluding certain variables in the following analysis. Generally speaking, the risk components were constituted from the neighborhood, demographic, and parental measures that were directly or indirectly linked to at least one of the outcomes of success explored in the three preceding chapters

Table 8.2

Multiple-risk score distribution (demographic, neighborhood, and caregiver's resources) and average outcome scores by number of risks

| Number of risks | Sample distribution | | Mean outcome scores by number of risks | | | |
	Percentage	N	Academic competence	Activity involvement	Mental health problems	Behavioral problems
0	7.6%	36	.36	.42	−.35	−.20
1	16.2%	77	.27	.08	−.21	−.17
2	17.4%	83	.08	.00	−.08	−.02
3	16.4%	78	.05	.06	−.11	−.09
4	13.9%	66	.09	.01	.04	.22
5	11.3%	54	−.48	−.23	.25	.20
6	8.8%	42	−.45	−.17	.39	.05
7	5.0%	24	−.05	−.07	.07	.34
8+[a]	3.4%	16	−.35	−.46	.75	−.02

Note: The multiple risk score includes demographic, neighborhood, and caregiver's variables, enumerating each variable as a separate risk.

a. There are ten variables in total, but the top category is collapsed to eight or higher, since there are only three observations in the higher categories.

with multivariate analysis. Appendix table A.8.1 presents the risk components and the ranges of risks. To transform the continuous variables into risk factors, we defined as "high risk" those falling in the lowest quartile.[1] For the categorical variables, such as a single parent or welfare receipt, high risk was defined as being in the risk state (i.e., single parent on welfare). To show the total number of risks that the adolescents face, we simply added the risks together across variables, so that each individual is assigned a multiple-risk score.

As table 8.2 shows, potential risk scores (number of risks) ranged from 0 to 10, though the relatively few cases with scores above 8 are grouped together because of small numbers. A huge variation exists within this inner-city sample of families, with fewer than 10 percent falling at each of the extremes: while nearly 8 percent of the sample have no risks, approximately the same percentage have seven or more risks at the high end. The mean risk score is 3.8, and the median number of risks is 3. The relationship of the risk score to each of the four domains of success generally conforms to expectations: with rising levels of risk, performance drops in each of the domains.

The variability of the cumulative risk score in relation to the outcome measures led us to consider an alternative measure of risk that is conceptually more congruent with the theory underlying our study. Instead of creating an overall risk score that disregards the site or source of the risk, we took into account the arenas in which the child was at risk, computing

Table 8.3

Group risk score distribution and average outcome scores by number of risks

	Mean outcome scores by number of risks			
Risk score	Academic competence	Activity involvement	Mental health problems	Behav- ioral problems
0	.20	.13	−.21	−.13
1	.02	−.02	.00	.03
2	−.35	−.15	.29	.13
3	−.42	−.52	.80	.31

Note: The multiple-risk score combines all the demographic, neighborhood, and caregiver's variables into one variable, which is then coded low to high risk, 0 to 3, based on the combined categories.

separate risk scores for each of the contexts explored in earlier chapters: the neighborhood level, the household level, and the individual level that measures the psychological resources of the child's principal caregiver. By aggregating risks within each context, we increased the stability of each measure. This approach is based on a somewhat different theory of risk. Severity of risk may not be simply judged by the *number* of risks but by their *distribution* in different realms of the child's life. Children, we posit, will be worse off when they experience high risk in many separate spheres inside and outside the home, even if their overall risk score is numerically lower than the scores of those at risk in only one or two contexts.

Appendix table A.8.2 provides the scheme for classifying risk levels and the distribution of cases in each category as the number who are at high risk in zero, one, two, or three or more contexts. Slightly more than a third of the sample is not at high risk in any context, almost the same percentage is at risk in one context; a fifth is at risk in two contexts, and only 3 percent are at risk in all three neighborhood, demographic, and caregiver contexts. Even in this urban sample, where most of the children are living in areas of moderate levels of poverty and neighborhoods with considerable urban blight, only a quarter of the children are in the category we have defined as severe risk (at high risk in two or more contexts).

Table 8.3 shows how the level of risk based on this more context-based measure is related to the four outcomes of success. We generated this level of overall risk by combining measures of risk from the three contexts—demographic, neighborhood, and caregivers' resources—and generating a composite measure based on the number of high-risk contexts children faced.[2] In the table we see how the differences in average outcome by group risk score show an even more regular pattern than what we observed in table 8.2. As the risks increase, the average outcomes are progressively worse. The worst outcomes are seen for the youths who come from high-risk neighborhoods, have high-risk demographic traits, and have poor caregivers' resources. The range in scores is large and linear, suggesting that the number of high-risk contexts is at least as important than the risk level based on a simple count. This global risk measure gives us a good way of testing family management techniques in mediating the effect of hazardous environments on adolescents' lives.

PROTECTIVE FAMILY FACTORS

Although other analyses (e.g., Sameroff, Seifer, and Bartko 1997) have suggested separate techniques for measuring risk and protective factors, here we examined them in combination. We are exploring whether positive family management practices offset negative risks associated with parent, household, or neighborhood conditions. Our measures of "protection" are similarly constructed by classifying the in-home measures of family management (parental warmth, support for autonomy, etc.) and the external measures (institutional connections, parental investment, public versus private schooling, etc.) into two separate indices. Appendix table A.8.3 provides the scheme we used for constructing the measures. Each family measure combines the various subscales that were a part of the analysis described in earlier chapters, maintaining the distinction between in-home and external management practices. For each of these items, we defined the families with particularly high scores as falling into the highest quartile on a particular scale. We then transformed the separate variables into one measure of protective family process and one measure of protective family management by aggregating the scores in each area, as we did for the neighborhood and demographic variables. The qualitative case studies provided validation that this coding scheme did a good job of distinguishing between families at the high end of effective management from those with average or low practices.

DOES FAMILY MANAGEMENT OFFSET RISK?

Turning now to the central question of whether risk is offset by the presence of skillful parenting and active management of the external world, we look at the data from several different vantage points. Figures 8.1–8.4 summarize the results regarding whether and how much in-home and external management practices mitigate the impact of risk. The bars on each graph show an adjusted risk score measuring how well a child is doing compared to the average of the entire sample—set at zero to create a common metric. This permits us to examine simultaneously the impact

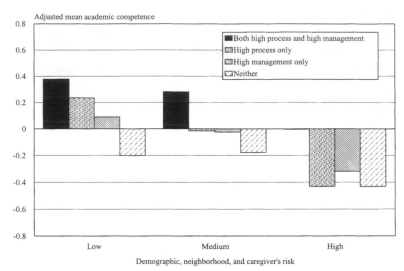

Figure 8.1 Academic Competence by Family Process and Family Management

of a negative risk environment and the positive family management practices for each separate outcome. Figure 8.1 shows the results for the outcome of academic competence. We notice that the risk level is strongly associated with academic competence when we compare the levels of all the bars in the low-, medium-, and high-risk environments respectively. In the low-risk environment, academic competence is clearly higher than in the medium- and high-risk environments. The different categories of parenting are shown by the four bars in each risk group. The leftmost bar (i.e., high academic competence) represents youth with both highly protective family processes and management techniques. The two middle bars represent the youth who have either high process or high management, but not both. The rightmost bar, and academic scores, are for youth with neither family protective mechanism. Effective parenting makes a large difference in low- and moderate-risk environments, especially when parents excel in practices both inside and outside the home. When they do neither, their children are significantly worse off. But the pattern is quite different in a high-risk environment. No matter how well the parents manage, their children have below-average scores in academic competence. Indeed, if the parents are very adept, their children are average at most, and with parents doing anything less than that, children perform very poorly. We suspect that these results reflect the parents' differential access to adequate schools and the limited resources they have to compensate for what the children do not receive from school.

At first glance, figure 8.2, referring to activity involvement, may seem

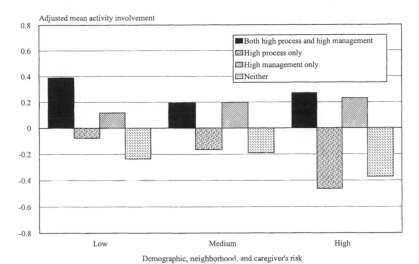

Figure 8.2 Activity Involvement by Family Process and Family Management

utterly confusing, showing the up-and-down relationship across different risk levels. The results are not as anomalous as they might appear, however. Generally speaking, activity level is somewhat related to risk environment, but the more important association is to parental ability to manage the external world. The bars showing strong family management skills, bars 1 and 3, are always higher for each risk environment, reflecting the fact that children are more involved when their parents are themselves more connected. This finding is consistent with the results presented in earlier chapters. Family process (the in-home dynamics) is not decisive in determining how youths fare in the realm of activity involvement.

The mental health outcome results, presented in figure 8.3, show that the in-home practices do account for the success of children's psychological adjustment. The higher bars for family processes, showing more mental problems (recall that this is coded the reverse of the two previous outcomes), persist in all risk groups. Overall, the risk environment contributes only minimally to the outcome. As we learned from earlier analysis, parental ability to manage the external world also makes only a trivial difference.

Turning finally to behavioral problems, we see yet a different pattern (see figure 8.4). The risk environment appears to have a greater influence on behavioral problems than does family management. The high-risk youths in all of the different family categories show more behavioral problems on average, and the low-risk youths show fewer problems, re-

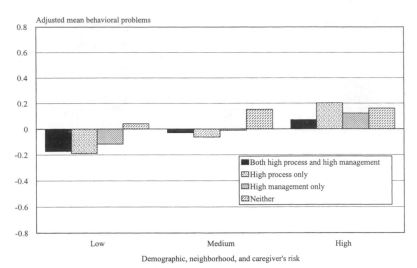

Figure 8.3 Mental Health Problems by Family Process and Family Management

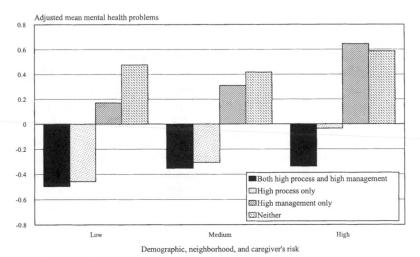

Figure 8.4 Behavioral Problems by Family Process and Family Management

gardless of family techniques (again, a lower score is better). This tells us that the demographic, neighborhood, and caregiver's resources that make up the risk contexts are more important in determining behavioral problems. Family management seems to have little or no impact in reducing the results. This result—that family management offsets environmental resource but differently for different outcomes—neatly summarizes the results of the multivariate analyses presented in earlier chapters.

Odds ratio, relative to "high risk" and "neither"

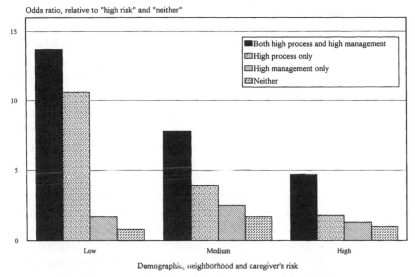

Figure 8.5 Relative Effect by Family Process and Family Management

A more coherent picture of the association of family management with adolescent success emerges when we turn to a summary measure of success that divides the sample into children who are generally successful and those who experience moderate or severe problems. This analysis relies on the cluster analysis that groups children by overall performance for the four discrete measures. The findings are presented in figure 8.5, which translates the results of the multivariate analysis into odds ratios of success depending on the level of risk and the degree of buffering provided by the family in the form of effective in-home and external family management.

Earlier in this chapter we observed that successful adolescent performance is strongly linked to risk environments. Now, we are able to see more precisely how those odds of success change when children are buffered by effective management in the home, outside the home, or both. For purposes of comparison, we set the odds at 1 in the worst-case scenario—for children who are living in a high-risk environment in families where parents provide poor or just ordinary levels of management. The graph illustrates how much the odds of success rise according to the level of risk and the presence of effective family management inside or outside the home, or when both are available to the child.

Children in a high-risk environment are almost *five* times as likely to succeed if families engage in highly effective in-home practices and are also highly successful at managing the external world. Doing only one of these increases the odds of success, but the improvement is not statistically significant. A similar pattern of enhancement occurs as we move to the moderate-risk environment. However, when families are highly effective in both in-home and external management practices, their children are almost *eight* times as successful as in the worst-case scenario. We can also see that either protective factor contributes to improved odds of success in the moderate-risk environment; in this case the differences are large enough to be statistically significant. However, if families offer neither effective management inside the home nor of the outside environment, children are likely to do no better than their counterparts at higher risk.

We observe a similar result among children living in the lowest-risk situation, where the absence of effective family process and management leads to equally poor odds of success even though the environment is relatively benign. This result contrasts strikingly with what occurs under the most favorable circumstances. When youth have everything going for them—both a highly effective family and a favorable life situation— they are almost *fourteen times* more likely to succeed than the youth living in the worst conditions.

The implications of these findings are that youth require *both* effective parents and benign environments to do well. They can succeed at relatively high levels if their families are very effective, even when they are living at high risk; they are only somewhat likely to succeed if their families are not very effective, even if they are residing in relatively benign circumstances. Still, environmental risk contributes enormously to the odds of making it. Youth are twice as likely to be successful by our global measure if they face only a moderate level of risk and three times as likely to be successful if they face a low level of risk, even when they receive the most effective parenting.

To sum up, our findings tell us that children are not able to reap the benefits of a better environment when their parents are incapable of or inept at capitalizing on those advantages. Nonetheless, disadvantage exacts its price even on children of the most skilled parents. We say more about this finding in the next chapter, when we discuss how children are faring in later adolescence.

B efore going on, we need to frame these results by referring to the introduction to this chapter. Effective parenting by itself does not occur in isolation; it is linked to the resources available to parents in the form of money, institutional support, social connections, and the like. We also know that more psychologically resourceful parents can make do with less. At the same time, we have learned along with other researchers that making do with less ultimately reduces the parents' reservoir of psychological resources. Parents operate in household and community contexts that can reinforce or erode their capacities to parent effectively. None of the conditions that we have examined is entirely independent of the others, but they make up the changing developmental context in which children reside.

Parents who are able to cope effectively in their immediate and more distal environments appear to greatly enhance their children's chances of success, assuming that this is the causal direction of the association described in the analysis presented in this chapter. Yet parents cope effectively largely because they are able to make use of the resources available to them. To separate the interrelated elements of this system is to misrepresent it in some respects. It is useful then—having featured separate units in this chapter—to put this system back together again, which is our aim in the next chapter.

Nine

Looking Ahead

Patterns of Success in Late Adolescence

With the assistance of
KAREN WALKER

Adolescence is marked by frequent turning points that bring opportunities for improving skills, such as entering a public magnet school, finding a good part-time job, or assuming a leadership position at school or in a youth group. It can also be a time of setbacks or negative events, such as an arrest, an unplanned pregnancy, or suspension from school. These transition points do not occur randomly to teenagers and their families; they arise out of prior experience. Youth who are not doing well in school rarely make it to magnet schools, and girls who are under-performing academically are also much more likely to become teenage parents. Youth from more affluent families who attend more select schools receive much more sponsorship and social support from mentors and social support for their academic careers (Furstenberg 1993; Cookson and Persell 1985; Cary 1991). Although the influence of family and community affects the trajectory of adolescence, teens also are becoming more active in selecting and responding to events as they enter their later teens.

We have argued in prior chapters that the advantages and disadvantages that youth and their families accumulate over time ensure a certain degree of personal continuity. However, we have also observed that many Philadelphia teens have only a tenuous hold on success, suggesting that maintaining their present trajectories will be difficult. Given the precarious circumstances in the lives of many teens, it is especially important to follow their transition from early to later adolescence, when inner-city youth begin to encounter critical turning points involving entry into the labor force or higher education. Our desire to know more about paths taken or foregone led us to speak informally with a small number of boys and girls and their parents in 1993, two years after we originally conducted the survey. We selected participants from four quite different neighborhoods: a community inhabited primarily by middle- and working-class African-American families; a socially stable, moderate-income, white community; a low-income, black community afflicted with severe problems; and the poorest white community in our sample (one of the poorest in Philadelphia). As we explained in chapter 2, within each of these areas we deliberately picked adolescents who were doing well or poorly according to our different outcome measures in order to compare children in different neighborhoods who were succeeding by multiple criteria and those who were not.

The qualitative follow-up interviews allowed us to track the success of the children as well as how parental management practices had changed during the two years following the survey. This chapter describes what we learned as the youth moved from early to later adolescence. Thus it provides a preview of how we might expect these people to be faring as young adults—the topic of a seven-year follow-up of the families that will be conducted in 1998.

Over the two-year period from 1993 to 1995, we carried out a series of extended conversations with parents and youths in thirty-five households equally divided among the four different communities. Karen Walker, who conducted the fieldwork, spent enough time in each community to become more familiar with important features of the neighborhoods and to watch how the focal families were managing their immediate environments. We were particularly interested in observing changes that occurred as children gained greater autonomy in their later teens. We also met periodically with a group of six adolescents from our four neighborhoods who served as informants, guiding us through the more recondite features of adolescent culture and serving as commentators, offering an insider's perspective on findings from the survey analysis.

Parts of the informal conversations we had with these families have appeared throughout this volume, and although they do not surface in the text, these case studies are nonetheless an integral component of the analyses presented. These reports have been used to corroborate the findings based on the survey. The naturalistic sightings proved extremely valuable, strengthening our faith in the interpretations or suggesting alternative explanations to ones we might otherwise have offered.

We were particularly relieved to discover, when we coded the results of our in-depth conversations and compared them to scales constructed from the interviews conducted two years earlier, in 1991, a remarkable degree of consistency in the parenting practices reported by parents and youth. (For details of this analysis, see appendix tables A.9.1 and A.9.2.) Parents, it turns out, are highly stable in descriptions of their practices.

Children, too, have coherent and stable ways of characterizing how they are treated over time, despite the real changes that occur in specific rules and practices. Naturally, as we will see in this chapter, parents altered techniques of management as their children entered their mid-teens, but they usually did so in ways that were generally consistent with the styles captured by measures used in the survey.[1]

The fieldwork reinforced the impressions from the survey that parents and children can and sometimes do live in different social worlds and may interpret each other's actions differently (see chapters 3 and 4). Both in the unstructured interviews with youth and in the group discussions, we heard a good deal about how parents struggle to maintain and reinforce their understandings of how their children should behave, even as the adolescents spent more time outside the household and became increasingly autonomous.

The changing balance of control is always a central feature of early adolescent development, but the issue of control takes on a different cast for inner-city parents in a way that has not been sufficiently recognized in the literature. Not only did parents expect and exercise less control inside the household as their children entered the middle-teens—as is generally true for all American parents—but many inner-city parents began to experience real limitations in what they could do for their children as they got older and became aware of the constraints of attaining success in terms of conventional standards.

Bear in mind that the families we were most closely monitoring were selected to provide diversity. And diversity we found: even within strata selected by neighborhood and outcome, we discovered a wide range of patterns linked to family circumstances, parental skill, and children's temperament. This chapter uses the qualitative case studies of the thirty-five families interviewed from 1993 to 1995 to examine how these trajectories of development are related to some of the key constructs explored in previous chapters: parental investment and involvement in their children's lives, social resources and opportunity in the immediate environment, and the ability of parents and children to take advantage of these resources.

PATTERNS OF ADOLESCENT SUCCESS

By the time we got to know the thirty-five families, most youth were in their mid-to-late teens; the oldest was approaching adulthood. It was striking to discover the high degree of continuity between how youth were doing in 1991, when they participated in the survey, and how they were doing in 1993–1995, when we conducted the in-depth interviews.

Table 9.1
Teen academic outcomes in 1995 by survey clusters

	Academically competent	Socially involved	At-risk	Delinquent	Total
High school students					
Good progress	4	8	0	0	12
Poor progress	1	0	3	1	5
Disciplinary school	0	0	1	0	1
High school graduates					
College or other training	1	2	3[a]	0	6
Employed	0	1	0	1	2
Unemployed	1	0	0	0	1
High school leavers					
Employed	0	0	1	1	2
Unemployed	0	0	2	2	4
Other outcomes	1[b]	0	1[c]	0	2
Total	8	11	11	5	35

a. One at-risk teen graduated from high school and has plans to attend college beginning fall 1995.

b. Teen left her father and stepmother's home. We do not know her current status.

c. After leaving a disciplinary school for boys (without a diploma or a GED), one teen joined the Job Corps and left the area.

Table 9.1 displays the progress of the teens in 1995 by their behavior profiles, based on the survey results collected four years earlier. Just over one-half of the small sample was originally classified as academically competent or socially involved. Table 9.1 shows the extraordinary level of continuity from early to later adolescence. Nearly all the youth that we had previously categorized as academically competent or social achievers were on track in school. None of the nineteen had dropped out of school, although one was in academic trouble, and another's whereabouts was unknown. All had entered high school, and many of the oldest had graduated by 1995. Several of the more academically successful had already entered college.

In contrast, few of the youth who were classified either as delinquent or at-risk as early adolescents were making good progress in school or in the labor market in their later teens. Several had dropped out because of pregnancy, problem behavior, or repeated school retention. One young woman was receiving public assistance. Some of the young men were having serious problems with the law, and several had been placed in disciplinary schools by the court. Other young women and men were at least temporarily disengaged from work, school, and family. JJ Newman, a young man whom we've come to know in this volume, spent his days "hanging" and gambling.

In sum, most youth experienced stability across the two points in time: of the thirty-five cases, twenty-nine remained either successful or unsuccessful. Of the six cases who had changed their status, two were doing substantially worse in later adolescence than they were earlier, and three others had improved dramatically. There was insufficient information to make a determination of the sixth case, a girl who had earlier been classified as academically competent. She had moved from her father's to her mother's residence under stressful circumstances and could not be recontacted.

It is tempting to ignore the continuities in favor of trying to understand the conditions that alter young people's course of development. However, it is no less important to understand what keeps youth in place as it is to understand what changes their course. So we begin by describing the circumstances of youth who stayed on track and then turn to those who were falling further and further behind. Then we take up the several cases of "downwardly mobile" youth who have fallen off a more successful path. Although they are few, they provide clues as to what may be in store for a minority of our participants whose families cannot protect them from the increasingly severe demands made on young adults. Finally, we examine the most anomalous cases—those youth who unexpectedly seemed to find their footing in later adolescence. These youth offer insight into how the grip of prior experience and future expectations can be loosened by deliberate intervention or fortuitous circumstance. As we will see, even the anomalous cases—both those teens who did worse than we would have expected and those who did better—can be understood in light of the parenting, community, and family processes we have discussed throughout this volume.

In reviewing these four patterns, we are not endeavoring to explain fully the developmental courses they represent, but to show how particular constellations of social conditions and personal attributes can produce similar or different outcomes. Of course, we understand that the interlinking of outcomes cannot be taken for granted. As we have discussed in previous chapters, the paths to particular outcomes are by no means identical. Though our emphasis here is on examining socioeconomic attainment, we will show that it may be traded off at some points for alternative ideals of success, especially when a reasonable level of attainment cannot be achieved.

Some cases, in fact, resist simple categorization as "success" or "failure," partly because of the fluidity of the adolescent years but also because so many youth in our study are straddling the lower reaches of the social structure. For reasons to be described in this chapter, we see signs that the successes in our sample may founder as they reach adulthood. On the other hand, we detect some glimmerings of hope for youth who are doing poorly, hope that they may right themselves in time. The notion that young people's prospects are permanently secured or irretrievably lost by late adolescence is highly questionable.

Staying the Course: Teens Who Do Well

It is remarkable how many youth in our study managed to stay on course in view of the tremendous changes that were taking place in their lives during the period in which we became acquainted with them. A number went through puberty, and their appearance often changed dramatically. It was a time when most reworked their relationships with their families, becoming much more autonomous and self-reliant.

Shifts also occurred in their peer groups: few had the same friends in their earlier and later teens, and how and where they spent their time changed as well. At twelve or thirteen, most teens played at friends' homes after school and on weekends. Between fifteen and seventeen, a number of them began to traverse the city to "hang" in the malls or to survey the prospects on South Street, where teens frequently congregate, or the Belmont Plateau, a favorite meeting place for African-American youth. Sports involvement among both boys and girls had changed: those who still participated in organized sports were increasingly competitive and devoted larger amounts of time to their sports. However, many had dropped out of organized sports and after-school activities in favor of work or hanging out. Most were experimenting with alcohol, and some with drugs. A majority had become sexually active, and a number had entered (and sometimes exited) serious relationships. What signaled problem behavior at twelve or thirteen carried a very different set of meanings for youth of sixteen and seventeen.

Family life continued to change too. A few adolescents experienced the death of parents; older siblings moved out; parents lost or found jobs; several families moved; and one family lost its home to fire—such events can have profound negative or positive consequences for the family's standard of living. To be sure, some of these changes had visible impacts on the success trajectories, but it was even more surprising that many of these reconfigurations of family life did not alter the circumstances of youth who were doing well. Most teens on track rarely suffered more than a slight depression in their achievement—either academic or social—in the wake of these transformations of family fortunes.

The adolescents who continued to do well were not immune to life changes, but they frequently resided in more protective families who sheltered them from some of the turbulence that marks the adolescent years. How does this happen? Again, the case of Robert James is instructive.

Robert did well in an accounting program in a business high school. During his junior year in high school he landed a desired internship in a pharmaceutical company and was asked to work beyond the official end of the internship. Determined to meet a number of realistic life goals, Robert seemed well on his way to adult success as he and his family defined it. He expected to have an active community and family life, to become an accountant, and to balance work and family so that he could support a family financially without compromising his other priorities. In short, he exhibited a high level of planning (Clausen 1993).

A member of our focus group, Robert was bemused by experiences of other members of the group, especially regarding their complaints about their families. Robert, a tactful and modest youth, generally listened quietly. During one group meeting, when others were extremely vocal about how much they had to do, the number of chores assigned to them, and their problems in getting along with their parents, Robert, as usual, was quietly taking it in. When Marcia, one of the girls in the group, referred somewhat bitterly to herself as the "little mommy" in her family and asked Robert if he was the daddy in his family, Robert replied,

> Nooo. [Chuckled] No, my mom, she's able to be home over the weekends and like watch [my younger brother and sister]. I get home late on the weekdays and so my mom and dad, they're home. I have my responsibilities but as far as having to really raise my brother and sister, I don't have to go through that. Plus, my weekends they're like planned in advance cause like I'm booked til like December. *So your parents give you space?* Uh huh, and I always tell them in advance, cause as soon as I know something's coming up, like Saturday, there's a party, and I'm tellin' them, "Oh, yeah, we will be going," so I went over to my buddy's house, and when it came time to go, I just called and asked my dad if he give us a ride up there, he's like, "All right." I'm saying cause he like already know. They respect me.

Robert had become increasingly independent over his adolescent years, but his mother, Michelle, had not given up control as much as ceded it to Robert incrementally. When she believed that Robert might be exposed to risk, she intervened. For instance, we offered Robert the chance to do some limited fieldwork in his neighborhood, drawing maps of playgrounds and streets and exploring how space was used. Before our appointment to talk with him about it, Michelle called us to find out if

Robert would be interacting with undesirable people in the neighborhood. She let us know that she would not allow him to do work that
would put him at risk.

Michelle's family management continued in a developmentally appropriate way. She was responsive to his increasing need for autonomy as
he got older, but she was also responsive to the conditions in which the
family lived. Like many of the African-American parents who lived in
neighborhoods with few resources, she was somewhat more restrictive
than white parents. Sensitive to the immediate climate of violence and
conflict on the street, she closely monitored her children's activities in
the neighborhood.

As we have said earlier, the James family is an ideal-typical case of a
family in which the teen is on a path to success, and the family is rich in
the social and personal resources that encourage success. Michelle James
was a highly skilled parent. The family was embedded in a community
that reinforced the parents' norms. Michelle and Nate, both skilled and
loving parents, were deeply engaged in their children's lives. The family's
income was modest, but it was enough for them to meet their needs.
Robert was fond of repeating, almost as a mantra, "We have everything
we need and some of the things we want."

Michelle James was not alone among efficacious parents in being able
to rely on a combination of personal, familial, and community resources
to raise successful children, even though the James's intensive religious
involvement set them apart from other families. Youth who stayed on
course toward success from the time of our survey through the end of
our interview study three or four years later tended to live in families
characterized by a particular set of beliefs and practices. Parents felt as if
they could make (and indeed had made) a difference in their teens' lives
by giving them opportunities, helping them through their troubles, and
guiding them toward the future. Also, relations between parents and
teens were generally good in these families; parents and their children
usually reported a sense of mutual respect and affection. Furthermore,
the parents in these families rarely reported having to discipline their
older adolescents: typically they reported that they had last disciplined
their children several years before. They also reported that they trusted
their teens to stay out of trouble. The teens in these families reported a
great and growing sense of autonomy.

Successful teens also tended to have parents who made good use of the
family management strategies of community involvement and parental
investment. As we demonstrated in the previous chapter, families were
characterized by high levels of community involvement, and if parents
invested heavily in their children and were efficacious, then their teens,

like Robert James, almost invariably remained on track toward success. These findings are, therefore, quite similar to the results of our survey analysis. The major difference appeared to be that parents of older, successful teens tend to report that discipline becomes less and less important as they are granted more responsibility and autonomy.

Most families, however, do not have the rich and multiple resources that Nate and Michelle James do: the James family was part of only a handful of families, both white and black, who possessed that level of personal and social capital. More typically, parents would be high in some, but not all, of the resources and skills we measured: most were relatively isolated from communities—whether neighborhood-based, church-based, or communities of extended kin; others lacked psychological skills that were important to parenting, and some were still responding inflexibly to new situations or exhibiting low parental efficacy. However, even in families with less-abundant social and psychological resources than the Jameses, close to half of the teens continued on their paths toward success.

Because some of the youth in families with several risks did reasonably well, while others did not, we looked more closely at processes, events, or situations that differentiated the families in which teens did well from those in which they did poorly despite facing similar levels of risk. Our case studies revealed how some parents could compensate for fairly high risk levels, a qualitative parallel to some of the statistical analyses performed in earlier chapters.

First, many of the teens from these families went to Catholic schools, which seemed to have a powerful protective effect; particularly as the teens got older, parental involvement in school declined, and peer influence increased. Parents sent their children to the parochial schools for two reasons: often they had gone themselves and were following family tradition; and/or they believed the parochial schools provided a better education than the public schools. Sending children to Catholic schools was thus a promotive family management strategy—an important way to manipulate children's social and academic environment. To parents and their children it also represented a considerable investment. Parents were choosing to spend their limited resources on their children's educations.[2]

Second, parents had different abilities to package effectively the resources that they had. Some parents overcame deficits by drawing adeptly on the resources that they could access. Some, such as one of the parents who relied heavily on church and kin ties to help her with her son, were highly skilled in family management strategies. Although she lacked important parenting skills such as support for autonomy or discipline effectiveness, she was able to parlay this social capital to good effect. Other parents exhibited especially strong psychological resources and were able to use them effectively to compensate for low social resources. A parent whose community and institutional connections were somewhat sparse recounted a dramatic example of parental intervention with her sixteen-year-old son. Frustrated with his school performance, this mother drove him to the poorest and most dangerous of Philadelphia's neighborhoods and told him to get out of the car:

> He said, "Get out?" I said, "Yeah, take this bag of clothes and get out of the car." "Why?" I said, "Because this how you wanna live." He said, "I don't wanna get out here." I said, "But you do because you don't listen to me, you complain when I ask you to come in. I'm going to look for you out in the street all the time? You want me to let you party all the time. You just wanna do whatever. You go to one of the best schools in the world. Here you come from the top-notch math student in the school down to nothing, and I'm just tired." And then finally we come on back home, and he's crying. He says, "Mom, I know you're not crazy, but I thought you were going to put me out."

In his last year of high school, the young man in question was on the honor roll; he subsequently entered a college nursing program and appeared to have settled into college. In some families, this strategy would not have worked, the parent's action would have driven the teen further into intransigence. In this family, however, it may have worked because the mother had previously invested heavily in her children. Her promotive strategies included taking her children on family vacations, guaranteeing that there would be money for college, finding good high schools, and encouraging them to join academic summer programs. The daughter in the family reported,

> [My mom] always wanted me to do things that she never did. Like going and live in the dorms. Like she said before, I'm spoiled. I have many things that she didn't have when she was younger. When I ask her for somethin' I always seem to get it.

Strong reciprocal obligations, created through the mother's long-term actions and investments in her children, were in place in this family. When one child acted out and threatened to upset his mother's plans, she was in a good position to point out how much he owed her, and she received a certain degree of compliance. She had accumulated a certain amount of family-based social capital which could be cashed in when necessary (Furstenberg and Hughes 1995).

If parents of successful teens did not possess a single set of common

assets, there were nonetheless some commonalities in their parental practices. Above all, these parents continued to be active agents looking out
for their children's interests throughout adolescence. For example, a
young man living in the Jameses' neighborhood was interested in doing
fieldwork for us. Like Michelle James, however, his mother decided that
it would require too much participation in the neighborhood and was
therefore unsafe. When Lakisha Wilkenson's cash register at work came
up short, her mother spoke on her behalf to the store manager. Several
mothers reported that they actively assisted their children in finding
work by canvassing local businesses to see if any needed help. Several
of the more middle-class parents took their teens on tours of colleges.
Therefore, even in very late adolescence, a time when support for autonomy is high, parents of successful teens often continue to invest time
and resources in their children: sometimes as advocates, sometimes as
protectors or sponsors. These parents contrasted strongly with those
whose children were on a trajectory of failure.

Persistently Problematic: Teens Who Do Poorly

Of the thirty-five teens in our in-depth interview study who were classified as at-risk or delinquent at the time of the survey, seven had stopped
going to school or officially dropped out by 1995. Another five continued
to have extremely serious scholastic problems, and, we suspect, will not
complete high school. Of these twelve teens, four were classified as delinquent at the time of the survey; the other eight fell into our at-risk category. Three of the delinquent teens continued to engage in problem behavior: one was a heavy drinker; one had been recently arrested for
shooting off a gun in his neighborhood; and the third, a girl, was deeply
involved with delinquent peer groups. The fourth delinquent teen in this
group is less obviously troubled now than he was in 1991, but remained
severely alienated from school and his parents.

Of the five at-risk teens who failed in school, three boys had become
delinquent: all ended up in disciplinary schools for boys, where they
failed or dropped out. One girl dropped out of school and bore her first
child. The fifth, a boy, also dropped out of school. At the age of sixteen,
he supported himself and his unemployed father for several months. He
also moved in with a young woman and became the "daddy" to her new-
born infant. As these teens head toward adulthood, their lives are becoming increasingly difficult. Educational deficits, the difficulty of finding
paid work, personal problems, and family responsibilities are taking
their toll.

Sean Grady's family provides a vivid contrast to the James family. A
good example is that instead of being rich in multiple resources, Sean's

family suffered severe shortages in personal, social, and financial resources. Sean's mother, Pam, attempted to alleviate these deficits by moving to a nearby suburb in the hope of improving Sean's prospects of finishing school. Sean, meanwhile, has not done well. He was extremely
unhappy in high school and explained to our fieldworker that the move
from his city vocational school to his suburban comprehensive high
school had been tough:

> At his high school in [the city] they teach ninth graders ninth-
> grade [subjects] and tenth-graders tenth grade [subjects]. When he
> went out to [the suburbs] they were teaching ninth graders tenth-
> and eleventh-grade [subjects] and [he said], "they expect you to
> keep up."

He reported that his grades were uneven, and more importantly, he found
the school socially unbearable. Our fieldworker reported,

> He didn't make friends all that easily. I suspected that there were
> class issues going on for Sean. He said that he went to the house of
> a kid from school once and it was like a mansion. The kid was one
> of his few friends and he didn't act like a rich kid—unlike many of
> the other students at the school. There were hardly any black kids
> there, and he found that strange, and the kids there were really
> prejudiced, they didn't like Blacks or Puerto Ricans. Sean looks and
> talks and acts very working class, and it doesn't surprise me that he
> had trouble mixing with middle-class kids in the suburbs.

Sean dropped out during the tenth grade. Six months later he left
home to live in his old urban neighborhood with two friends for several
months. During that period he and his friends made money doing odd
jobs during the week and saved as much as they could to buy beer and
pot on the weekends. He then moved in with his girlfriend and her father.

In our three visits with Pam between 1993 and 1995, we noted that
the family continued to have problems, owing in part to Pam's social isolation and her difficulty in managing relationships with outside institutions. Pam also began to withdraw and, perhaps, give up on Sean. The last
time we spoke to her, she reported that she rarely saw Sean. Although the
family had moved out of the city, their new house remained crowded and
chaotic. Though physically affectionate with her children and grandchil-
dren (her daughter had also dropped out of high school and had two children before she was twenty), she had little good to say about them, even
in their presence. Emotionally withholding and socially awkward, Pam
was unable to garner the knowledge and resources to help her children
in the outside world.

Given the importance of parents as role models, we can see perhaps both why Sean was socially uninvolved as a youth and why the family's move to the near suburbs of Philadelphia did not work out as Pam had envisioned. Pam occasionally used preventive and restrictive discipline (keeping Sean in the house over the weekend instead of allowing him to visit friends in his old neighborhood), but he responded poorly to her efforts. Sean's opportunities for increasing self-confidence or developing his own sources of social support with responsible adults and teens remained low. It seems as if the deficits were simply overwhelming and the capacities of the family to respond were simply inadequate. Eventually, we see parents like Pam begin to give up, sometimes turning their attention to other children in the family.

In several other instances in which youth are struggling, parents seem not to have much emotionally to invest in their children. One boy's widowed mother was an alcoholic who supported the family financially but did little else for her sons. By her own account, she comes home from work and sits "in that chair over there, and I'm smoking a cigarette and drinkin' a beer. I'm tired. I'm usually upstairs around eight o'clock." She saw the home as a private haven against the outside world and would not allow her sons to bring friends in: "I don't like a lot of extra children in my house. [And so I say] 'You can't bring friends in because you don't know these people.'"

Her oldest son did large amounts of family work: he shopped, paid the bills, cleaned house, cared for his brothers, and cooked. This parent respondent knew little about the youth's school or outside activities, and she reported that he was currently involved in an after-school science and a sports program. In fact, his involvement in those programs had taken place in prior years. The boy did poorly in school and continued to fit the profile of an at-risk teen—socially uninvolved, unsure of himself, having poor grades, but not yet in serious trouble.

Another male, who lived primarily with his grandmother because his mother's living arrangements were often unreliable, reported a misunderstanding with his high school over his program and grades. He said that his mother had promised to talk with the school but never did. He thought he was supposed to be in summer school, which his mother was supposed to arrange. But by mid-July he was still not attending classes and confessed that he no longer thought it would happen.

Unlike the mothers of successful teens, more of these parents were underinvolved in their teen's lives: they neither intervened in the outside world on their childrens' behalf nor enabled them to manage their external environments. As we saw in the previous chapters, teens did not fare

well when their parents were unable to involve them in normative communities outside the home, had low psychological resources, and did not
know how to communicate effectively with schools and legal institutions.
These parents were both white and African-American, and they lived in
both high-resource and low-resource neighborhoods. Just as teens whose
parents were rich in skills and resources generally did well, those whose
parents had exceedingly few or no positive resources generally did poorly.

However, most parents were not as unskilled and isolated as Pam and
a few other parents whom we observed. The vast majority were, in fact,
doing relatively well by our parenting measures. Further, not all the
teens who were struggling had unskilled parents: some teens in our in-
depth interview study did poorly despite having seemingly competent
parents. As we have reiterated throughout this volume, cause and effect
are difficult to unravel when it comes to explaining why some children
do well while others do not. Although some teens, such as Robert James,
clearly benefited from their parents' practices, others appeared to resist
parental attempts to steer their development toward success. In these
cases an overemphasis on family dynamics is likely to lead to false conclusions about the causal relations between parenting actions and child
outcome. Because teens live in multiple contexts, it is essential to look
beyond the level of the family to the teens themselves, their schools,
and their peer groups to understand why some fail and others succeed.
Although we have focused in this volume on the family, we are fully
aware that development is only partly shaped by this context, especially
in the adolescent years.

When Teens Fail Even Though Parents Are Doing the Right Things

Several teens in our qualitative study failed in school or became delinquent (or did both) despite their parents' considerable efforts. When we
spoke with Eleanor in the fall of 1993, it appeared that she was an engaged parent who used both promotive and preventive strategies to raise
her son. Over the course of two years, however, Leon, already classified
as delinquent in the 1991 survey, became more seriously delinquent, and
Eleanor appeared to be using increasingly preventive strategies. Thus the
child's "outcome" and a parent's practices were reversed from those that
we have previously been discussing. Instead of Leon's outcome being the
result of Eleanor's reliance on preventive strategies, Eleanor's response
was a result of Leon's behaviors. It is, after all, very difficult to promote
a child who acts out consistently and who shows little or no interest in
prosocial activities of any sort. Describing this process, Eleanor said,

When he was little I [made him go] to the Cub Scouts and the Boy
Scouts and I had him in an after-school program and they did a lot
of different things. And um, he went to Sunday school, and I took
him around a lot. I always pushed him. When he got old enough, I
mean, he badgered me so bad the last year of Boy Scouts that I said,
"This is it. I'll let him out." So he finally came out of that. What
happens is that they become their own people, and when they don't
want to do something, they on you and on you and on you. Or, for
instance, in his case when I did force him to do things. Okay, he
would go and do it right? But he would be so disinterested. Really
not participating, you know?

Eleanor went on to recount the ways that Leon had, much to her frustration, resisted her best promotive efforts:

Our church has a tape ministry where they do the video as well as
the audio, they teach you how to do these things and so forth. And
I thought that that would be nice. And he agrees with me, but then
when it comes time I say, "Well, come on, Leon, let's either go and
see what we have to do to do it." Or, "just go and get involved." Or,
"the date's coming up where you can go and do it." And he'll say,
"Not today mom." Or "not tonight." Or, "I'm not gonna give up
my Friday."

Eleanor engaged in few promotive strategies with Leon mostly because Leon's behavior limited her opportunities to use promotive strategies. As his behavior became more problematic, the energy Eleanor ex-
pended on prevention increased dramatically—indeed, it was exhausting
to listen to her detail the calls she made to schools, outside programs,
probation officers, counselors, and lawyers. Her attempts to employ promotive strategies met with considerable resistance from Leon and had all
but ceased by 1995.

Eleanor appeared to be at least as competent as most parents in the
study. She was articulate, well-educated, and energetic. She had a strong
family network helping to care for Leon. But Leon faced considerable
risks, and neither he nor Eleanor were equipped to deal with them. His
best friend, who lived across the street, was more delinquent and delinquent at an earlier age than Leon. Leon disliked his local high school so
much that he asked to be sent to a disciplinary school for boys after his
first arrest. Eleanor reported,

He actually requested to go to [the disciplinary school]. He has
been hollering all along, "I don't wanna go [to the local comprehensive school]. I never really wanted to go to it, and I don't wanna

have to go back there in September." He told his probation officer the same thing: "I never really wanted to go there. I know too many people over there, and I can get in trouble easy."

Leon faced a number of risks, but none appeared to derive primarily from Eleanor's parenting or the family's dynamics. Rather, it seemed that the neighborhood friends to whom he was exposed undermined Eleanor's best efforts to keep him out of trouble. Leon had friends who engaged in delinquent activities and none who participated in prosocial ones. Apparently, he was getting little support for the messages received at home. In a different neighborhood setting, Eleanor's parenting skills might have had more effect.

This book has not examined school contexts in great detail, and we cannot document just what kinds of troubles teens may be facing in their schools. Just as teens who attended Catholic schools tended to do well, teens in certain public schools tended to do poorly. In one neighborhood, four teens from our study—two girls, two boys—attended a particular high school that their parents agreed was especially bad. All four eventually dropped out. In three of these cases, all faced multiple and overlapping risks coming from neighborhood, school, and demographic factors of their family. This presented overwhelming obstacles to success. Youth in these circumstances were facing overwhelming odds against succeeding.

As in Leon's case, skillful parenting is typically a necessary but not sufficient condition for successful adolescence. The relationships between parenting strategies and teens' outcomes may become even weaker in late adolescence as parents of both successful and unsuccessful teens disengage from actively managing their lives. Parents with older adolescents who are doing well generally trust their children to signal their needs. These parents may spend more time with younger children whose trajectories are not yet stable. Parents with older adolescents who are confronting failure may declare their inability to help their teens further, as Eleanor increasingly did over the years. Eleanor's pain was palpable when she described the heartbreak of being unable to help Leon. In response to her frustration and pain, she withdrew and gave up as Leon's delinquent behavior became more serious.

By late adolescence, what parents do seems to matter less than how teens have done in the past and how successful they are at dealing independently with the world outside the family. Increasingly, the fate of teens is located less in the parents' hands and more in their own actions and peer groups or in institutions outside the family. The accretion of apparently small missteps—on the part of parents, teens, and communities— over the years makes problems more and more difficult for teens, much less their parents, to reverse. The problems associated with failure in school, encounters with the law, and families in the labor market all become more consequential. As we have emphasized throughout this book, teens are active participants in their own lives, not simply the passive recipients of good or bad parenting. Like Leon, they can wreak havoc in their own lives even as their parents struggle to create order and help them achieve.

Managing Children Who Are Not Succeeding

It is possible to distinguish analytically, as we have done above, between teens who fail because parents do not do well, teens who fail because they are resistant to conventional behavior, and teens who fail because their schools and peer groups are inhospitable environments for achievement. In reality, however, interactions between teens and parents exacerbate the problems of failing youth (cf. McCord 1990; Patterson 1976; Peterson and Hamburg 1986). Once teens begin to fail in earnest, parents—even the most committed, such as Eleanor—begin to lower their expectations considerably.

In addition, not only parents' skills but their perception of the broader economic context shape the dialogue and dynamics of parent-adolescent interaction. Thus it is important to take into account the part played by the economic context in which families live and parents' interpretations of that context to understand what may happen to youth development in inner-city communities. Popular as well as academic discourse (Brooks-Gunn, Duncan, and Aber 1997a, 1997b; Jencks and Peterson 1991; Kasarda 1985; National Research Council 1990; Wilson 1996) emphasize that stable, manufacturing and other blue-collar jobs that pay well have largely disappeared from large northeastern cities and that technical or professional training beyond high school is necessary to ensure the future well-being of youth. A large majority of the parents we interviewed were culturally literate in these discourses, and sensitive to the implications for their children's futures because they themselves had observed and sometimes been victims of the flight of good jobs from their communities. One black father spoke eloquently when he said,

> He won't get the opportunity to play around like I did because, see, I had a lot of opportunities, you know. Westinghouse was open, RCA, Navy Yard. And all those things are downsizing, you know? So the opportunity's not there.

Parents worried greatly about their teens' opportunities under current economic circumstances. In response to their anxieties, they hoped that their teens would become sufficiently educated for success in a techno-logically demanding employment structure. In our 1990 survey, 53 per-cent of the African-American parents and 47 percent of the white parents reported that they expected their children to finish college.

As we have seen, however, parents of youth who were doing poorly were often unable to do much to help their teens, whose life chances continued to diminish through academic failure or delinquent behavior. About one-third of the teens in the in-depth interview study had little prospect of attending college because they had dropped out of, or were failing in, high school. Another sizable group was unlikely to attain a higher degree, either because they attended vocational high schools or because their families had no concrete plans for their attending college. Some parents were unable to afford college for their teens and unsure of how to locate and secure the little financial aid possibly available to them.

Despite poor educational and financial circumstances, some parents found it difficult to lower their expectations, because doing so meant los-ing hope in their teens' futures. In the social and economic context in which the families lived, parents reacted to the possibility of their chil-dren's failure in different ways.

Some interpreted failure as the result of their child's intransigence, thus relieving themselves of the burden of guilt and placing the blame directly on the adolescent. Bella's daughter Amanda, for instance, had failed ninth grade in a public school. Bella sent Amanda to a private reli-gious school out of state, where she did much better. But Bella was un-willing to pay for a second year of private school and reenrolled Amanda in the public school, where she failed and eventually dropped out. Bella, overwhelmed with a number of family demands, disengaged, saying of her seventeen-year-old daughter, "I have told her that she will make her life decisions, and school was part of it." By this she meant that Amanda could choose whatever alternative school program she could find either to finish high school or to get a G.E.D. A year later, Amanda had com-pleted a G.E.D. program and Bella said, "She finished the course as far as I know. I didn't see anything official, but since she was the one that was paying for it, I felt like her accountability to me was minimal." Bella and Amanda had participated, over a period of several years, in a process of mutual disengagement that ultimately left Amanda isolated and without adequate resources for making life decisions. We saw this same scenario replayed in several other families: the adolescent's failure is followed by the parent's recriminations; then the youth promises to do better but is unable to do so in the face of enormous deficits and meager supports. Parents and children find themselves trapped in a cycle of frustration, anger, and retaliation. Eventually, exhausted by the effort of trying to get them to achieve, parents shift the responsibility and blame for making major decisions to their children. Over and over we heard such comments as "He has to do it himself."

One father kicked his eighteen-year-old son out of the house because he was sleeping his days away, neither working nor going to school. Although the son responded positively by joining the Job Corps, he broke off all contact with his father. It is hard to know what the consequences of such ruptures in family ties will be for the teens. Will they fare better on their own or with other family members, especially in cases where the previous caregiver had been demanding and abusive? Will they fare worse because they have been deprived of a potential source of support? Typically, in these instances, adolescents were socially isolated before their parents or step-parents washed their hands of them. It seems likely, however, that highly punitive responses will result in a downward spiral in the youth's life chances, considering the limited alternatives available in the labor market and the difficulty of making up lost ground through educational remediation.

A second group of parents followed quite a different strategy: instead of withdrawing from their children, they reluctantly lowered their expectations. Linda Ellis is a good example of a parent who adopted this approach to her son's low school performance. Neither Linda nor her husband had gone to college, but when interviewed in 1990, they had high hopes that Greg—a socially involved teen and a relatively good student in a Catholic school—would go. By January 1994, when Greg was sixteen and a sophomore in high school, Linda's expectations had fallen, along with Greg's grades. Linda no longer expected him to go to college. We asked her if she had thought about college for Greg, who maintained that he wanted to be a fireman:

> I've asked him. I don't know. Greg's been changing around lately, but especially since he's been with the restaurant and bussing [tables], he seems to be feeling out the restaurant field a little bit. *So you asked him?* Yeah, but somehow I don't really think so. He doesn't seem to be like the college type, you know? We'll be perfectly happy the day he graduates. The little one, she's my college-bound one.

Linda still wanted Greg to get some training beyond high school, but she was unsure if he would do so: "I don't think the job opportunity is all that great for the Fire Department anymore. I just want him to have some sort of background, some sort of technical trade, I guess, besides just wantin' to be a fireman." Like all the parents in our study, Linda still worried that without post–high school training, good job opportunities would be out of reach for Greg. At least, however, lowering her expectations relieved the strain that would have resulted had she continued to place demands on Greg that he was unwilling or unable to meet. Lowering expectations was almost as problematic as parental disengagement. Neither course of action adequately ensured the teens' future success.

A third option that parents took when teens did not live up to their original expectations was to redefine and expand the meaning of success. Of the various strategies for managing failure, this was the most common. Many years ago, Talcott Parsons (1954) noted that in an achievement-oriented society there is a risk that parents will use withdrawal of love to punish children who fail. Many parents chose instead to redefine the meaning of success to encompass their children, softening the disappointment that their teens would not fulfill their earlier dreams. In doing so, they retained love and respect for their children. By stretching the boundaries of success to include positive social behaviors such as responsibility and caring, parents avoided defining their children by their accomplishments in school or in the workplace. Emphasizing character, they compared their children favorably to others who were disrespectful or unreliable. Linda Ellis, for instance, told us with pride that Greg's friends called him their "guardian angel" because, while they drank, Greg remained sober and made sure his friends returned home safely. Similarly, when asked how Jesse was doing in the summer of 1993—he was attending summer school for having failed high school chemistry—Lucy Park replied:

> He's been doing fine. He, um, looking for a part-time job, you know, for after school and for now. He just went to interview. And um, he's learning to drive. He been keeping busy. He got a girlfriend and stuff like that. So he been pretty well busy watching over the house with his mother. *So he's pretty responsible?* Yeah, he's more grown up than the rest of them.

Unlike mothers who emphasized their children's school performance, Lucy spoke at great length about Jesse's kindness. She talked about how respectful he was with his girlfriend. Her assessment of his success was based on his interpersonal relationships and his reliability, not scholastic success.

The mother who most eloquently described the social psychological processes that lead to a redefinition of success had a very troubled son. Considered delinquent at the time of the survey, he later failed the eleventh grade because he did not attend the last two months of school. He considered both the Job Corps and a G.E.D. program, but eventually decided to return to high school because he did not want to be the only person in his family not to finish. However, he appeared to have serious emotional problems as well and was terrified of being out on the streets. It appeared as if this young man had little hope of graduating. When asked to reflect on how her child was doing, his mother replied,

> I would have to really say that I guess that's normal for parents, you always want more for your kids, you know? Than what you had. And you be disappointed when it don't turn out like that. Because you have high expectations. I mean, you're glad that your children never went to jail or they never hurt anybody, different things like that. You're glad that they're like, for the most part, decent. Like never got into trouble. You really are glad about that. But you would have wished maybe that um, they would have got their degree, had a better job, a better-paying job.

This mother's world view incorporated two definitions of success: achievement in school, work, and family, and success in basic standards of social behavior. Although she hoped for the former, she was willing to settle for the latter. Seemingly unaware of her son's earlier delinquent behavior, she worried about his prospects, but was glad that he was staying out of trouble with the law.

Changing Course

Not all the teens in the sample continued along the same trajectories of success or failure on which they had been at the time of the survey. Some who were doing well began to do even better academically or in their social involvement, while others who were at risk were doing much worse by 1995. In six of the thirty-five families that we interviewed in depth, the teens' trajectories toward success or failure changed direction altogether. In these families, how the teens were doing differed noticeably from what we would have predicted given their previous cluster classifications and the number of risks that they faced at the time of the survey.

That only six teens have completely switched direction is a powerful testament to the importance of the influences on successful development that are manifest even by early adolescence. We will examine these exceptions closely to see what made the difference in their turn of fortunes. These "deviant cases" can provide important clues to the conditions that alter the life course.

From Success to Failure

Jeanette Sullivan, an academically competent teen, was struggling in school when we returned to interview her two and a half years later.

We were puzzled by Jeanette's drop in school performance because, if anything, the family's risk factors had diminished. Cathy, her mother, had older children who had moved out of the house, thereby relieving some of the strain on the budget: "This is the first that we really felt that weight off our shoulders where, if [Jeanette] needs a pair of shoes, I can probably afford to buy her a pair of shoes right away instead of [saying] you gotta wait." Further, through years of involvement in the Boy Scouts, Cathy had become a more efficacious parent with greater self-esteem.

Despite these improvements, Jeanette, who had done well in school through the eighth grade, failed the ninth grade in an academic magnet school that she did not like. The next year she transferred to the local comprehensive high school, where her performance was uneven. Sadly, Jeanette's faith in her abilities plunged; she told us on several occasions that she "used to be smart."

Because Cathy interpreted her own upbringing by an overly strict and restrictive mother as deficient, she placed great emphasis on independence in her children: "I tried to get them to be really, really independent and come up with their own ideas and have enough confidence in themselves to go out and do what they wanna do." Cathy said that she would help her teens get what they wanted, but they first had to find programs and activities on their own. The approach was problematic. Jeanette often seemed lost and unsure of herself. Cathy said, "She knows kind of where she wants to go, she's just not quite strong enough in following up on what she wants to do."

Although we have noted that older teens often find programs on their own, the most efficacious parents, such as Michelle James, who had the most efficacious teens, remained instrumental in helping them find and take advantage of programs, even when they were in late adolescence. Despite her obvious affection and respect for Jeanette, Cathy did not effectively employ promotive strategies with her older children. Her support for autonomy was poor—not because she was overly restrictive as some parents were, but because she provided too little support.

In a second case in which a teen was doing much worse than previously, we suspect that the opposite patterns may have occurred: parents were inappropriately restrictive and reactive in late adolescence. Tamika Blake lived with her father, stepmother, and half-sister in a middle-class neighborhood. She had only two risk factors, was a good student, and reported having a very close relationship with her stepmother at the time of the survey in the spring 1991. When we returned to interview her in the summer of 1993, we found that she had run away from home in the summer of 1992 and had gone to live in a housing project with her mother, who had lost custody of her years before for neglect. Tamika tried to contact her father on several occasions, but her stepmother refused to let her speak to him and told her not to call the house again.

We interviewed Glenda Blake, Tamika's stepmother, and she reported that, as far as she and her husband were concerned, Tamika no longer existed. It is our understanding that, Tamika and her stepmother had gotten into a cycle of escalating punishment, restriction, and acting-out behavior. The more her parents restricted her to the house for acting out, the more she rebelled. Finally she ran away, after refusing to write a summary of a newspaper article that Glenda insisted she do on a daily basis during the summer. She first ran to a friend's home and told the family there that she would "get a beating" if she returned to her father's house. The family called city officials, who called her father, who confirmed that he would beat Tamika when she returned home. Tamika went to her grandmother's house, and two weeks later she ran away to her mother's apartment in the bleakest and most dangerous of Philadelphia's housing projects. Her present whereabouts are unknown.

These negative cases reinforce the survey finding that adjusting the level of autonomy granted by parents is an extremely important and delicate feature of managing adolescents. Cathy Sullivan allowed great autonomy to Jeanette but did so without providing adequate support. And Glenda and Jim Blake were restrictive and reactive and did not give Tamika enough autonomy, apparently resulting in Tamika's withdrawal from the family.

From Failure to Success

Three teens who were struggling at the time of the survey were doing better when we returned to interview them in 1993. Their cases also illustrate the importance of familial and outside social processes in influencing the direction of trajectories. Two teens who changed for the better had powerful psychological reasons for doing so. Social capital within their families was well developed, and their parents were able, more or less explicitly, to make them feel indebted; and important sources of social support outside the families had helped affect the course of the adolescents' lives. Not coincidentally, all three teens attended Catholic high schools, where abundant support was available to aid teens who were faltering. Just as important, teens attending parochial schools did not encounter the subversive peer groups that were present in the comprehensive public schools. The combination of psychological motivations and the existence of social support enabled these teens to improve their chances for mainstream success—a combination that was not present for other teens who were faring poorly in early adolescence.

Jesse Park, an African-American youth, was classified as delinquent in our survey. He was among the teens most exposed to street culture. Living in a beleaguered neighborhood, he "hung with his crew" on the street corner and the local playground, sometimes drinking beer. His life was dangerous. In a period of six months Jesse reported to us that his friends were held up at gunpoint, that he himself was held up walking home alone from his girlfriend's house, and that a neighborhood friend was found murdered in a cemetery. In focus group meetings, Jesse reported these events calmly and without drama.

Despite the fact that he was held up one night, Jesse generally avoided trouble in a way that we found truly miraculous. Further, he seemed to do so quite consciously: he valued his relationship with his girlfriend in part because it kept him out of trouble.

Why was Jesse able to stay out of trouble and, in fact, do fairly well despite his exposure to risks? The answer seems to lie in the family's organization, his mother's investments in Jesse, and Jesse's Catholic school attendance. Jesse's mother, Lucy, invested considerably in her children. She stretched the family income to send Jesse and his brother to Catholic schools. The combination of Lucy's investment and her promotive and preventive strategies in drawing on the help of her brother to influence Jesse seemed to turn the tide. Remaining in Catholic school considerably reduced Jesse's risks of increasing problem behavior. He said that he had wanted to go into the neighborhood comprehensive high school after the eighth grade, but the paperwork did not go through in time. In retrospect, Jesse reported that he was glad that he had stayed in Catholic school, believing that it had been safer for him. His brother succumbed to risks despite a similar investment and exposure to Catholic schools. Jesse refers to his brother's troubles with the law as part of the reason he was able to get himself together. Jesse's mother was a tired and hard-working widow who depended heavily on Jesse to help her out in the household—both emotionally and financially. She showed tremendous pride in Jesse, and Jesse believed that he must avoid trouble so that his mother had at least one good son. The last time we spoke to Jesse, he proudly reported that he had found a part-time job as a dishwasher in a restaurant, had quickly been put on full-time, and then had been promoted "over everyone else" to being a cook. The pay was not as good as he wanted, and he had been talking to men he knew about undergoing training as a welder. It appears that Jesse could be on a successful trajectory in early adulthood.

In another case, Paul Polaski, whom we classified as an at-risk teen when we interviewed him in 1991, became academically competent, graduating from a Catholic high school with high grades and entering college. In his first semester he took a fairly rigorous academic program and made straight A's. His physical transformation from his senior year in high school to the semester break his first year in college was truly remarkable. From being a pale, thin, mumbling kid in an oversized T-shirt, he had become a solid and socially adept young man. His aspirations and self-confidence rose. After one semester, he said that he planned on transferring to the main campus of the state university system after two years, having chosen a secondary campus because he thought he might be overwhelmed by the large main campus. By the end of that year, he had decided to transfer even sooner, and planned to begin classes at the main campus in the fall semester.

Paul's parents scored low on parental efficacy in our survey, and Paul himself perceived them as ineffective, stating that "I guess I should respect [my parents] more, [but] they just don't have enough respect for themselves for me to respect them." Nonetheless, Paul's parents worked very hard to provide him with a Catholic school education and the material goods that American teenagers value so much. Paul interpreted his parents' hard work as sacrifices for him, and he felt tremendous pressure to do well academically. Furthermore, the family lived in a highly cohesive neighborhood in which support for Polish immigrants was high. When he applied to college, he said, "I just read the directions most of the time and just did it myself, and I went to the counselor and my principal and he just helped me out."

Paul's case provides an interesting counterpoint to the teens who dropped out of the public school. Like them, Paul had a constellation of risks in his background, which suggested that he might not do well in later life. Unlike other teens, however, he had access to social support in domains outside his family in the form of school and neighborhood. And even though strains remained within the family, Paul's parents were willing to pay for his education, first in private high school and then in college.

The third teen whose trajectory changed for the better was a girl who lived in Paul Polaski's neighborhood. We classified Sharon Smith as at risk at the time of the survey; her grades were mediocre in a parish school (mostly C's) and she was uninvolved in activities. Like Sean Grady, she had several risk factors on family processes: support for autonomy, parental investment, and family climate were all low.

Despite the number of risk factors in her family and her mediocre school performance, however, Sharon had just finished her first year of college in the summer of 1995. Although Sharon's progress continues to be uneven, she does seem committed to staying in college. In addition, her mother, Beverly, is determined to do everything in her power to help her daughter make it through college. Aware of the negative family climate (she has repeatedly told us that her husband is "too hard" on her kids), she tries to compensate by smoothing the relations between Sharon and her father. She generally manages her husband's working-class doubts about the importance of college in response to their daughter's lackluster performance. She also believes that Sharon has been overly dependent and needs support for autonomy and not the restrictiveness that characterized her earlier parenting. Beverly reports that she wants Sharon to have a job that pays well so that, should Sharon find herself in an abusive marriage, she will be able to support herself:

> I want her to have a good education, and I would like her to have a really good job because if she's . . . and this sounds really horrible, but I've seen so many people that are stuck in a marriage because they aren't financially able to support themselves. I want her to be able to take care of herself. For all I know, when [she] gets married [her husband] could be a son of a gun. And I want her to be able to leave if she has to and be able to support herself.

When we look at the rare cases in which teens changed trajectories, we do not necessarily see exceptional people. Instead, we see families in which a confluence of social and psychological support (or lack of it) work to help or hinder teens' development. Jesse's, Paul's, and Sharon's mothers were determined to continue to provide for their children despite their difficulties. Tamika's stepmother, in contrast, had given up on Tamika. And Cathy, although she loved and cared for Jeanette, did not believe that an older teen needed much support or guidance. Jesse, Paul, and Sharon also attended Catholic high schools and were not exposed to the risks experienced by teens who attended public schools. And Paul and Sharon lived in a highly cohesive neighborhood. Although Jeanette, too, lived in that neighborhood, her mother's earlier poverty had marginalized the family, so that they could not benefit from its cohesion. The distribution of risk factors across social domains helps us to understand why some teens change course, whereas others do not; the risk factors help us to understand, even if they do not completely predict, successful outcomes. We also see how important personal agency on the part of both mothers and teens is in determining the course of the teens' trajectories.

Glimmers of Hope, Forebodings of the Future

In this chapter we have emphasized that most of the teens who were doing well in 1990 continued to do well in 1995, just as most who were at risk of failure or delinquent in 1990 have more problems than they did. We suspect that, as time passes, the number of changers will increase. Unfortunately, some teens who were doing well throughout the years of this study will be faced with problems that have no easy solution. Consider Trisha, for example. During the first several years of our study, she was tremendously successful. She did well in school; she was a serious athlete; she was involved in a local church group for teens and often mentored younger teens; and her sense of personal efficacy was very high. In our first in-depth interview with her, we noted that she "exudes confidence."

Despite her personal competence, Trisha was being seriously undereducated for college at the vocational school where she was studying electronics. Although she originally wanted to get further training in electronics, she chose a school that was both out of state and not accredited. Her mother resisted Trisha's plan and instead supported Trisha's second plan, to go to a local Bible college that the family could not afford. Trisha failed all courses but one in her first semester and dropped out in the first few weeks of her second semester. In the eighteen months since, she has held a series of low-paying jobs for which she has little tolerance. Her self-esteem has dropped; she has no firm plans for the future. Trisha is also drinking alcohol and becoming drunk with some regularity. Her involvement in sports, always tremendously important to her, has dropped off precipitously. In addition, she has come out of the closet as a lesbian—which has had mixed results. On the one hand, Trisha seemed much happier to declare herself, and found her new identification with a lesbian community very exciting. On the other hand, her family relationships have become extremely strained. Her mother reports being "ashamed": She moved out of her mother's household because, even though she was hardly ever home, when she was home her mother yelled at her "constantly" and told her she should "go talk to the pastor."

What happened to Trisha, a young woman with tremendous potential? First, the family finances posed a serious problem. Even though she attended one year of a private college, both Trisha and her mother reported that the family could never afford a second year. Second, there was a disjuncture between her vocational high school program and her academic college plans that neither she nor her mother recognized. She may well have done much better had she received more training in electronics. Alternatively, she might have been better off in an academic high school. Third, her gender and her mother's apparent expectations about gender roles meant that her mother pushed her toward the Bible college and said that she hoped that Trisha would get a job "working with kids." Finally, Trisha's developing sexuality has meant a serious shift in identity, which has been somewhat disruptive for her and has deprived her of support in her family.

Youth on the Margin

Trisha may yet succeed; she has obvious personal talents. But her current road is rocky, and her problems are exacerbated by poverty. Other teens in our sample face different problems associated with limited financial resources. One girl, for instance, is currently doing very well on an honors track in a Catholic school and wants very much to go to college. Her parents have made it clear to her that she is expected to get scholarships, and they will not be able to help pay her expenses because they have several other children to put through Catholic schools. A boy, who graduated first in his class from a vocational school in a cooking program, wanted to go to culinary school. His parents, however, who are paying his older sister's tuition in college, urged him to work for a couple of years. He is currently unemployed. Lakisha Wilkenson is doing well in school and is very responsible, but whether she will remain on track is far from clear, given the family's financial problems.

The shortage of various resources within households, schools, and communities makes it likely that some successful teens may face serious constraints in the near future. Even if they graduate from high school with reasonably good grades, limited family resources may put up barriers that they cannot surmount. White, working-class parents, in particular, indicated that they would not be able to afford college. Others appeared to have no clear idea of how much college cost or how they would pay for it. Teens who are not college bound seem to have few people to turn to for help in getting jobs. Despite considerable competence on the part of many parents when their teens are in school, the future of the teens is uncertain.

Moreover, many of the teens are struggling against the odds, and neither they nor their parents seem to know how to reverse trajectories of failure. Although the teens are becoming increasingly independent, they clearly need continued support from their parents, schools, and communities. Without such support, they are at risk of failure or delinquency. Parents frequently lack the knowledge necessary to navigate the increasingly complex pathways into higher education or the labor market.

Despite these bleak prognoses, we should note that as teens head into adulthood, they may become capable of efficacious action on their own behalf. Good parenting, as we have emphasized, is usually necessary for successful adolescent outcomes, but may be less essential for success in adulthood. Sean Grady, for example, may manage to do better than his current circumstances suggest. Although he has taken on enormous family responsibilities by moving in with his girlfriend and helping to support her and her baby since he dropped out of high school, he has also gained in self-esteem and has landed a good job: his girlfriend's father offered him an electrician-trainee position in his contracting company. Sean reports that he is much happier now that he has well-paid employment, and he has much more energy than he ever did in school. He has proved to himself that he is a responsible young man. Our fieldworker observed that his level of planning impressed her, despite the continuing problems that he faced.

We should note, however, that we do not feel as hopeful for the African-American teens, particularly the young men. They are having greater difficulty in finding jobs than are their white counterparts. Jesse managed, but his story indicates the kinds of problems facing the teens. His first job was in a dollar store, where he became the night manager after proving his reliability. The owner closed the store because it had been robbed and one of the employees killed. Jesse spent several months looking for other employment. Eventually a neighbor, who worked in a mall restaurant, told Jesse that one of the dishwashers had been fired, and there was an opening. Jesse took public transportation to the mall (an hour away) and applied for the job. After waiting for an hour and a half, he was told to return the next day for an interview because no one had time to see him that day. The next day he showed up and was given a part-time job (two days a week) washing dishes and, as we have seen, was soon promoted to full-time cook. When asked why he had gone back the next day, Jesse, an exceptionally proud and reserved young man, allowed himself to smile ever so slightly: "I knew they was testing me to see if I would be reliable."

We cannot overemphasize how unusual Jesse was compared to many of his counterparts; his sense of personal efficacy is exceptionally high. He is prepared to wait, to work hard, to take poor jobs because he believes that his personal qualities will eventually lead to respect. He has a high school diploma and a work history with solid references. If finding a job as a dishwasher is so difficult for such an impressive young man, how can we believe that others lacking Jesse's personal qualities and educational accomplishments will find success in the near future?

Despite the modest number of shifts in trajectories, the primary story of this chapter has been continuity from early to later adolescence. Successful youth generally remained successful despite temporary setbacks and detours. Teens with problems only occasionally showed marked improvement. We sense beneath this stability a disturbing trend whereby the slope of success may flatten in early adulthood, while the slope of failure may become ever steeper. If we are correct, the racial divide may become much wider, especially for the black males in our study.

In many respects, this qualitative chapter echoes the findings of the previous chapter that quantified risk and protective factors. We see that youth and their families are in a balancing act in trying to traverse a difficult passage. By late adolescence, successful youth have acquired the personal attributes (skills, stamina, and discipline) and the social resources (informal support, institutional involvements, and social connections) that keep them on course. Unsuccessful youth frequently have none of these and face bleak prospects of improving their situations.

We have argued throughout this book that these personal and social resources, although often clustered together, are in fact relatively independent of one another, in part because they may be context-specific. Youth with strong families may not live in neighborhoods with ample resources or attend schools that adequately equip them with skills for higher education or for securing a good job. Understanding patterns of success, then, involves seeing how personal and social resources are packaged together as well as how they cumulate or cancel out over time. Chapter 10 explores the implications of these results for inner-city youth and all those who want to improve their life chances. It also reveals how a paucity of resources jeopardizes the chances of the young people in our study to maintain a successful course of development. Unlike middle-class youth, who are typically afforded time to wander and second chances if they go off track, the adolescents in our study are operating with a thin margin of error.

Ten

Managing for Success
Lessons from the Study

Ideally, science is about finding simple and elegant solutions to complex problems. It often seems, however, that social scientists do just the opposite: making seemingly simple matters more complex. That practice has not always endeared us to politicians, policy makers, members of the media, or the public who are clamoring for *answers* to vexing social concerns. Unfortunately, simplifying matters such as the ones explored in this book—What is good parenting in bad neighborhoods, and how do features of the neighborhood shape the course of adolescent development?—run the risk of producing wrong answers and misguided remedies.

This final chapter pulls together the findings of this study and explores the implications of what appears to promote successful adolescence in disadvantaged communities. Certain results contradict popular impressions of family life and adolescent behavior in urban communities. Others provide a more complicated picture of how families are managing risk and opportunity in difficult environments and the consequences of these management practices for children's well-being than we had imagined at the outset of this study. The evidence rarely leads us to the conclusion that if only parents did x or y—or even both x and y plus z—their children's prospects in later life would be vastly enhanced.

To be sure, the family is a powerful and essential influence in setting children on a successful course, but parenting practices are only part of the ingredients that produce successful development in early adolescence. Moreover, good parenting itself comes in many forms and must be responsive to children's changing capacities and varied circumstances. This understanding led us to consider how parents' actions are shaped in part by their personal, social, and material resources—in particular how these resources depended on local institutions and informal social ties.

Our research is neither based on the premise that parents (or children) are inevitably victims of their circumstances nor on the opposite premise that committed and capable parents will invariably produce successful youth. Personal agency as exercised by parents and children is an important element in establishing and maintaining a successful life path, but agency without opportunity can produce paradoxical developments, as the sociologist Robert Merton (1968) observed in his famous essay "Social Structure and Anomie."

Personal agency *combined* with social opportunity is a potent formula for successful development, but implementing this prescription is no easy matter. Still, we do not despair of discovering the means to do so. In the final part of this chapter, we make a case for strengthening the capacities of families to assist their children. We are persuaded that policies and programs that build both a greater sense of agency and a context in which personal agency counts can enhance the prospects of successful development during adolescence. Along these lines, we offer some specific suggestions for how these twin goals can be achieved. Before doing so, let's first recap the results of the Philadelphia Study.

RECAPPING THE FINDINGS OF THE PHILADELPHIA STUDY

Growing out of an in-depth study of how parents functioned in neighborhoods with different levels of resources, opportunities, and dangers, the Philadelphia Study surveyed parents and children from nearly five hundred families located in sixty-five census tracts that were randomly selected from low-income sections of the city. The objective was to examine how parents managed children both within and outside the confines of the household. Family management practices, we speculated, may provide important linkages between the neighborhood, family, and the course of adolescent development.

Our theoretical perspective, laid out in chapter 1, provides a rationale for why and how community organization and resources may be connected to how parents operate in the world beyond the household. In particular, we examined how different features of neighborhoods and different characteristics of parents and family organization might act in concert to shape the success trajectories of younger adolescents. We contended that certain neighborhoods promote the development of greater social capital, which draws families into more collective strategies of childrearing because it makes available a broader scope of institutional resources. More advantaged families, regardless of where they live, can isolate their children from dangers and provide them with opportunities by sending them to private or parochial schools. Disadvantaged families must rely more on effective parenting practices.

The results reported in this book draw on the survey information described in chapter 2 that was provided both by the parents and by their young adolescents. We also carried out extensive qualitative case studies of several dozen families who were selected to maximize variation in neighborhood and children's success on the basis of a set of indicators that included measures of academic and cognitive performance, social involvement, problem behavior, and psychological adjustment. We worked back and forth between looking at the survey data and the case studies and considering individual constructs as well as more global assessments based on varied measures. Our aim was to avoid the pitfall common to survey analysis of losing sight of the whole families or the multiple contexts in which children develop.

The analysis elaborates the descriptive findings presented in chapters 3, 4, and 5 showing the range of variation in family management strategies and adolescent success. The second part of the analysis examines how the link between the two is altered by different features of the family and the neighborhood. We revisit the findings of the multivariate analysis presented in the middle part of the book in the final chapters, which attempt to weave the results together, first by using a risk-and-resiliency perspective and then by returning to the qualitative case studies.

Our approach does a better job of broadening the question of how features of the neighborhood are connected to styles of family management than it does of showing that variations in neighborhoods are linked to patterns of success. Our explicit intention is to provoke further research on how families, neighborhoods, and—we hope in the future—schooling and informal peer relations operate in tandem to shape trajectories of development. This has been the agenda of the MacArthur Network, which sponsored this project. However tentative our findings, they point to some intriguing lessons—some that were anticipated and others that were unexpected.

THE LESSONS LEARNED

The Myth of Bad Neighborhoods/Bad Parents

One of our most important results emerged from the descriptive analysis presented in the early chapters of this book. Judging from the measures of family process that we constructed or that we borrowed from previous studies, the great majority of the nearly five hundred families that we surveyed were functioning reasonably well—some might even say very well considering that close to a quarter of the families were living in poverty and another quarter were experiencing chronic economic strain. Typically, these families lived in problem-ridden neighborhoods, localities where the residents themselves had considerable fears about having their children walk around at night. These areas—dotted with abandoned dwellings and often with unemployed males hanging out on street corners—fit most outsiders' definition of "bad neighborhoods." Many Philadelphians would feel uneasy about going into these communities even during daytime hours.

Yet we discovered that parenting skills, especially when measured by the standard scales that assess warmth, commitment, discipline, and control, varied in only trivial ways by the quality of the neighborhood as measured by its resources and social climate. Inadequate parenting, as measured both by quantitative measures derived from the surveys of parents and children and by qualitative assessments based on in-depth interviews with parents and children among a subset of thirty-five families, was far more often the exception than the rule. Most parents were committed, reasonably skilled, and strongly invested in their children's welfare. The generally good quality of parenting applied to households with two resident parents as well as those with a single parent.

To be sure, parents exhibited a range of competencies, and few scored high on all dimensions of parenting. In this respect, however, we doubt that they differ greatly from parents outside the inner city, although our sample did not include affluent areas of Philadelphia or the surrounding suburbs. Expected differences related to the education of the parents did occur, but they are relatively small compared to variability that is related to personal characteristics of parents arising, no doubt, from individual differences in temperament and upbringing.

Undeniably social-class differences appear in parenting styles and practices, but existing research sometimes produces the mistaken impression that low-income parents are less caring, concerned, or invested, and are generally unskilled caregivers. The important message that emerges from our data is that the great majority of low-income parents are competent caregivers—neither insensitive to their children's needs nor unskilled in meeting them. This result no doubt will surprise some readers; however, it is not idiosyncratic to the Philadelphia sample. It is replicated in several ongoing studies of companion projects undertaken by the MacArthur Network on Successful Adolescence. We cannot assume, then, that poor parenting is more common in poor neighborhoods. Parenting, our study indicates, is not the main reason why children from disadvantaged communities do not fare as well as those from better-off neighborhoods in later life.

Neighborhoods Do Influence Family Management Practices

Our research identified a somewhat different province of parenting than the traditional dimensions of warmth, authority, and discipline emphasized in most research on childrearing. Concern with the beliefs that parents hold and the actions that they take to advance their children's development has typically been confined to the study of face-to-face interactions occurring within the household. Traditional theories of socialization have largely ignored the direct and indirect ways in which parents organize their children's life chances: the choice of neighborhood and school, which greatly affect peer involvements; the strategies devised by parents to shield their children from dangers when they are outside the home; the contacts that parents make to enhance their children's opportunities; the sponsorship and advocacy provided outside the home; and the networks in which parents are embedded that build social capital and extend it to their children.

We used the term *family management* to encompass both in-home practices designed to develop children's capacities to manage the world outside the household and the strategies that parents employ to cultivate, oversee, and influence the external world in which children participate, including the neighborhood, social agencies, the school, peer relationships, and the workplace.

On the basis of previous exploratory fieldwork in five communities, we speculated that family management practices might vary by features of the neighborhood. Both the survey and the qualitative interviews provided support for this assumption, although these domains of parenting also varied much more within than across the neighborhoods, as we reported in chapter 7. Families residing in more dangerous neighborhoods and black parents regardless of where they lived were more likely to employ restrictive measures to shield their children from hazards in the immediate environments. White parents and well-off parents relied on two broad strategies of family management: choice of residential area and choice of school. Our sample excludes most of the families who resorted to the first of these strategies, because many families would have moved out of the neighborhoods in our study if had been financially able to do so. However, the strong association between neighborhood quality and the use of private schools testifies to the large number of parents who resorted to the second strategy. More than half of the parents in better-off neighborhoods sent their children to select schools—

private, parochial, or magnet programs in the public school—compared with just 14 percent of those in the least-advantaged communities. Moreover parents in the better-off neighborhoods also made more use of local resources in their communities—extracurricular activities at school, youth clubs, organizations, and the like—that are more typically close at hand (see chapter 4).

Thus parents with greater access to material and social resources within their communities were able to make use of collective and institutional ways of protecting their children from negative influences and promoting their achievement. Impoverished families, in contrast, were compelled to rely upon individual and in-home techniques of management unless they took special steps to find institutional resources outside their communities. We return later to this central finding.

The range and intensity of family management practices varied to some extent with the personal characteristics of parents, as shown in chapter 5. Parents with greater efficacy and better psychological resources were more able to read and respond to their immediate environments, and were more adept at garnering institutional resources for their children. In general, however, we found in chapter 7 that these parents' psychological resources were similarly distributed in all communities, despite the very uneven distribution of the institutional resources available to parents in their local milieus.

Neighborhood Advantage and Children's Well-Being

We had expected to find that neighborhood advantage would be linked to success in early adolescence, but we were surprised to find that this was not so. *We found virtually no neighborhood-level differences in academic competence, acting out, parents' assessments of their children's adjustment, or the children's self-assessment of their mental health.* The single exception to this pattern was involvement in prosocial activities, which was moderately associated with neighborhood quality and level of advantage. Children from communities with more local organizations were, not surprisingly, more likely to participate in sports, clubs, or after-school activities than those in communities less endowed with institutional resources. Their organizational involvements may be associated with improved prospects of long-term success, but in early adolescence they are not strongly associated with the other domains of well-being.

The absence of neighborhood differences in markers of success does not reflect the lack of variation in these measures of well-being within our sample of pre-adolescent and early adolescent children. It merely tells us that children living in the same census tract or even within a small set of blocks are as likely to be well or poorly adjusted, engaged or not engaged in problem behavior, and so forth as children who live in different census tracts or block groups in the same census tract.

This result surprised us because it is widely believed that children are not functioning as well in more-impoverished and disorganized neighborhoods. Naturally, the result made us wonder if our measures could have been insensitive to subtle behavioral differences. However, nothing from the qualitative interviews led us to suspect the quality of the measures from the survey. Indeed, a substantial correlation existed between the survey and qualitative measures, even though the case studies were conducted two years after the survey, as described in chapters 2 and 9.

We also considered the possibility that our discrete measures of success might not have captured differences that would have appeared had we used a more global measure of success. Using a cluster technique, we classified youth by their overall patterns of success into four groups: (1) competent (doing well, especially in school); (2) involved (above average on social involvement and not exhibiting problem behavior); (3) at-risk (below average but not experiencing serious problems); and (4) delinquent (more than experimental substance abuse and involvement in crime). Again, we found only slight evidence of neighborhood clustering, except in the instance of involved youth, who were overrepresented in neighborhoods with abundant institutional resources and higher income.

A more plausible explanation for the absence of across-neighborhood variation could be connected to the design of the study. Two features of the sampling procedure may have suppressed neighborhood effects. First, the range of neighborhoods was somewhat restricted by the absence of affluent communities and the underrepresentation of extremely poor communities. Second, the use of telephone screening procedure may have excluded very poor and perhaps very disorganized families. If these families without phones were concentrated in certain communities, this, too, might have dampened variation across neighborhoods.

Even acknowledging the likelihood that the study design could have led to an underestimate of variation between neighborhoods in children's well-being (and perhaps family functioning as well), we suspect that the results are not far off the mark. In Prince Georges County and in Denver and Chicago, where neighborhood studies are also being conducted in a wide range of census tracts with data collected at school or in the home, the amount of variation in youth adjustment at the neighborhood level is quite small among children in their preteens and early teens.

As we speculated in chapter 7, changes in mobility, transportation, communication, and the location of jobs are likely to have produced less tightly bounded local communities. And neighborhoods are probably less capable of generating and sustaining distinctive social norms than they once were. Indeed, we found strong evidence from the qualitative study that so-called neighborhoods were often ambiguously defined and frequently perceived differently by members of the same block and even members of the same household. In short, we are inclined to conclude that we may be overestimating neighborhood as a potent source of influence, at least in early adolescence.

Even if we are correct, this conclusion must be confined to the age group we have studied. In chapter 9, which brought us up to date on thirty-five youth with whom we have remained in contact since the survey, we found intimations that neighborhoods may begin to exert more influence as the youth in our study move into middle and later adolescence, and parents relinquish influence. Ongoing research in Denver and Chicago by our colleagues Del Elliott and William Julius Wilson also provides evidence that different levels of success across neighborhoods become more conspicuous in later adolescence. Along with their growing autonomy from parents, older teens may become more resistant to efforts intended to keep them in mainstream activities. The transition to high school, especially to standard public schools in the inner city, often confronts youth who have accumulated academic deficits with an indifferent and unrewarding environment. Street life and involvement with peers present more alternatives and, accordingly, more dangers along conventional paths to adulthood. Thus the distinct possibility exists that place of residence may yet come into play in shaping the trajectory of success. We will have an opportunity to examine this possibility in Philadelphia when our follow-up data become available.

Family Management Practices and Adolescent Success: No Simple Association

We found consistent and compelling evidence that parental practices were linked to how the teens in our study were doing. However, the results complicate our understanding of the conventional wisdom that more capable and resourceful parents invariably raise more successful children. We found that discrete patterns of success among the children were, in fact, linked to discrete parental practices. Warmth, discipline effectiveness, and respect for autonomy, as well as particular family management practices in and outside the home, were all associated with particular outcomes of success. Simply said, no single parental practice or set of practices results in success in all the domains of well-being that we examined in this study.

The "good parent" is an ideal type or an abstraction of what occurs in social life; in reality parents possess particular qualities or competencies that may work well in certain circumstances (and, no doubt, for certain children, although an examination of siblings was not part of this study) and may be problematic in others. Parenting also comes in packages, and in some respects the packaging of parental qualities may affect children as well as the particular components. This could be one reason why discrete measures or even all measures together are only moderately related to particular dimensions of children's well-being.

Both the survey results presented in chapter 6 and the qualitative case studies discussed throughout this book indicate that children are affected by a complex interplay of parents' psychological, social, and economic resources, which are translated into daily routines, responses, and initiatives. These resources, for example, shape and are shaped by marital dynamics or the absence of a marriage. They influence the style of parenting, which itself is partly a response to the parents' own experiences of their childhood.

Parenting practices, however, are neither determined nor fixed. Normally they are fluid and emerge from family experience and a historical relationship with a child. Adolescence requires parents to alter previous practices or adopt new ones as children need and often demand greater autonomy. Parents must ease up on the brakes as children move out of the home. This developmental sequence has been long recognized, but social scientists are only now beginning to appreciate how much it may be affected by the specific context in which the family is situated. Getting it right for adolescence involves parents as well as their children's ability to read and respond to the world outside the home. The capacity to engage in this task constructively depends on the preparation that children have received from parents as well as the ways in which parents continue to monitor and assist their efforts to move out in the wider world.

This study has situated the process of adolescent development in urban neighborhoods that presented different levels of opportunity and danger. We found that parents' repertoire of management techniques, such as their face-to-face interactions with their children, were linked to certain specific domains of success, but again one approach did not necessarily fit all of them. By virtue of considerable sacrifice, some parents were able to send their children to parochial or private schools that provided, in effect, the equivalent of a "social neighborhood," or what has been referred to as a functional community (Coleman, Hoffer, and Kilgore 1982). Others created a community through religious ties or, occasionally, community organizations. Although such investments did not invariably pay off in the form of academically successful or well-adjusted children, they generally reduced the level of risk to young people and may be even more potent weapons against failure in the future.

Despite the fact that parents used different sorts of management strategies depending on where they lived and the level of resources available, we found little evidence that resources at either the household or the neighborhood level affected the success of parenting practices. We had expected to find that parents might have more success with certain practices than with others, depending on the type of neighborhood in which they resided. And we speculated that greater parental quality and skills might be required in more-impoverished environments. Parents would have to "overachieve" by using more innovative techniques, supervising more closely, and investing more to produce successful children in poorer neighborhoods. Evidence for these sorts of "interaction effects" was slim.

Parents who displayed warmth and discipline effectiveness, and granted appropriate levels of autonomy, found ways of investing time and resources in their children inside and outside the home. They were able to locate opportunities for their children and advocate on their behalf in school or in the community, and these qualities and skills in various combinations improved their children's chances of doing well regardless of where the parents lived or their demographic characteristics. So neighborhoods matter regarding access to schools and community organizations, but adept and resourceful parents have about the same likelihood of having children do well regardless of where they live—at least when their children are in primary and middle school.

The analysis in chapter 7 did reveal several neighborhood-level differences in parenting styles consistent with the earlier ethnographic work done in Philadelphia. Parents in the neighborhoods that were better off, especially the whites, relied more on private schools than in-home techniques to monitor and control their children, while residents of less advantaged communities generally used more restrictive techniques to shield their children from dangers. The consequences of these differences may become quite significant over time as children in more advantaged communities experience more promotive parenting, while those in the least-advantaged neighborhoods experience more preventive attention. To the extent that these parental styles contribute to expanding or restricting future opportunities for sponsorship, entry into educational programs, or the acquisition styles that may be more compatible with mainstream success, neighborhood-based norms may insinuate themselves into patterns of success in later life.

We discovered that in primarily black communities, regardless of socioeconomic level, parents were generally more restrictive in monitoring their children. Controlling children's movements outside the household, no doubt, is consistent with higher perceptions of crime and the dangers associated with street life. These collective responses may or may not have long-term consequences for children's behavior in later life, but evidently black youth are exposed to a higher level of scrutiny, including those in the more middle-class areas. Understandably, parents are more sensitive to the risks of unsupervised movement outside the home.

Cumulative Risks and Adolescent Success

We have described family management practices as a deliberate (though not always explicit or articulated) effort to keep children on course, accomplished under varying degrees of risk. Chapter 8 provides strong support for the idea that cumulative risks steadily increase the likelihood that children will encounter problems. Risks may be present at the neighborhood, household, or individual level. And, although our evidence cannot speak to the issue, they probably mount up over time, as well.

Because risks no doubt cluster together—for example, single-parent families are more likely to be poor and live in poor neighborhoods—the risks are also sufficiently independent that we found each to be more or less equally related to the probability of poor outcomes. This may be why we found that resourceful parents who have at their command an array of family management practices are more likely to succeed regardless of where they live.

At the same time, the aggregation of risks within certain households and communities helps to account for the sharply different patterns of overall success. In the least-advantaged neighborhoods, youth were only a third as likely to be successful as in the most advantaged areas. Within each of these neighborhood groupings, we discovered that the combination of family processes and management practices was also associated with a huge variation in overall success. Youth residing in the best neighborhoods and experiencing high-quality parenting practices were fourteen times more likely to be successful than youth who came from the worst neighborhoods and received little support from their parents. Considering that our sample excluded the most advantaged areas of Philadelphia and the most advantaged families, these differences are startling indications that the combination of neighborhood risks and parenting practices is quite important in understanding why some youth are on a successful track and others are not.

Socioeconomic conditions are thus linked to adolescent success through both the level of opportunity and danger encountered in the immediate neighborhood and the increased ability of parents to employ more promotive management strategies when they have more material resources. Lower levels of economic resources erode marital relations, which in turn undermines effective in-home parenting practices. Parents with more limited resources thus experience handicaps in raising children even though they are no less committed or skilled as caregivers.

We surmise from the qualitative data presented in chapter 9 that, over time, parents' efforts matter less and their children's own capabilities and support systems outside the home begin to matter more. The case studies provide an ominous glimpse of what may be in store for youth who were struggling in their early and mid-teens. Their capacity for self-management may be limited, and their parents' ability to keep them on the right track is likely to diminish as they approach adulthood.

The cost of economic disadvantage may also be compounded over time because poorer youth are exposed to higher levels of danger, attend worse schools, and are more often exposed to peers who engage in antisocial behavior. Thus we anticipate that as the parents' influence diminishes during adolescence, their children will begin to do less well despite their best efforts. This is what we observed in some of the case studies in chapter 9.

It is still too early in our study to detect in most cases the tipping points at which children move from being at risk to becoming problem youth—when they fail school for a second time and drop out, when they are arrested and sent to jail, when they have children and are forced to seek public assistance. How many of the half of the youth whom we classified as at risk will complete school, stay out of serious trouble, avoid an unintended birth, or become economically independent? Or even more to the point, how many can expect to find rewarding and remunerative employment, form a lasting and gratifying partnership, or become contributors to their community—the essential elements of middle-class aspirations?

Managing for Success

Only time will answer these questions, but from what was foreshadowed in our case studies, these dreams will elude many participants in our study. No doubt, as we concluded in chapter 9, parents will continue to exert an influence on the directions of adult pathways, but many—especially those with meager social and financial resources—will be able to do less and less to influence their children's prospects with the passage of time.

Our current indicators of success—academic competence, personal contentment, interpersonal skills, social involvement, and staying out of trouble—accorded well with the definitions of what it meant to do well that were volunteered by parents and youth in the qualitative interviews. Yet these standards may be applied differently across the social strata and may also change over time.

The fieldwork suggests that some families with limited economic resources and information about the social requirements for making it in a middle-class sense were applying "good enough" standards. Whether the children performing adequately in the preteens and early teens are actually being prepared for the challenges of higher education or gaining the requisite skills to find a job that pays a living wage is open to question.

Most parents in our study devoted their attention to the here and now, believing that the future would take care of itself if their children managed to remain in school and stay out of trouble. Not unlike the teachers in many of the neighborhood schools attended by children in this study, parents were applying expectations appropriate for a past rather than a future economy. Not that parents didn't worry about what would become of their children if they didn't go to college: almost all did. However, many parents simply didn't have adequate knowledge of the middle-class world to guide their children in how to succeed, and they rarely had the resources to subcontract with those who did have that knowledge. Similarly, most of the youth did not sufficiently understand that they were being vastly underprepared to perform in the middle-class world—a realization that often only dawns upon them when they reach adulthood.

WHAT CAN WE DO ABOUT IT?

National debate focuses largely on how to help families help their children. Americans strongly adhere to the ideal of a family system protected from government interference, in which children's fates are almost entirely in the hands of parents. When children succeed, we credit their parents, and when they fail, we find the parents to be at fault. Of course, there is more than a grain of truth to these attributions. However, our family-centered political culture does not recognize how much parental success itself is interwoven into a system of opportunity and inequality of life chances that are set by economic and political priorities.

Ours is a free market system where parents, theoretically at least, can make choices for their children about where they live and go to school, the range of adult mentors and sponsors to whom they are connected, and the peers with whom they can associate, not to mention the immediate and broader culture to which they are exposed. Failing to notice that these choices are constrained by existing economic and social opportunities, however, amounts to being blind to the way that social advantage is perpetuated and maintained in America. Thus parental choice, whether at the community or family level, is a construct that conceals socially structured differences in access and knowledge. In the fashionable parlance of today, we might say that family differences in social and cultural capital are in turn a by-product of economic advantage and education. Unless children have fair access to the educational system, choice is a political pretense for maintaining privilege. How then are we to enlarge parents' capacities to help their children take advantage of existing opportunities, and how can we expand opportunities so that poor parents may indeed have a wider range of choices for their children?

MAKING CHOICES REAL

Throughout this book we have observed that while privilege is linked to both parental agency and social opportunity, parents feel differently empowered and are unevenly able to help their children surmount inequality. We saw this first in our findings on family management practices in chapters 4 and 5, but limitations in parents' abilities to work the system are painfully evident in the qualitative evidence presented in chapter 9. Equipping parents with the beliefs and skills to manage scarce opportunities is likely to have some impact on how their children will do in later life.

Strengthening Families' Capacities to Manage the External World

Family management practices can be cultivated to children's advantage. Parents can become more knowledgeable about the social world in which their children are situated. Specifically, many parents are poorly informed about the educational tracking that takes place in high school, the courses their children must take to enter a four-year college, sources of academic support outside the high school, and ways of financing higher education. Knowledge and social connections of this sort may help to make preparation for college less abstract and more attainable. In Philadelphia and elsewhere there have been some efforts to create better linkages between schools and families. For the most part, these programs have been more symbolic than real.

Similarly, parents can be assisted in directing their children to health resources, social support, and recreational programs in the community. Many children must find their own way to these agencies, leaving parents unconnected, ill-informed, and sometimes even suspicious of these potential structures of opportunity. We are reminded of one of the Latino parents in our pilot study who was unwilling to allow her academically talented child to attend a private school on a scholarship because she was fearful of his leaving the neighborhood (Furstenberg 1993). Her fears were real but might have been assuaged had the school done a better job of reaching out to and reassuring this apprehensive parent.

Institutions—typically outside impoverished communities—do a generally poor job of connecting to parents. Home visits, phone calls, and chauffeured events are typically not part of the repertoire of schools, youth clubs, health clinics, and so forth. Furthermore, these institutions often deal with children for a brief span and have neither time nor resources to build a relationship with parents. Their efforts to promote children's capacities and relationships with adults outside the home may be viewed by parents with a wary eye.

Building Social Connections

In all the neighborhoods we studied, there were parents who lacked the management skills required to connect their children to outside institutions, champion their interests, and look out for them when they were at school, and there were parents with modest resources. The latter group, having the management skills that made them effective advocates for their offspring, might be identified and channeled to the former group. Parents with special skills could be attached to or housed in settlement houses, libraries, schools, or health agencies. These local parent advocates might be older parents, church leaders, respected community figures— what Eli Anderson refers to as "the wise heads" (Anderson 1990). They are present in virtually every community and need to be designated and aided to do what they already may be doing on a modest scale.

Some existing institutions are committed to reaching out to parents, but too many others rely on an active consumer mentality that simply is not widespread within the population in this study. Public schools in urban areas, in general, are conspicuously poor at engaging parents as active participants in the schooling of their children. Parental disengagement foreshadows disengagement of children. School personnel blame parents for lack of involvement, and parents, in turn, feel excluded from the educational process. No doubt, parents could be made more responsible, and schools could take an active part in bringing parents in, demystifying what happens at school, and assisting parents in the learning process. This model of soliciting parental involvement requires commitment and resources on the school's part, rare commodities in urban school systems (see, for example, Epstein 1981; Ryan et al. 1995).

Building Social Capital

The middle school is an underutilized resource in most urban areas, often isolated physically and socially from its constituency. Only a tiny fraction of the parents in our study were actively involved in their children's schools. This was most true for the parents who might have had the most to gain from a closer connection to the school. Indeed, in some areas, the school is the only publicly funded local institution. Isolated examples exist of schools in Philadelphia that have extended their institutional resources to provide a safe haven for children beyond the hours of instruction, to build an extracurricular program that contributes to youth development, to provide a hub for health and social services, and to give parents a place to find a supportive network of like-minded caregivers (Ryan et al. 1995; Schneider and Coleman 1993).

Schools might also provide a place during the summer where teachers could offer enriched curriculum, life skills, and mentoring frequently not afforded during the overcrowded academic year. Typically, more affluent parents purchase schooling in the summer by sending their children to camp, classes, or organized experiences aimed at cultivating skills, segregating them into favorable peer environments, and building social networks that promote their life chances. Mounting evidence suggests that children are greatly disadvantaged by the absence of summer and after-school programs (Entwisle and Alexander 1992; Heyns 1978). The children in our study were largely left on their own to find what meager public or private resources existed for low-income urban youth. In Philadelphia, funding barely exists to keep the swimming pools and libraries open, and privately organized youth programs are financed on shoestring budgets for limited populations. The most engaged and resourceful parents can make do, but their options are severely limited.

The stripping away of community-based services in disadvantaged neighborhoods has taken place during the last several decades as government funding at all levels has been reduced for neighborhood-based institutions in the inner-city. Most publicly funded institutions such as schools, libraries, and community centers have suffered severe cutbacks, and privately funded service institutions have been unable to pick up the slack. The steady decay of the urban infrastructure has been hastened by the loss of population, especially middle income families who pay taxes and vote disproportionately to their share of the population. And, of course, as the population ages, families with dependent children who make use of these services represent a smaller share of the population than they once did.

Our research calls attention to the costs of this public downsizing of supportive services to families and communities. We need to rethink ways of rebuilding these institutions as a means of stabilizing communities and providing overburdened parents with support. Communities that once helped to co-socialize children and youth no longer can offer much assistance. One promising strategy for strengthening families, tried in some communities, is to make local institutions multifunctional, whether they be schools, churches, settlement houses, or health services, and multigenerational, that is, designed to serve whole families rather than target populations of youth or adults. The concept of social capital refers to the way in which individuals and families are embedded in a larger community based on social ties and obligations that reinforce a common set of beliefs and commitments. Most of the families in our study possess low levels of social capital (Garbarino 1992; National Research Council 1996). Unlike parenting skills, this resource was unevenly distributed across the neighborhoods in our study. Certain neighborhoods—principally the white ethnic areas—show greater levels of trust and normative agreement. These features of neighborhoods are, no doubt, linked to a willingness to take responsibility for the welfare of other people's children.

Communities of this sort, however, need not be geographically bounded. City neighborhoods only rarely take the form of urban villages. More often, parents are able to find what James Coleman and Thomas Hoffer (1987) referred to as functional communities, institutions that provide a collective purpose that reinforces parents' beliefs and values. Churches and private schools are the most common forms of functional communities, but other institutions could be constructed intentionally to involve the family as a social entity.

Functional communities potentially provide reinforcement to parents by making it possible for their children to associate with peers of like-minded parents as well as allowing those parents to reinforce their values. They offer "high observability" for parents who cannot be in close proximity to their children (Merton 1972). A large system of dense social ties provides collective scrutiny while strengthening parental authority. It widens the array of mentors, sponsors, and advocates for children without undermining the family. As such, it is attractive to Americans wedded to social programs that strengthen local institutions.

As Robert Putnam (1995) has argued, functional communities thrive under conditions in which voluntary associations are plentiful. He claims that over the past several decades these associations have been in decline largely because of the pervasiveness of television. Although his thesis is controversial, many scholars agree that local institutions have not thrived in the second half of the twentieth century. The workplace, in the words of Rose Coser and Gerald Rokoff (1974), has become a "greedy institution" crowding out family and community concerns (Hochschild 1997).

We offer no simple solution for institution building, but we are suspicious of the popular argument that local ties have been frustrated by the growth of government. The strategy of strengthening local institutions is not inimical to government; we would argue that it is impossible without an alliance between government at all levels and local communities (Schorr 1997). That the current devolution of federal and, to a growing extent, state government will promote more active partnership at the local level strikes us as a dubious proposition. The withdrawal of government support may only hasten the demise of fragile community institutions.

Changing the Rationing System

Making more information available to parents and expanding their capacity to cultivate local resources cannot significantly improve their children's chances without expanding educational and developmental opportunities for children. Unless adequate resources exist, improving parents' skills at locating opportunities only changes their place in the queue. If the places at the front of the line are always purchased in advance by those with means, then parents with limited economic resources will not have much success in gaining a favorable position for their children, regardless of how hard they try.

Again, it is instructive to think about a key finding in the Philadelphia Study. The more affluent parents, especially if they are white, largely send their children to private or parochial schools. Black parents rely more on the public school system, trying to get their children into magnet schools or select programs within the comprehensive public schools. However, there are many more applicants than places in these select public schools. In some of the programs, fewer than one in twenty-five are admitted, a ratio far more selective than the admission policy of any Ivy League college. Thus many students who might otherwise be prepared for higher education are relegated to programs that simply do not offer the curriculum or the skills to enter college or to qualify for many entrance-level jobs.

As we said earlier, the same is true of activities outside school. Extracurricular programs within schools have largely been eliminated in the past several decades, along with publicly funded recreational services and privately funded institutions such as the YMCA, YWCA, Scouts, and youth clubs. The rationing of resources for children means that only a fortunate few are granted entrance to programs providing the adult supervision, skill training, and prosocial contacts that serve some of the same functions as are routinely purchased by those with the means to do so.

As with health care, an excellent system exists for those with the resources to purchase services. The uninsured must make do with public clinics and, increasingly, with emergency room visits. Families, in effect, are put in the same position when it comes to finding opportunities for formal and informal education. Too often, families are having to make do with an inadequate system that leaves them too few real chances and choices. We have constructed a system that can only increase economic inequality while maintaining an ideology that professes to do just the opposite.

Although we believe that we ought to enhance parents' capacity to manage the external world in ways that may benefit their children, greater managerial skills cannot compensate for a paucity of opportunity. Faulting parents for their failure to promote their children's chances under such circumstances is morally reprehensible.

Changing the allocation system that currently assigns less public support to those who need it most is not on the political agenda. Indeed, in the last decades of this century we have moved in the opposite direction—away from public to private financing of education, health, recreation, and social services. This private-allocation system is consistent with American political and cultural beliefs about how families should control their children's destinies. Far more than our European counterparts, we underplay the role of the state and even the community in collaborating with parents as childcare and socializing agents, believing that childrearing practices are among the private choices that individuals make. However, this belief system collides with the growing demands placed on parents to shoulder the responsibilities of work and family while bearing most of the costs of raising children. Parents are being confronted with impossible and conflicting choices, creating problems that are detrimental to their children and the larger society.

This system of belief promotes agency by insisting that families are responsible for helping their children overcome economic and social disadvantage, and indeed our research findings support this belief. But the results of this study also show that parents are aided by community support and social institutions—when a system is in place that helps to co-socialize children.

Rather than seeing parent initiative and community support as disconnected alternatives, our findings indicate that personal agency and social ecology are mutually interdependent. Parents manage the external world better when it invites them to be involved and supports their efforts. In turn, their investment in the community helps to sustain the institutions that are critical to their children's welfare. Institution building and parental involvement go hand in hand. The political dialogue that views public support as the enemy of private initiative falsely divides institutional support from the promotion of a sense of personal agency. We must think about whether the cultural model that assigns almost exclusive responsibility to parents is in need of revision.

A poignant lesson of our study is that most parents are investing in their children, and those with limited means who live in impoverished neighborhoods hardly differ in their aspirations, their concern, and the energy that they devote to the task of childrearing. Good parenting appears to be more available than good neighborhoods, good schools, and good social services.

Appendix

QUALITY OF DATA

The development of the interview schedules was lengthy and demanding because of the complexity of the study, the number of investigators, and the feedback provided by our colleagues on the full committee. The draft interview schedules were far too long; we were forced to balance competing demands of gathering data on a full range of constructs and measuring each in sufficient detail. Our respective disciplines— not to mention our varying professional interests and background—often led us to assign different weights to the importance of the amount of detail required and the centrality of certain constructs. So our meetings were alternately animated and tedious. The process of developing the interview schedules took over a year. The final version of the in-person interviews lasted approximately an hour with parents and forty-five minutes with children.

The fieldwork commenced in the fall of 1990 and was not completed for nearly six months.[1] In all, 486 interviews were conducted by twenty interviewers, We found no evidence that interview quality varied greatly by interviewer.

Although originally intended to precede the evaluation survey (referred to as the Philadelphia Teen Survey, or PTS) that shared the same screening procedure, the two studies actually ended up overlapping in the field. The PTS drew a much larger and broader sample of census tract and targeted families with older teens between the ages of fourteen and eighteen. The survey itself was much briefer, conducted by telephone, and by a different research group. As it happened, nearly a fifth of the

1. The reason for this protracted period was the difficulty of tracing families, the instability of the fieldstaff, and the requirement of multiple visits to obtain interviews from both parent and child.

families in this study also participated in the PTS, affording an unusual opportunity to examine the reliability of similar or identical items in the two studies.

A few months elapsed between the studies on average, creating the possibility that changes in responses to similar questions may have resulted from real changes in circumstances or opinions. Appendix table A.2.1 arrays the items asked in both surveys along with cross-study correlations and the percent of same response. The status characteristics and demographic data are quite reliable; most correlations are in the range of .9 or higher. As one might expect, much lower correspondence exists for more subjective or variable items such as neighborhood features, child-rearing practices, and participation in neighborhood services. For most of these items, correlations range between .3 and .6 with a few falling outside of that band.[2]

Items that could be scaled show somewhat higher levels of concordance. The scales with reasonable levels of reliability (.8 or more) revealed respectable correlations of .6 and above across the two studies. The reliability of items across the surveys is about as high as the association of separate items within each study.

Still, the measurement errors in some constructs in the study (such as perceptions of the neighborhood, reports of childrearing practices, and, no doubt—had we happened to measure them at both points in time—indicators of children's well-being) suggest that we will not be spared from a problem familiar to social science researchers: relying on imprecise measures to examine our central research questions. Clearly, the results reported in earlier chapters are likely to understate the findings that we might have obtained had our measures been more reliable. In this regard, we face the same obstacles as other behavioral researchers in attempting to discern patterns through the haze of our measures.

2. In some cases, slight differences in wording, placement in the interview schedule, and mode of interviewing could have produced response variation. Respondents may also have shifted opinions or had different experiences between the two surveys. When the response categories were dichotomous, agreement usually occurred in 70 percent or more of the cases.

Table A.2.1

Correlations of Responses to Questions Asked in both MacArthur and William Penn Wave 2 Surveys

Questions asked	Corr. with Wm. Penn	Percent with same response	N	MacArthur variable	Wm. Penn variable
		Objective questions			
Gender	n/a (all female)	100.00	92	p2801	pgend
Race	.9354	96.70	91	p2757	race
Month born	.9709	96.67	90	p1446	birthmm
Year born	.9930	96.67	90	p1448	birthyy
Relationship to teen	1.000	100.00	45	p1452	relt1
Religion (recoded to Catholic/not Catholic)	.9357	97.53	81	p2725	p58
How often do you attend church or religious services?	.6344	58.54	82	p2727	p59
Highest grade of school completed	.7543	67.42	89	p1825	p50
Do you have a job for which you get paid?	.6341	87.78	90	p1961	p51
Do you or family members receive supplementary income from the following?					
Social Security	.6451	89.98	89	p2029	p54a
Public assistance	.5448	86.52	89	p2028	p54b
Food stamps	.6796	89.01	91	p1918 p1923	p54c
Do you have any of the following?					
Car, van, or truck	7320	85.71	91	p2021	p55a
Medical or dental insurance	.4959	89.01	91	p2023 p2024	p55b
Savings account or savings bond	.5840	79.78	89	p2017	p55c
Credit card	.7234	85.39	89	p2018	p55d
Checking account	.7544	88.76	89	p2019	p55e
Current marital status	.9198	92.31	91	p1244	p61
Are you currently living with someone in a marriagelike relationship?	.2778	89.74	39	p1416	p62
Is your spouse/partner the biological parent of TC?	1.000	100.00	21	p1444	p63
What is the highest grade your spouse/partner has attained?	.8474	73.33	45	p1811	p65
Does your spouse/partner have a job for which he or she gets paid?	.3800	85.42	48	p1813	p66

Table A.2.1
continued

Questions asked	Corr. with Wm. Penn	Percent with same response	N	MacArthur variable	Wm. Penn variable
Have you or anyone living with you ever participated in the following?					
Community family health service or counseling center	.3288	86.81	91	p245	p18a
Community watch program	.4483	81.32	91	p233	p18b
An active community organization or tenants council	.5708	81.52	92	p239	p18c
Local politics	.3907	86.81	91	p251	p18d
An after-school recreation program for children	.1968	59.78	92	p257	p18e
An organized summer recreation program for children	.2861	66.30	92	p310	p18f
An active scouting troop or youth group	.4162	72.83	92	p319	p18g
Community athletics or drill team	.4097	73.91	92	p328	p18h
Literacy, GED, or tutoring program	.3809	76.09	92	p337	p18i
An organized center like the Y, city programs in parks, or boys' and girls' clubs	.5557	82.61	92	p401	p18j
Subjective questions					
Does your neighborhood have a name?	.4373	78.89	90	p101	p1
When you think about your neighborhood, you think about (geographical area)?	.2925	41.11	90	p104	p3
How much do you agree or disagree with the following statements about your neighborhood?					
You worry about the kind of people your children will meet in your neighborhood.	.5326	76.09	92	p215	p5c
Your neighbors generally have similar views about how to raise kids.	.4488	64.10	78	p216	p5d
This is a close-knit neighborhood.	.3324	48.89	90	p218	p5e
People around here are more willing to ask for help than give it.	.3847	50.60	83	p219	p5f

Table A.2.1
continued

Questions asked	Corr. with Wm. Penn	Percent with same response	N	MacArthur variable	Wm. Penn variable
Schools around here are so bad that you can't blame kids for not going.	.3365	74.42	86	p221	p5g
People in the neighborhood gossip too much about each other.	.5178	61.84	76	p222	p5h
If you want decent health/ social services, you can't find them around here.	.2021	55.84	77	p224	p5i
There are a lot of adults that your children can look up to in neighborhood.	.5971	59.66	89	p225	p5j

How much of a problem are each of the following in your neighborhood?

High unemployment	.5421	54.55	88	ps101	p6a
Different racial/cultural groups not getting along	.1589	59.78	92	ps102	p6b
Vandalism, buildings and personal belongings broken or torn up	.3436	57.61	92	ps103	p6c
Little respect for the rules, laws, and authorities	.5244	57.14	91	ps104	p6d
Abandoned homes	.5510	53.26	92	ps106	p6e
Open drug use and dealing	.4673	53.93	89	ps114	p6f
Unsupervised children	.3837	55.43	92	ps116	p6g
Medical services too far away	.3349	74.16	89	ps120	p6h
Poor schools	.4313	52.27	88	ps122	p6i
Teenage mothers	.4295	48.86	88	ps117	p6j

Have you ever talked to your child (TC) about the following?

Biological facts of sex and pregnancy	.4329	85.11	47	p856	p10a
How to decide whether or not to have sex	.3678	76.60	47	p857	p10b
Different methods of birth control	.2653	61.70	47	p860	p10c
Where to get birth control	.4710	68.09	47	p861	p10d
How to avoid getting VD or AIDS	.2468	78.72	47	p864	p10e

How far would you like to see your child (TC) go in school?	.5236	57.78	45	p1157	p20

Table A.2.1
continued

Questions asked	Corr. with Wm. Penn	Percent with same response	N	MacArthur variable	Wm. Penn variable
How far do you think your child will actually go in school?	.5692	61.36	44	p1158	p21
Does child have a set time to be home on school nights?	(no var)	68.09	47	p952	p22
Does child have a set time to be home on weekend nights?	.4216	76.92	47	p957	p23
If child did not come home by the set time, would you know?	.0612	84.62	39	p962	p24

Table A.2.2
Target youth scales

Scale description	Sample items in scale	Source of items[a]	α	Scale mean	Scale SD
Neighborhood constructs					
Neighborhood problems	How much of a problem is prostitution? assaults or muggings?	CSA	.91	2.11	.55
Probability of success for kids in neighborhood	In your neighborhood, what are a teenagers chances of graduating high school? finding a stable job?	CSA	.78	2.99	.90
Neighborhood social control	Would anyone do something if someone were breaking into your house in plain sight? if someone were trying to sell drugs to children?	CI	.59	3.05	.52
Family constructs					
Family-child shared activity	How often do you do homework or a school project together? go shopping for something together?	CI	.73	3.02	.96
Sense of significance/ family expectations	Agree/disagree: My family needs my help around the house. My family counts on me at home.	CSA	.66	2.42	.65
Parent-child constructs					
Constructive problem solving	How often does your parent listen to your ideas about how to solve the problem? have good ideas about how to solve the problem?	CI	.83	4.01	.86
Destructive problem solving	How often does your parent just seem to get angry? ignore the problem?	CI	.60	4.29	.66
Disagreements	Do you argue with your parent about who you can hang out with? where you can go?	CI	r = .44	2.64	.53
Involvement w/ primary caregiver	How often do you and your parent do things together that you enjoy? How close do you feel to your parent?	CI	.64	3.71	.74
Involvement w/ absent father	How often do you and he do things together that you enjoy? How close do you feel to him?	CI	.79	2.66	.99
Involvement w/ absent mother	How often do you and she do things together that you enjoy? How close do you feel to her?	CI	.70	3.02	.83

*Table A.2.2
continued*

Scale description	Sample items in scale	Source of items[a]	α	Scale mean	Scale SD
Involvement w/ spouse of primary caregiver	How often do you and (spouse of pcg) do things together that you enjoy? How close do you feel to (spouse of pcg)?	CI	.78	2.24	.90
Communication	How often do you talk to your parent about problems you are having with your friends? about your plans for the future?	CI	.68	3.72	1.28
Identification with parent	Agree/disagree: I respect my parent a lot. I want to get away from home as soon as I can.	CI	.71	3.98	.92
Overprotectiveness	Agree/disagree: Your parent tries to protect you too much. Your parent has too many rules for you.	CI	.74	2.67	.55
Parent supervision	How many days in the past week did someone make sure you got breakfast? make sure you got to school on time? (for parent help only)	CI	.58	2.78	.91
Individual constructs					
Depression/ symptoms	How much have you felt angry? felt hopeless?	CSA	.87	3.65	.78
Satisfaction with self, close relations	How happy are you with the kind of person you are? your closest friends?	CSA	.73	3.23	.70
Popularity with peers	Agree/disagree: I am not liked by other girls/boys. I have a hard time getting along with other children.	CSA	.65	3.24	.64
Resourcefulness/ resilience	Agree/Disagree: I am very good at carrying out plans that I make; learning from my mistakes.	CSA	.67	2.27	.39
Satisfaction	How happy are you with the kind of person that you are? How popular you are with boys/girls?	CSA	.74	2.87	.54
Self-efficacy	How well can you get teachers to help when you get stuck on schoolwork? get adults to help when you have personal problems?	CSA	.81	5.22	.55
Significant school figure	How much does this person look out for you and help you? care for you?	CI	.67	4.33	.62
Help w/problems from school staff	When you have a problem, how often can you depend on your teachers to help you out? your parents to help you out?	CI	.70	3.01	1.08

Table A.2.2
continued

Scale description	Sample items in scale	Source of items[a]	α	Scale mean	Scale SD
Values and attitudes					
Life chances	What are the chances that you will get involved with drugs? go on welfare?	CSA	.84	5.39	.47
Ways to get ahead/applied values	How much would each of these things help you get ahead in life graduating from high school? church?	CSA	.72	3.15	.47
Costs and gains of engaging in problem behavior	What are the chances of your getting injured or killed? getting arrested?	CSA	.92	2.71	1.08
Attitudes toward delinquency	How wrong is it to cheat on school tests? use alcohol or drugs?	CSA	.87	3.45	.46
Moral disengagement	Agree/disagree: Okay to skip school if friends are doing it. Smoking marijuana is no worse than drinking alcohol.	CSA	.83	3.59	.55
Prosocial peers	How many of your friends did well in school? did community or volunteer work?	CI	.73	3.00	.84
Antisocial peers	How many of your friends suggested that you do something that was against the law? damaged or destroyed property that did not belong to them?	CI	.85	4.69	.40

a. For Source of items: CSA = target-child self-administered schedule; CI = target-child interview schedules.

Table A.2.3
Parent scales

Scale description	Sample items in scale	Source of items[a]	α	Scale mean	Scale SD
Neighborhood constructs					
Rating of block relative to neighborhood	Is your block safer than most, about the same, less safe? Does your block have more neighbors who help each other? about the same? less?	PSA	.76	2.19	.46
Probability of success for kids in neighborhood	In your neighborhood, what are a teenager's chances of graduating from high school? completing college?	PSA	.84	2.83	.79
Programs for children in community	Do you have any of the following in your community: an after-school recreation program for children? an active scouting or youth club?	PSA	.78	1.56	.34
Consumer resources	Do you have the following in your community: a bank? a supermarket?	PSA	.73	1.80	.32
Community services	Do you have the following in your community: a community day care service? a literacy, GED, or tutorial program?	PSA	.67	1.58	.32
Community political organizations	Do you have the following in your community: a community watch program? an active community organization?	PSA	.67	1.52	.39
Neighborhood problems	How much of a problem is high unemployment? assaults and muggings?	PSA	.92	1.94	.46
Social control	Would anyone do anything if someone were breaking into a house in plain sight? if someone were trying to sell drugs to children?	PI	.82	3.19	.64
Neighborhood cohesiveness	Agree/disagree: You and your neighbors have similar views about how to raise your children. This is a close-knit neighborhood.	PI	.76	3.27	.83
Negative affect in neighborhood	Agree/disagree: Neighbors often ask too much of you; People in the neighborhood gossip too much about each other.	PI	.72	3.23	.70
Barriers to services	Agree/disagree: Unless you know the right people, you can't get services in this neighborhood. You can't find decent health/social services for your children here.	PI	.62	3.48	.74

Table A.2.3
continued

Scale description	Sample items in scale	Source of items[a]	α	Scale mean	Scale SD
Family constructs					
Family problem solving	Agree/disagree: My family solves most of the everyday problems that we have. We usually do what we decided to do to solve it.	PSA	.77	3.12	.45
Family interaction style (positive)	How often do family members support each other? care about what happens to each other?	PSA	.79	4.25	.65
Parent-target child constructs					
Parent-child disagreements	How often do you and your child have disagreements about how he/she spends money? his/her report card?	PSA	.77	2.58	.79
Parent-child shared activity	How often do you and your child do homework or a school project together? go shopping for something together?	PSA	.82	3.35	.65
Positive humor	How often do you and your child enjoy a good laugh? joke with one another?	PSA	.78	3.64	.64
Negative humor	How often do you make fun of your child in front of others? yourself when you are around your child?	PSA	.33	3.77	.58
Fear of child	How often do you hesitate to enforce the rules with your child because you fear he/she might harm someone in the household? feel that you must be careful not to upset your child?	PI	.58	2.85	.32
Parent-child communication	Agree/disagree: My child and I talk about his/her plans for the future. My child and I talk about the things that make him/her feel bad.	PSA	.79	3.74	1.16
Parent's sense of target child's significance	Agree/disagree: I expect my child to do things around the house. I count on my child's help at home.	PSA	.55	3.65	.56
Self-sufficiency of TC	How often does your child prepare food that requires cooking for him/herself? do household chores for the family?	PSA	.73	3.60	1.09
Constructive problem solving	How often does your child listen to your ideas about how to solve the problem? have good ideas about how to solve the problem?	PSA	.82	3.74	.68
Destructive problem solving	How often does your child just seem angry? blame others for the problem?	PSA	.75	3.36	.71

Table A.2.3
continued

Scale description	Sample items in scale	Source of items[a]	α	Scale mean	Scale SD
Child resourcefulness	Agree/disagree: My child is very good at figuring out problems and planning how to solve them. Carrying out the plans he/she makes for solving problems.	PSA	.76	2.94	.41
Parent–older sibling constructs					
Parent's sense of older sib's significance	Agree/disagree: I expect my older child to do things around the house. I count on my older child's help at home.	PSA	.67	2.69	.62
Constructive problem solving	How often does your older child listen to your ideas about how to solve the problem? have good ideas about how to solve the problem?	PSA	.89	3.77	.79
Destructive problem solving	How often does your older child just seem to get angry? blame others for the problem?	PSA	.88	3.93	.84
Resourcefulness	Agree/disagree: My older child is very good at figuring out problems and planning how to solve them; carrying out plans he/she makes for solving problems.	PSA	.87	3.01	.49
Competence	Agree/disagree: My older child makes me proud; is a good student.	PSA	.78	3.27	.50
Self-sufficiency/ responsibleness	How often does your older child prepare food that requires cooking for himself/ herself? do household chores for family?	PSA	.79	4.03	1.21
Family management constructs					
Strategy for worries	How often did you talk to him/her about it? keep him/her away from these dangers?	PI	.65	2.34	.38
Discipline	How often do you let your child get away with things? If child is punished, how often does the punishment work?	PI	.59	2.55	.39
Discipline effectiveness	How often do you feel child's behavior gets worse if you punish him/her? have difficulty controlling your child?	PI	.68	2.67	.42
Responsiveness	How often do you and your child have disagreements about how he/she spends time outside of school? Do you ask your child what he/she thinks before deciding on family matters that involve him/her?	PSA	.75	3.62	.61

Table A.2.3
continued

Scale description	Sample items in scale	Source of items[a]	α	Scale mean	Scale SD
School-related constructs					
Perception of delinquency at TC's school	How much of a problem is the use of alcohol? the use of drugs?	PI	.84	3.43	.68
Perception of disaffection at TC's school	How much of a problem is fighting among the students? poor discipline in the classroom?	PI	.86	2.98	.77
Satisfaction with TC's school	How satisfied are you with interest/competence of teachers? your child's safety at school?	PI	.80	2.36	.50
Individual constructs					
Resourcefulness/ planfulness/ resilience	Agree/disagree: I feel that I have a hard time getting things done. I am very good at carrying out the plans I make for solving problems.	PSA	78	3.68	.56
Costs of social support	Do people count on you to listen to their problems when they are feeling down? to help them with small favors?	PI	.76	2.71	.59
Economic indicators					
Assets	Do you have any of the following: a savings account or savings bonds? a department store charge card?	PI	.76	1.56	.35
Insurance	Do you have health benefits or medical insurance? dental insurance?	PI	.59	1.81	.34
Subjective economic state	How much difficulty have you had with paying your bills? Generally, at the end of the month do you end up with more than enough money left over?	PI	.72	2.58	.84
Economic adjustments	In the last 12 months, has your family made any of the following adjustments because of financial need: used savings to meet daily expenses? postponed medical or dental care?	PI	.72	6.04	2.25
Marital indicators					
Positive marital relations	In the last year, how many times has your spouse/partner asked your opinion about an important matter? acted loving and affectionate to you?	PI	.84	4.74	1.30

Table A.2.3
continued

Scale description	Sample items in scale	Source of items[a]	α	Scale mean	Scale SD
More severe negative relations	In the last year, how many times has your spouse/partner hit/tried to hit you with something? pushed, grabbed, shoved you or threw something at you?	PI	.83	5.67	.76
Less severe negative relations	In the last year, how many times has your spouse/partner berated you or put you down on purpose? yelled at you?	PI	.75	4.13	1.35
Marital Adjustment	How do you and your spouse get along? How often do you and your spouse argue about how to discipline your child?	PI	.77		

Attitudes and values

Scale description	Sample items in scale	Source of items[a]	α	Scale mean	Scale SD
Attitudes toward delinquency (related to someone TC's age)	How wrong is it for someone your child's age to use marijuana or hashish? break into a vehicle or building to steal something?	PSA	.91	3.89	.75

a. For Source of Items: PSA = parent self-administered schedule; PI = parent interview schedule

Table A.3.1
Qualitative Sample Teen Characteristics

Teen characteristics		Comments
Name	JJ Newman	Teen is a poor student; he was suspended from school six times between eighth and ninth grade. He has been known to threaten violence. He says his mother doesn't trust him. Mother is an inconsistent parent.
Gender	Male	
Race	African-American	
Neighborhood	Low-resource/African-American	
Age at survey	14	
Family structure	Lives with single mother and her partner	
School	Public	
Name	Robert James	Teen gets mostly A's in his honors classes, has close relationships with adults, is happy with himself, and is a strong athlete. Family belongs to Jehovah's Witnesses. The teen has an active community life organized by parents.
Gender	Male	
Race	African-American	
Neighborhood	Low-resource/African-American	
Age at survey	12	
Family structure	Lives with both parents	
School	Public	
Name	Lakisha Wilkenson	Teen is a mediocre student, getting mostly C's. She is very involved in extracurricular activities including "Students Against Drugs," student council, singing in the school choir, etc. No problem behavior.
Gender	Female	
Race	African-American	
Neighborhood	Low-resouce/African-American	
Age at survey	14	
Family structure	Lives with single mother, grandmother	
School	Public	
Name	Dwight Williams	Teen is a very poor student who spends a good deal of time and energy caring for dying mother. He has no adult guidance or care and never gets into trouble at school or with the law.
Gender	Male	
Race	African-American	
Neighborhood	Low-resource/African-American	
Age at survey	14	
Family structure	Lives with single mother	
School	Public	
Name	Lamar Jackson	Teen is a poor student. He was suspended four times during eighth and ninth grade and arrested once for hitting a teacher. He hangs out with good group of kids who get good grades, expect to go to college, and do not get into trouble. Teen reports being very close to his parents. Parents use ineffective discipline strategies, provide little (or inconsistent) structure.
Gender	Male	
Race	African-American	
Neighborhood	Low-resource/African-American	
Age at survey	14	
Family structure	Lives with both parents	
School	Public	
Name	Darren Coupe	Teen gets mostly A's in accelerated classes, is a school officer, and volunteers on the school newspaper. He is described as cooperative and engaging. He has high expectations of himself. Remarkably close to mother and father, who are attentive and loving as parents.
Gender	Male	
Race	African-American	
Neighborhood	Low-resource/African-American	
Age at survey	14	
Family structure	Lives with both parents	
School	Parochial	

Table A.3.1
continued

Teen characteristics		Comments
Name	Derek Jacobs	Teen is poor student, receiving C's and lower. He failed sixth grade and was suspended three times in past two years.
Gender	Male	
Race	African-American	
Neighborhood	Low-resource/African-American	
Age at survey	12	
Family structure	Lives with grandparents	
School	Public	
Name	Rasheedah Powell	Teen gets generally high grades (A's), with occasional slips (one F last year). He was suspended once and is sexually active. No drugs or drinking. He is managing well enough, but reports being very lonely and unhappy.
Gender	Male	
Race	African-American	
Neighborhood	Low-resource/African-American	
Age at survey	12	
Family structure	Lives with single mother	
School	Public	
Name	Jamal Hutchins	Teen gets mostly C's (occasional B's, one F), and was suspended once. He claims that he has no special talents or interests. Grandmother says he is obedient and well behaved.
Gender	Male	
Race	African-American	
Neighborhood	Low-resource/African-American	
Age at survey	12	
Family structure	Parents divorced; lives with grandmother	
School	Public	
Name	Terrance Gavin	A quiet boy who does not get into trouble, does moderately well at school, and enjoys it. Mother drinks heavily since father's death in 1987. She has a limited social network, but manages to provide a reasonably routine and functional home life for her son.
Gender	Male	
Race	African-American	
Neighborhood	Low-resource/African-American	
Age at survey	13	
Family structure	Lives with single mother	
School	Public	
Name	Mark Sanders	Teen says he is in a gifted program at school; however he also reports getting mostly D's and C's. Friends with group of teenagers who drink, fight, and steal. Mother lives with her partner (not children's father) and gets limited help as a parent. She seems to be a confident parent who organizes activities for her children and monitors them reasonably well.
Gender	Male	
Race	European-American	
Neighborhood	Average-resource/European-American	
Age at survey	15	
Family structure	Lives with single mother	
School	Public	
Name	Greg Ellis	Teen is a solid student and is involved in many extracurricular activities. He does not get into trouble at school and obeys parents at home. Parents are active in neighborhood and local politics, provide structure and routine for their children. Household is organized and functions well.
Gender	Male	
Race	European-American	
Neighborhood	Average-resource/European-American	
Age at survey	14	
Family structure	Lives with both parents	
School	Parochial	

Table A.3.1
continued

Teen characteristics		Comments
Name	Matthew Maloney	Teen does not do well at school and was
Gender	Male	suspended three or four times. Reports
Race	European-American	being very unhappy. Parents are
Neighborhood	Average-resource/European-American	divorced; teen spends weekends with
Age at survey	13	father. Teen does not drink or do drugs
Family structure	Lives with mother and her boyfriend	and is not yet sexually active. Home life
School	Public	is a bit chaotic, but in fundamental ways, it is functional.
Name	Stephanie Clark	Parent reports that teen makes mostly
Gender	Female	A's, while teen reports that she makes
Race	European-American	mostly B's, but got four F's and one D
Neighborhood	Average-resource/European-American	last year. She participates in few
Age at survey	14	activities. Catholicism very important in
Family structure	Lives with both parents	family life.
School	Parochial	
Name	Marcia Lawrence	Teen excels at school (enrolled in a gifted
Gender	Female	program at school) and leads an active
Race	European-American	life. She has close relationships with
Neighborhood	Average-resource/European-American	peers and adults. Teen and family alike
Age at survey	13	are very involved in Catholic church.
Family structure	Lives with both parents	Parents are active in local community;
School	Parochial	they are encouraging and resourceful parents who provide a good deal of structure.
Name	Trisha Collins	Teen is a good student, involved in
Gender	Female	sports, very active in her church, and
Race	European-American	spends a good deal of time baby sitting.
Neighborhood	Average-resource/European-American	She has a strong sense of right and
Age at survey	15	wrong and does not engage in delinquent
Family structure	Lives with mother and stepfather	behaviors. Relationship with parent is
School	Vocational	not problematic, but not particularly close.
Name	Timothy Ross	Teen is self-motivated and does
Gender	Male	reasonably well at school. He is involved
Race	European-American	in many activities (e.g., boy scouts and
Neighborhood	Average-resource/European-American	drama club). Mother is attentive to
Age at survey	12	children and runs an orderly and routine
Family structure	Lives with both parents	household.
School	Parochial	
Name	Shaneesha Walks	Teen receives mostly B's in accelerated
Gender	Female	program at school. She is involved in
Race	African-American	many activities and sports. She has close
Neighborhood	Average-resource/African-American	relationships with a number of adults.
Age at survey	13	She is close to her mother, who is an
Family structure	Lives with single mother	involved and active parent. Mother
School	Public	communicates a great deal of confidence in her daughter.

Table A.3.1
continued

Teen characteristics		Comments
Name	Kevin Morton	Teen receives C's and lower (two F's last year). He frequently skips school and was suspended five times in two years.
Gender	Male	
Race	African-American	
Neighborhood	Average-resource/African-American	
Age at survey	14	
Family structure	Lives with single mother	
School	Public	
Name	Michael Richards	Teen is a sporadic student, sometimes doing extremely poorly. His mother is a "take-charge" parent and is very on top of her son's life. She pushes her son incredibly hard, not always to a good end. Interviewer writes that teen is intelligent, cooperative, and likable.
Gender	Male	
Race	African-American	
Neighborhood	Average-resource/African-American	
Age at survey	14	
Family structure	Lives with single mother and grandparents	
School	Vocational	
Name	Jesse Parks	Attends accelerated classes for gifted children, but has also failed some classes. Teen hangs out with a gang of about twenty-five boys who get in a fair amount of trouble. Some of them deal drugs; many of them are sexually active. Teen was arrested once for writing graffiti. Mother knows little about what her son is up to.
Gender	Male	
Race	African-American	
Neighborhood	Average-resource/African-American	
Age at survey	15	
Family structure	Lives with single mother, father died in '87	
School	Parochial	
Name	Tanisha Lennet	Teen is a poor student. Mother reports increasing behavioral problems, including skipping school, getting suspended, failing classes. Mother's attempts at discipline are unsuccessful. Mother sent her away for awhile to live with grandparents during part of 1989–90 school year, but little changed in her behavior or school performance.
Gender	Female	
Race	African-American	
Neighborhood	Average-resource/African-American	
Age at survey	15	
Family structure	Lives with mother and stepfather	
School	Public	
Name	Tamar Anderson	Teen was suspended from school eight times in two years and is generally a poor student. He hangs out with a bad crowd of kids and has been in trouble with police. Father has sought professional advice, and tries to keep his son in organized activities, but his attempts do little. Overall, father does not monitor son very closely.
Gender	Male	
Race	African-American	
Neighborhood	Average-resource/African-American	
Age at survey	15	
Family structure	Lives with father	
School	Public	
Name	Traci Kinsley	Teen gets mostly B's in honors classes at magnet school for gifted children. She is very involved in activities both inside and outside school. She plans to go to college. She is "extremely close" to both parents.
Gender	Female	
Race	African-American	
Neighborhood	Average-resource/African-American	
Age at survey	15	
Family structure	Lives with single mother	
School	Magnet school	

Table A.3.1
continued

Teen characteristics		Comments
Name	Moya Kirk	Teen and parent have different reports about teen's well-being. Teen says that she gets mostly B's (with one D), and her mother says that teen gets mostly C's (and one F). According to mother, teen has "gotten involved with wrong kinds of kids," has run away from home, and been suspended from school three times. Mother claims she did "nothing" when her daughter did these things.
Gender	Female	
Race	African-American	
Neighborhood	Average-resource/African-American	
Age at survey	14	
Family structure	Lives with single mother	
School	Public	
Name	Tarissa Hawkins	Teen gets mostly B's. She is "extremely close" to her stepmother and father, has a very positive picture of herself and a lot of self-confidence.
Gender	Female	
Race	African-American	
Neighborhood	Average-Resource/African-American	
Age at survey	13	
Family structure	Lives with father and stepmother	
School	Public	
Name	Ryan Hart	Teen is a solid student. He wants to study cooking after high school. He is Catholic, and religion is very important to him. He is very close to his parents. Teen is severely overweight.
Gender	Male	
Race	European-American	
Neighborhood	High-resource/European-American	
Age at survey	15	
Family structure	Lives with both parents	
School	Parochial	
Name	Christine Lang	Teen is an excellent student and is involved in many extracurricular activities. She has close relationships with parents and other adults, has many friends (who are also good students), and does not get into trouble.
Gender	Female	
Race	European-American	
Neighborhood	High-resource/European-American	
Age at survey	13	
Family structure	Lives with both parents	
School	Parochial	
Name	Sheryl Dobbs	She is a good student who sometimes lapses into not doing so well. She doesn't get into trouble, though she does skip school sometimes. Mother works in the evening and on an irregular schedule, so teen's older sisters often take over the job (not always so well) of caring for teen.
Gender	Female	
Race	European-American	
Neighborhood	High-resource/European-American	
Age at survey	13	
Family structure	Lives with single mother	
School	Public	
Name	Douglas Harwood	Teen is a good student, plays a lot of sports, and hangs out with kids who don't get into trouble. Mother is fairly active at her son's school.
Gender	Male	
Race	European-American	
Neighborhood	High-resource/European-American	
Age at survey	13	
Family structure	Lives with both parents	
School	Parochial	

Table A.3.1
continued

Teen characteristics		Comments
Name	Kate Harvey	Teen is a good student, participates in
Gender	Female	sports, and sings in church choir. She is
Race	European-American	close to her mother but not to her father
Neighborhood	High-resource/European-American	(who she appears not to like). She does
Age at survey	13	not get into any trouble and is not yet
Family structure	Lives with both parents	sexually active.
School	Parochial	
Name	Pam Koller	She is an honors student, likes to dance,
Gender	Female	play flute, and is involved in church
Race	European-American	youth group. Friends are good students
Neighborhood	High-resource/European-American	who are active in school programs.
Age at survey	12	Mother is involved in child's school,
Family structure	Lives with both parents	though mother and daughter report
School	Parochial	being only "fairly close."
Name	Megan Forman	Teen is a very good student and is
Gender	Female	incredibly active (church youth group,
Race	European-American	girl scouts, volunteers as a tutor, plays
Neighborhood	High-resource/European-American	flute and piano, etc). She has many
Age at survey	13	friends, does not get into trouble, and
Family structure	Lives with both parents	feels that she gets quite a lot of affection
School	Parochial	and encouragement from her parents.
Name	Paul Pulaski	Teen is a very strong student and athlete.
Gender	Male	He doesn't get into much trouble, though
Race	European-American	he does sometimes drink alcohol.
Neighborhood	High-resource/European-American	
Age at survey	15	
Family structure	Lives with both parents	
School	Parochial	
Name	Sarah Sullivan	Teen is an average student and not
Gender	Female	involved in activities except for church
Race	European-American	youth group. She does not have access to
Neighborhood	High-resource/European-American	many adult resources. Her parents are
Age at survey	14	strict; however she says she is close to
Family structure	Lives with both parents	them.
School	Parochial	

Table A.6.1
Parental competence and health by social and economic factors:
regression coefficients in standard form

Social factors	Parental efficacy		Resourcefulness		Lack of mental health problems	
	r	Beta	r	Beta	r	Beta
Total family income	.08	−.00	.13	.07	.05	.02
Welfare dependence (1 = yes)	−.09	−.09	−.06	.05	−.16	−.01
Education of parent	.08	.02	.18	.17***	.02	.01
Household size	−.01	−.05	−.11	−.05	.05	.04
Race (1 = black)	−.00	.05	−.01	−.02	.07	.09*
Single parent (1 = yes)	−.10	−.17***	−.00	−.09	−.03	−.17***
Weak marriage (1 = yes)	−.03	−.13**	.16	−.19***	−.16	−.24***
Age of caregiver	−.13	−.16***	.15	.16***	.15	.14***
Age of child	−.14	.13***	−.02	−.01	.00	−.01
Gender of child (1 = female)	.08	.10**	.15	−.12***	−.05	−.03
R^2		.08		12		.07
N		486		486		486

*$p < .10$; **$p < .05$; ***$p < .01$

Table A.6.2

Family process and management strategies by social and psychological factors: regression coefficients in standardized form

| | Family processes | | | | | | Family management strategies | | | |
| | Support for autonomy | | Discipline effectiveness | | Positive family climate | | Institutional connections | | Parental investment | |
Social and psychological factors	r	Beta	r	Beta	r	Beta	r	Beta	r	Beta
Controls										
Age, child	-.02	.02	-.05	-.01	-.05	.01	-.15	.11***	-.17	.12***
Gender, child (1 = male)	.02	-.01	.01	.03	.03	-.02	.02	.01	.04	.05
Psychological, parent										
Efficacy	.41	.28***	.34	.28***	.39	.24***	.18	.11**	.30	.23***
Resourcefulness	.44	.30***	.28	.09*	.49	.32***	.17	.07	.23	.14***
Mental health problems	-.36	-.18***	-.36	-.23***	-.38	-.16***	-.08	.00	-.14	-.03
Social factors										
Total family income	.11	-.02	.03	.03	.09	-.03	.20	.13**	-.03	-.06
Welfare dependence (1 = yes)	-.17	-.11**	-.06	-.04	-.09	-.02	-.10	-.01	.00	-.02
Education, caregiver	.04	-.06	.01	-.04	.11	.01	.32	.22***	.10	.03
Household size	-.08	-.06	.03	.06	-.15	-.13***	-.15	-.10**	-.16	-.15***
Race (1 = black)	-.09	-.05	.15	.14***	-.04	-.03	.12	.14***	.16	.16***
Single parent (1 = yes)	-.11	-.04	.00	.01	-.04	-.14***	-.00	.01	.04	-.02
Weak marriage (1 = yes)	-.04	.01	-.12	-.05	-.21	-.19***	-.07	-.03	-.08	-.01
Age of caregiver	.03	-.04	.11	.09*	.04	-.04	.01	.01	-.00	-.03
R² minus psychological variables		.05		.06		.11		.16		.09
R² change		.28***		.18***		.26***		.02**		.09
R²		.33		.24		.38		.18		.18
N		486		486		486		486		486

*p < .10; **p < .05; ***p < .01

Table A.6.3
Successful and problem behavior of adolescents by social and psychological factors: regression coefficients in standard form

Social and psychological factors	Successful and problem behavior							
	Activity involvement		Academic competence		Mental health		Problem behavior	
	r	Beta	r	Beta	r	Beta	r	Beta
Controls								
Age, child	−.07	−.04	−.06	−.02	.03	.08**	−.32	.29***
Gender, child (1 = male)	.13	.12***	−.15	−.14***	−.01	−.02	.16	.13***
Psychological, parent								
Efficacy	.11	.06	.26	.20***	.43	.32***	−.34	−.27***
Resourcefulness	.19	.12**	.09	−.03	.41	.27***	−.05	.03
Mental health problems	−.06	.01	−.10	−.07	−.33	−.15***	.11	.05
Social factors								
Total family income	.19	.17***	.20	.05	.07	−.03	−.07	−.07
Welfare dependence (1 = yes)	−.07	−.01	−.26	−.18***	−.10	−.07	.10	.06
Education, caregiver	.23	.13**	.22	.15***	.07	−.01	.02	.07
Household size	−.11	−.05	−.12	−.10**	−.03	.01	−.13	−.13***
Race (1 = black)	.04	.07	−.09	−.05	−.02	−.01	−.03	−.04
Single parent (1 = yes)	.03	.10*	−.08	.01	−.04	−.02	.09	.02
Weak marriage (1 = yes)	−.05	.01	.00	−.01	−.10	−.05	.02	.04
Age of caregiver	−.02	−.03	−.03	−.05	−.01	−.06	.04	.00
R^2 minus psychological variables	.10		.14		.04		.17	
R^2 change	.02**		.04***		.27***		.07***	
R^2	.12		.18		.31		.24	
N	483		483		479		478	

$*p < .10; **p < .05; ***p < .01$

Table A.6.4
Activity involvement of adolescents by parent behavior and social factors: regression coefficients in standard form

Parent and social factors	Activity involvement of adolescent		
	Total	I	II
	r	Beta	Beta
Controls			
Gender of child (1 = male)	.13	.12***	.10**
Age of child	−.07	−.06	.01
Social factors			
Total family income	.19	.17***	.10**
Education of caregiver	.23	.17***	.04
Single parent (1 = yes)	.03	.12**	.08*
Psychological, parent			
Efficacy	.11	—	.00
Resourcefulness	.19	—	.05
Family management			
Institutional connection (with private school)	.48		.40***
Investment in child	.28	—	.13***
Restrictiveness	−.05	—	−.09**
Adjusted R^2		.08	.2
R^2 change		—	.19***
N		483	483

*$p < .10$; **$p < .05$; ***$p < .01$.

Table A.6.5

Academic competence of adolescents by parent behavior and social factors: regression coefficients in standard form

Social influences	Total	I	II
	r	Beta	Beta
Academic competence of adolescents			
Controls			
Gender of child (1 = male)	−.15	−.15***	−.13***
Social factors			
Welfare dependency (1 = yes)	−.26	−.21***	−.11**
Education of parent	.22	.18***	.15***
Household size	−.12	−.09**	−.06
Psychological, parent			
Efficacy	.26	—	.13***
Resourcefulness	.09	—	.10**
Family process			
Support for autonomy	.30		.21***
Institutional connection	.22	—	.08***
Selective school placement	.28	—	.20***
Investment in child	.12	—	−.01
Adjusted R^2		.12	.24
R^2 change		—	.12***
N		483	483

*$p < .10$; **$p < .05$; ***$p < .01$.

Table A.6.6

Child's psychological adjustment by parent behavior and social factors: regression coefficients in standard form

Social influences	Parent report on child's psychological adjustment	
	r	Beta
Controls		
Age of child	.03	.07**
Psychological, parent		
Efficacy	.43	.17***
Resourcefulness	.41	.11***
Mental health problems	−.33	−.03
Family Process		
Support for autonomy	.61	.39***
Discipline effectiveness	.42	.14***
Positive family climate	.42	.07
Adjusted R^2	.45	
N	479	

*$p < .10$; **$p < .05$; ***$p < .01$.

Table A.7.1
Tract-level correlations (N = 45)

Variable	1	2	3	4	5	6	7	8	9	10	11	12	13	14	15	16	17	18	19	20	21	22	23	24	25	26	27
Percent college grads																											
Percent poverty	-.39																										
Percent white	.20	-.34																									
Percent female head HH	-.48	.68	-.76																								
Neighborhood orgs.	.34	-.37	.38	-.37																							
Neighborhood climate	.43	-.37	.40	-.47	.62																						
Neighborhood network	-.08	-.28	.56	-.46	.43	.27																					
Social capital composite	.29	-.42	.56	-.55	.83	.79	.74																				
Child age	-.05	-.09	.05	-.06	.09	-.13	-.07	-.08																			
Race	-.05	.03	-.86	.47	-.18	-.24	-.47	-.38	-.01																		
Income	.48	-.60	.56	-.71	.32	.48	.28	.44	.10	-.40																	
Parent education	.62	-.44	.01	-.32	.20	.26	-.20	.08	.08	.19	.58																
Welfare dependency	-.44	.48	-.56	.56	-.33	-.54	-.14	-.43	.09	.42	-.68	-.46															
Household size	-.24	.21	-.12	.19	.33	-.40	.07	-.25	.12	.06	-.14	-.18	.31														
Single parent	-.29	.32	-.63	.47	-.33	-.33	-.35	-.45	.13	.63	-.57	-.11	.57	.21													

Psychological resources	.29	−.15	.13	−.25	−.27	.01	−.07	−.14	−.16	−.14	.3⁻	.35	−.17	−.09	−.08												
Positive family climate	.31	−.16	−.04	−.08	.34	.40	.09	.34	.06	.0⁵	.20	−.30	−.43	−.15	−.04												
Autonomy	.07	.04	.07	−.04	.04	.15	.19	.18	−.21	−.17	−.0⁻	−.17	−.21	−.34	−.08	.12	.46										
Discipline effectiveness	.10	.11	−.40	.16	−.17	.05	−.13	−.07	−.09	.48	−.0⁶	.00	.02	.13	.24	−.09	.17	.21									
Institutional connections	.63	−.43	−.05	−.19	.34	.43	.01	.33	−.19	.16	.4⁻	.52	−.41	−.39	−.24	.21	.49	.34	.28								
Investment	.06	.02	−.30	.14	−.2⁰	−.07	−.12	−.12	−.26	.35	−.2⁰	.05	.00	−.13	.24	.22	.27	.43	.47	.39							
Positive social network	.57	−.48	.04	−.40	.22	.42	−.07	.22	−.12	.51	.59	−.26	−.23	−.05	.24	.32	.08	.12	.57	.21							
Restrictiveness	.21	−.44	−.63	−.53	.43	.59	.42	.61	.06	−.52	.54	.16	−.58	−.35	−.45	.12	.30	.22	−.13	.36	−.02	.28					
Private/magnet schools	.01	−.41	−.70	.62	−.14	−.17	−.55	−.35	−.18	.54	−.50	−.11	.30	.04	.33	.08	.01	.00	.29	.12	.29	−.11	−.43				
Mental health	−.03	−.10	.15	−.09	−.02	−.08	−.01	−.07	.08	−.10	.11	.16	.07	.12	−.11	−.12	−.37	−.75	−.39	−.26	−.45	−.02	−.10	−.25			
Acting out	−.03	−.03	.10	−.03	.16	−.08	.22	.11	.25	−.13	−.07	.05	.12	.04	−.13	−.16	.11	−.04	−.32	−.16	−.14	.02	.04	−.15	.08		
Academic performance	.30	−.13	.11	−.22	−.03	.19	−.14	.00	.03	−.14	.31	.36	−.40	−.50	−.14	.48	.14	.36	−.02	.41	.09	.27	.03	−.35	−.30		
Activity involvement	.25	−.49	.00	−.26	.29	.23	.26	.35	.05	.17	.42	.39	−.28	−.03	−.10	.25	.20	.20	.28	.57	.39	.42	.31	−.10	−.28	−.02	.26

Table A.7.2
Neighborhood-level characteristics

Variable	Mean	SD	Minimum	Maximum	N
Percent college graduates	9.56	9.38	0.00	43.86	45
Percent in poverty	23.86	12.90	5.00	62.00	45
Percent white	28.15	35.24	0.31	98.90	45
Percent female-headed household	19.17	7.56	6.07	35.17	45
Neighborhood organizations	−0.04	0.31	−0.91	0.64	45
Neighborhood climate	−0.04	0.38	−1.05	0.97	45
Neighborhood networks	−0.06	0.40	−0.68	0.78	45
Neighborhood social capital composite	−0.04	0.29	−0.74	0.58	45
Child age	12.52	0.48	11.60	13.60	45
Race	0.66	0.40	0.00	1.00	45
Income	3.61	0.87	2.17	5.36	45
Parent education	12.49	0.97	9.50	14.83	45
Welfare dependency	0.57	0.21	0.09	1.00	45
Household size	4.63	0.64	3.60	6.33	45
Single parent	0.44	0.20	0.00	0.83	45
Psychological functioning	0.01	0.23	−0.71	0.52	45
Positive family climate	0.03	0.28	−0.68	0.69	45
Autonomy	−0.02	0.27	−0.68	0.45	45
Discipline effectiveness	0.02	0.25	−0.72	0.59	45
Institutional connections	3.02	1.03	0.89	5.80	45
Parent investment	0.02	0.25	−0.66	0.54	45
Positive social networks	12.40	2.92	6.43	20.55	45
Private/magnet schools	0.25	0.21	0.00	0.75	45
Restrictiveness	0.12	0.88	−1.93	1.73	45
Mental problems	−0.01	0.29	−0.96	0.63	45
Behavioral problems	0.00	0.26	−0.41	0.82	45
Academic competence	−0.02	0.36	−0.99	0.75	45
Activity involvement	−0.01	0.27	−0.50	0.68	45

Table A.7.3

Cross-model hierarchical linear model: family management

| | Family management processes | | | | | | | | | |
| | Positive social network | | Institutional connections | | Investment | | Restrictiveness | | Private/ magnet school | |
Predictor	Beta	r	Beta	r	Beta	r	Beta	r	Beta	r
Neighborhood level										
Percent poverty	−.061**	.029	−.013	.012	−.000	.003	.016*	.009	−.003	.002
Percent white	−.018*	.011	.000	.006	.000	.001	−.017***	.004	−.000	.001
Social capital	1.373	1.466	1.210**	.584	−.099	.143	.154	.419	.198*	.105
Individual/neighborhood										
Age	−.387**	.196	−.195**	.079	−.060***	.022				
Gender								.168		.071
Black	.835***	.192	.866**	.374	.235**	.101	−.558***	.304	−.159**	.040
Income/					.054	.037	.121	.064	−.007	.001
Percent poverty					−.003*	.002	.052		.000	.001
Percent white									.001**	.000
Social capital									.032	.058
Education/	.715***	.136	.510***	.116	.006	.015	−.095	.097	.033	.025
Percent poverty			−.009***	.004			.002	.003	−.000	.001
Percent white			.000	.001			.001	.002	−.000	.000
Social capital	.982**	.472					.516**	.235		
Welfare					−.037**	.019			−.110**	.044
Household size			−.139**	.067						
Single	2.363***	.561	.606***	.203			−.398**	.190		
Psychological resources/social capital	1.082**	.500			.199***	.059				
Positive family climate					.244***	.041				
Autonomy										
Discipline effectiveness										
Percent between neighborhood variance explained	69.4		52.4		96.1		99.7		88.9	

*p < .10; **p < .05; ***p < .01.

Table A.7.4
Cross-level hierarchical linear model: child outcomes

Variables	Behavioral problems		Activity involvement		Academic competence	
	Beta	SE	Beta	SE	Beta	SE
Neighborhood level						
Percent in poverty	.001	.003	−.003	.003	.003	.004
Percent white	−.001	.001	−.002	.001	.001	.001
Social Capital	.202	.174	.373	.143	−.306	.186
Individual/neighborhood						
Age	.165***	.024				
Gender	.263***	.060	.132**	.057	−.261***	.070
Race						
Income			.044**	.022	.039	.027
Education			.073	.016	.048**	.019
Welfare					−.154*	.082
Household size						
Single parent			.124**	.063		
Psychological resources/	−.108*	.062	.073	.058	−.021	.075
Social capital					−.318	.261
Positive family climate						
Autonomy					.225***	.050
Discipline effectiveness/	−.201***	.049				
Social capital	−.636***	.171				
Institutional connections/	.010	.017	.128***	.017	−.057	.040
Percent in poverty					.004**	.002
Percent white	−.001*	.000	−.000	.000		
Social capital					.184***	.061
Investment/						
Positive social network			.112	.049		
Restrictiveness/	−.048	.037	−.072**	.035		
Percent in poverty	.002	.002	.002	.001		
Social capital	.069	.063	.100*	.059		
Private/magnet schools					.171***	.039
Between-neighborhood variance explained	31.4		97.2		90.5	

*p < .10, **p < .05, ***p < .01

Table A.8.1
Creation of risk categories from explanatory variables

Variable	Range	Lowest quartile
Demographic variables		
Age of child[a]	10.0–15.0	11.0
Gender of child[b]	1.0–2.0	2.0
Race	1.0–2.0	1.0
Parent education	3.0–19.0	11.0
Single parent	0.0–1.0	1.0
Household income	1.0–7.0	2.0
Welfare	0.0–1.0	1.0
Number of children in household	1.0–8.0	≧4.0
Neighborhood variables		
Percent of families in poverty, 1990 census	5.0–62.0	≧25.0
Institutional resources	1.0–16.0	≦6.0
Climate	−1.6–1.3	≦ .38
Caregiver's resources		
Resourcefulness	1.4–5.0	≦3.25
Self-efficacy	1.4–4.5	≦3.33
Mental health	1.0–4.7	≧2.73

a. In the final models, age, gender, and race are not included in the cumulative risk scores, but are controlled for separately.

b. Girls are coded as 1.0, and boys are coded as 2.0.

Table A.8.2
Risk factors by sets of variables

Groups of variables	Risk range	Risk level		
		High	Medium	Low
Demographic traits	0–5	3–5	2	0–1
Neighborhood traits	0–3	2–3	1	0
Caregiver's resources	0–3	2–3	1	0

Families by number of high risk levels				
	High risk levels			
	0	1	2	3
Number of families	178	183	99	16
Percentage of families	37.4	38.5	20.8	3.3

Table A.8.3

Creation of Protective Family Factors from Separate Family Variables

Scoring of family variables	Range	Lowest quartile
Family management		
Institutional connections	0.0–12.0	≤ 1.0
Social networks	0.0–30.0	≤ 8.0
Parental investments in child	−2.6–1.7	≤ -0.35
Private schooling	0.0–1.0	0.0
Family processes		
Positive family climate	−3.6–1.8	≤ -0.46
Support for autonomy	−3.1–1.5	≤ -0.47
Discipline effectiveness	−3.1–2.4	≤ -0.33

		Protection level		
	Risk range	Low	Medium	High
Protective family factors				
Family management	0–4	3–4	2	0–1
Family processes	0–3	2–3	1	0

Table A.9.1
Case Summary Coding ($N = 35$)

Survey instrument scales	Case summary coding			
	Parental competence	Financial resources	Social capital	TC outcome
Parenting				
Parent/TC involvement	.32	.15	.36	.29
Parent positive use of autonomy	.58	.35	.60	.70
Parent investment	.34	.07	.28	.28
Parent discipline effectiveness	.31	.25	.39	.33
Positive family relations	.44	.21	.55	.62
Positive interactions with TC	.44	.19	.38	.43
Negative interactions with TC	−.50	−.33	−.41	−.48
Financial resources				
Parent felt constraint	.39	.54	.49	.47
Household SES	.31	.72	.44	.38
Household income	.46	.76	.54	.40
Social capital				
Positive opportunity networks	.29	.06	.24	.17
Informal networks	.20	.41	.24	.29
Institutional ties	.41	.10	.16	.31
Target-child outcome				
Acting out	−.69	−.34	−.55	−.68
Academic problems	−.51	−.57	−.59	−.71
Involvement in activities	.21	.00	.31	.23

Table A.9.2
Qualitative Interview Scales (*N* = 35)

Survey instrument scales	Qualitative interview scales		
	Parental competence	Financial resources	Social capital
Parenting			
Parent/TC involvement	.35	.28	.42
Parent positive use of autonomy	.29	.27	.17
Parent investment	.20	.11	.24
Parent discipline effectiveness	.29	.43	.39
Positive family relations	.35	.32	.32
Positive interactions with TC	.33	.40	.18
Negative interactions with TC	.47	.45	−.14
Financial resources			
Parent felt constraint	.17	.52	.33
Household SES	.29	.43	.27
Household income	.41	.62	.39
Social capital			
Positive opportunity networks	.32	.28	.46
Informal networks	.29	.42	.38
Institutional ties	.33	.25	.41
Target child outcome			
Acting out	−.47	−.43	−.07
Academic problems	−.28	−.35	−.15
Involvement in activities	.29	10	.35

Notes

CHAPTER ONE

1. The theme of Jay Macleod's *Ain't No Makin' It* (1987) now stands in contrast to studies of pathways out of disadvantage, such as Chase-Lansdale and Brooks-Gunn's *Escape from Poverty: What Makes a Difference for Children?* (1995) and South and Crowder's "Escaping Distressed Neighborhoods" (1997). The psychology of these pathways centers on the process of resilience in which children overcome setbacks and rise above the limitations they face. This process is enhanced by protective factors, such as religious involvement and support from friends and teachers, that minimize the adverse effect of risk factors such as chronic poverty, drugs, and violence. Examples of this work include that of Michael Rutter (1988), Norman Garmezy (1985), and Smith et al. (1995).

CHAPTER TWO

1. Systematic cross-site comparisons were being undertaken as this book was being completed.

2. About the time that the MacArthur Network on Successful Adolescent Development was setting its research agenda in 1988, Furstenberg was in the midst of conducting an evaluation of a community-based intervention program located in a large number of Philadelphia neighborhoods. When the ethnographic study was contemplated the following year, Furstenberg volunteered to supervise the fieldwork and eventually located the sites in some of the same communities that were included in the ongoing evaluation. Once the ethnographic work was completed, it made sense to remain in Philadelphia, especially because a survey could be piggybacked onto another study of families residing in several inner-city neighborhoods. For no additional cost, we could sample households in which younger adolescents were present at the same time that we screened for eligibility for the other study.

3. Respondents were asked about the size of their neighborhood in this study and in the overlapping evaluation study. The question was, When you think about your neighborhood are you thinking about (a) the block or street you live on, (b) the block or street you live on plus several blocks or streets around you, (c) the area within a 15-minute walk, or (d) an area larger than all of these? For the

ninety adults who were interviewed in both studies, we were able to compare responses to this question over a period of averaging four months. Only 41 percent
of the respondents gave the same response twice. The correlation between responses in each study was .29.

4. Within each of the sixty-five randomly selected tracts, we drew a subset of
block groups, which became the sampling frame for screening households. A
street address listing was compiled using census maps of the selected block
groups. From a reverse telephone directory, we enumerated all listed phone numbers from those addresses. We also randomly drew a supplementary list of 981
households with unlisted phones or without phones in order to include households that would have been otherwise omitted from the sample. Those addresses
were screened in person by the fieldwork staff for eligibility.

5. The proportion of eligible families is somewhat lower than was originally
estimated from census data on the number of families with children in the appropriate age range residing within the sample of block groups. We surmise that
some parents (or other household members answering the screening question)
deliberately opted out of the study by inaccurately reporting that the household
contained no eligible children. While we cannot be certain that these "soft refus-
als" did not introduce some bias in the data, we know that these families opted
out of the screening process before they were informed about the study or invited
to participate. Thus, they did not knowingly decline to participate because of the
interview content.

6. In the screening instructions, we asked to interview the parent who knew the
most about the child. Not surprisingly, in most cases (84 percent) this person
turned out to be the child's biological mother. Parent surrogates included 5 percent
grandparents, 6 percent fathers, and 4 percent other relatives or foster parents.

7. The families without phones or with unlisted numbers were less well educated and poorer on average. It seems likely that our underrepresentation of very
poor families from very poor census tracts is at least in part due to the telephone
screening procedure. This result is consistent with other evidence showing that
very poor families are less likely to have listed numbers and much more likely to
have no phone in the household, though relatively few families (5 percent) in
Philadelphia do not have a telephone in the household.

8. We also collected a self-administered questionnaire from an older sibling
when one was present in the home. These data are not used in the analyses that
follow.

9. In all but a few families, a complete set of interviews was obtained. Where
this was not possible, families are excluded from the data analyses that follow.

10. In some cases, slight differences in wording, placement in the interview
schedule, and mode of interviewing could have produced response variations. It
is also entirely plausible that respondents shifted options or had different experiences between the two surveys. When the response categories were dichotomous,
agreement usually occurred in 70 percent or more of the cases.

CHAPTER THREE

1. We generally used scales that had reliabilities of at least .7 or greater.

2. While we made some efforts to assure ourselves that the measures them-

selves were internally consistent, we lacked information from schools or records that might allow us to validate these measures. Prior attempts in delinquency research suggest that self-reported data are reasonably well correlated to record data (Hindelang, Hirschi, and Weiss 1981; Huizinga and Elliott 1986).

3. See appendix table 9.1 and the discussion in chapter 9 for specifics.

4. We used a statistical procedure known as cluster analysis to identify groups of adolescents who were similar to each other across the five domains of successful development: academic performance, psychological adjustment, self-competence, prosocial involvement, and problem behavior. Cluster analysis is a powerful procedure that yields homogeneous groups of individuals by taking into account their functioning on a range of indicators, in essence producing unique profiles of typologies of youths (Aldenderfer and Blashfield 1984; Blashfield and Aldenderfer 1988).

5. This point is particularly important in this study, given the potential for artifactual results due to the method variance created by relying entirely on mother's reports. Here, the adolescents' own reports of psychological well-being can serve in a confirmatory capacity.

6. Perhaps this difference in factor structure reflects the fact that academic competence and activity involvement are more readily accessible to direct, objective observation than psychological adjustment, which by its nature is a more subjective construct, less readily accessible to dual-informant convergence (Achenbach, McConaughy, and Howell 1987). To the extent that this is true, then, these constructs may have formed different indices because they represent different reporters. However, it is also possible that the parent and child reports formed separate factors because they tapped somewhat different aspects of the child's psychological experience; the mothers' reports by and large assessed their perceptions of the absence of dysfunction in their children; in contrast, the adolescents' self-reports were more representative of the presence of positive psychological functioning. This distinction is consistent with Kazdin's (1993) recent assertion that mental health should be defined in light of both the absence of dysfunction and the presence of positive functioning, or competence.

7. The adolescent outcome variable "problem behavior" is constructed from several subscales assessing different domains of problem behavior. These were delinquency; engagement in illegal activities; aggression; the use of physical force against peers, parents, and teachers; substance abuse, primarily alcohol and cigarettes; and school truancy, high absenteeism, and school suspensions. To describe further the characteristics of the adolescents in our clusters, we examined how these separate subscale behaviors were distributed across the four groups. What we found was that our small group of delinquents was at the extreme on each of these subscales. They were the only group significantly above average in delinquency, aggression, substance abuse, and school truancy.

CHAPTER FOUR

1. The *Parent Shared Activity* scale consisted of seven items like the following: "How often do you go out to the zoo, a museum, or libraries together?" "How often do you work on something together around the house?" Alpha for this scale was greater than .70.

2. These items are modified versions of the Epstein and McPartland (1977) Family Decision-Making Scale used by Eccles and her colleagues with middle- to lower-middle-class samples. The internal consistency is .81.

3. This scale (alpha = .75) was measured with a 5-point response format anchored toward increasing disagreement. Representative items: "How often do you and your child have disagreements about how he/she spends time outside of school? How he/she spends money?"

4. Both of these scales were measured by a 5-point Likert response format with 5 = almost always. Cronbach's alpha for the constructive-problem-solving scale was .82, with a mean of 3.73. Cronbach's alpha for the destructive-problem-solving scale was .76, with a mean of 2.1 (Cronbach 1951).

5. Items were measured on a 3-point Likert response line anchored with 3 = often for the effective end point. Representative items: "How often do you feel you have difficulty controlling your child?" and "How often do you feel child's behavior gets worse if you punish him/her?"

6. Each item was measured via a 3-point Likert response line that was anchored in the direction of more consistency. Representative items: "If you warn your child that he/she will be punished if he/she does not stop doing something, how often do you actually punish him/her if he/she does not stop?" and "Does the kind of punishment you give the child depend on whether you are in a good or bad mood?"

CHAPTER FIVE

1. For the most part, the parenting and family management measures used in this study were adapted from those used previously in the Iowa Youth and Family Project (Conger and Elder 1994), The National Youth Survey (Elliott, Huizinga, and Menard 1989), and the Adolescent Transitions Project (Eccles et al. 1989). Many of the items originated from the Thornberry et al. (1995) multisite study on the causes and correlates of delinquency.

2. The four measures of consistent and effective discipline (monitoring, discipline effectiveness, discipline consistency, and fear of child) loaded on the same factor (discipline effectiveness). The alpha for this composite was .64. Similarly, the four measures of developmentally appropriate support for autonomy (involvement in decision-making, constructive and destructive problem solving, and disagreement) loaded on the same factor (support for autonomy) and yielded a composite scale with an alpha of .74. Positive family climate stood alone as its own indicator with an alpha of .78.

Most of the quantitative scales tapping child-centered management (verbal encouragement, enroll in programs, work with child, praise child, proactive prevention, shared activities) also loaded on a single factor. We have labeled this factor *parent investment,* since it included the one indicator we had for parent involvement as well as the quantitative promotive and preventive management strategies. This composite had an alpha of .78. The control scale for the preventive management strategies did not load with this factor and had rather a poor alpha itself (.50). However, since this component of family management emerged as such a critical factor in Furstenberg's (1993) ethnographic study of family management, we created a composite scale reflecting a count across several of the more qualitative indicators of restrictive strategies. This composite reflected the parents' restrictive response to the following questions: "Does (Child) have a regular time to come home on school nights?" "Does (Child) have a regular time to come home on weekend nights?" "Where does (Child) go after school?"

3. The *economic adjustments* measure was constructed to represent affirmative responses to any adjustments the parent has had to make due to financial need. Representative items: cut-back on social entertainment, changed eating habits to save money, and reduced household utility use. The Cronbach alpha for this summated scale was .70.

4. Institutional connections is a composite measure reflecting parents' involvement in community organizations, school, and religious organizations. Social networks indicate access to work and other models. *Informal social networks* are indexed by summation of friend and kin support across types of need situation.

5. The total amount of variance accounted for by these measures ranges from 6 percent to 44 percent. Both the lowest and highest percentage probably reflect method bias. The highest (44 percent) occurred for parents' reports of their children's mental health. This is the only model in which the same informant provides all of the information on both the predictors and the outcome measure. In contrast, the lowest percent (6 percent) occurred for the adolescents' reports of their self-competence. Although this is not the only model in which the adolescent is the sole reporter of the outcome measure, mental health is much harder to assess in someone else than activity involvement and problem behavior—both of which are overtly visible, while mental health must be inferred. What is more important in these two regression equations is that they manifest the same pattern of association. Both measures of psychological adjustment are most strongly predicted by traditional measures of family socialization: support for autonomy, discipline effectiveness, and positive family climate—in that order, with support for autonomy being particularly important in both equations.

6. This association may also reflect the fact that parents infer the effectiveness of their discipline (another of the subscales making up this composite) from the lack of psychological problems in their adolescent children.

CHAPTER SIX

1. Family residential instability is reported to be high among inner-city residents, so we initially explored the impact of such change on both parent and child in the sample. We asked the mother or caregiver how frequently they had moved since the child was born, a period of at least eleven years. Slightly more than half of the mothers reported three or more moves, but only a tenth of the mothers had moved more than five times. These figures do not reflect unusual rates of instability, and we were unable to find any family or child effect of more frequent changes. Frequent residential changes can be thought of as indicating a context in which effects of economic hardship are magnified. However, this line of inquiry also proved to be unproductive.

2. Marital conflict was measured by two indicators: marital adjustment and marital relations. The first measure (alpha = .77) taps the extent to which parents report arguing in each of seven areas, from child discipline to money (response

from 1 to 3, high). All scales were unit-weighted and apply to partnerships as well as to marriages. Unmarried parents currently living with a partner were included in the intact family sample. Marital relations represent a composite of positive relations minus negative relations. Positive relations refer to such behaviors as "acted loving and affectionate toward each other." Negative relations are illustrated by physical abuse and the like. The alpha coefficients for the two measures are virtually the same (average .85).

3. The three scales are based on reports by the adult respondent in the interview and questionnaire. A sense of parental efficacy (alpha = .91) represents the mean of the three subscales: child's sexual activities and drug use, positive activities, and potentially dangerous situations. The first subscale is an average of five items (e.g., How much can you do to get your child not to use drugs or alcohol, to practice safe sex, to not get involved in selling drugs?); the second index represents an average of six items (e.g., How much can you do to get your child to do his/her homework, to get a good job, to stay healthy?); and the third is also an average of six items (e.g., How much can you do to get your child to stay out of trouble in school, to stay away from the wrong kids, etc.?). The range of the subscales varies from 1 (nothing) to 4 (a lot).

Parental resourcefulness (alpha = .77) is measured as a mean of eight items, such as "I am good at learning from my mistakes, I am very good at bouncing back from bad experiences, and I am very good at figuring out problems and planning how to solve them." Scores range from 1 (almost never) to 5 (almost always).

Parental mental health problems represent the mean of four subscales: depression, anger, anxiety, and exhaustion. The parents are asked how much during the past couple of months they have felt a certain way. Depression is assessed as the mean of eight items (e.g., felt hopeless, lonely, unhappy); anger as the mean of seven items (e.g., felt angry, been ready to fight); anxiety as the mean of three items (felt that something bad is going to happen, felt uneasy, felt suddenly scared for no reason); and exhaustion as the mean for four items (e.g., felt drained, tired, exhausted). The four subscales vary between 1 (almost never) and 4 (almost always).

4. Only four factors predict the use of a selective school. The parent describes herself as more efficacious ($p < .05$), and she is not likely to be dependent on welfare ($p < .01$), to be black ($p < .01$), or to be low on total family income ($p < .10$).

5. Most of the variation has not been accounted for by socioeconomic factors, parental social factors, parental social ties, and investments in children. Some adolescents are more active than one would expect from knowledge of these predictors, and they are identified by positive residuals above the median from the analysis reported in appendix table 6.3. Other youth with negative residuals above the median are less active than one would expect. In an effort to describe youth who were doing better and those doing worse, we selected for this regression analysis all social and personal factors that did not significantly predict the involvement of youth as reported in appendix table 6.3.

Two social factors identify youth who are doing better than one would expect on their social involvement—education of mother and dependence on public welfare. Youth who are doing more activities than one would expect tend to have better-educated mothers (beta = .30; $p < .01$), and come from households that are not dependent on public assistance (beta = .28; $p < .01$). No other factor proved to be statistically significant. Among youth who are less involved than expectations would predict, those who have better-educated mothers tend to be more involved (beta = .41; $p < .001$). Clearly educational advantage in a family is a major factor in the social involvement of youth.

6. Among whites in our sample, the effect of female status is twice as strong for youth in below-average-income households as compared to higher-income families (beta = −.29 vs. −.14). The coefficients for black youth are −.15 versus −.07, for low versus high income. The elements of family nurturance for academic success appear to be similar among boys and girls. That is, we find no difference in the effects of family influences between boys and girls that could explain these gender effects.

7. We deleted "weak-marriage" households because our interest was in two-parent families that were functioning effectively. Single, white parents were too scarce to support this line of analysis. The first statistical model included gender, parent's education, and welfare dependence; the second added parental efficacy, support for child's autonomy, and institutional connections.

8. The basic measurement model estimated by LISREL 7 (Joreskog and Sorbom 1989) used a single index for each of the three constructs: the boy's problem behavior, ineffective parent discipline, and lack of parental efficacy. This means, of course, that we assume perfect measurement for each construct. The multigroup option of LISREL 7 enables us to test whether or not a single model fits the data for both groups. Goodness-of-fit measures indicate that the two groups are significantly different, as theory suggests.

9. Using an analysis of deviations from the grand mean, we find that these groups also rank well above average on measures of socioeconomic disadvantage. They are most likely to have experienced low family income and welfare dependence. Furthermore, single-parent status distinguishes the at-risk and delinquent groups, but the variation is modest at best. All three factors vary significantly across the groups. The value is $F > 2.8$; $p < .05$. However, after other factors such as income are added as controls, single-parent status is no longer significant.

10. The F-ratios exceed 11.5 across the three factors; $p < .01$.

11. The F-ratios for teachers and principals exceed 2.8 and the .05 level.

12. Each set is represented by the most potent factors with independent effects in the analysis up to this point: social factors by low income and single-parent status; parent attributes by the sense of parental efficacy; management strategy by parental investment and institutional connections; and family process by support for autonomy, family climate, and discipline effectiveness. To ascertain group differences, we set up all possible controls: (1) the competent, involved, and at-risk youth in relation to the delinquent cluster; (2) the competent and involved youth compared to the at-risk youth; and (3) competent youth compared to the socially involved.

13. Cumulative advantages and disadvantages are also illustrated by the sibling relations of older Philadelphia boys (age thirteen or more). Youth who are doing well in school are not only generally surrounded by prosocial friends but

often have a supportive older sibling (average $r = .26$). The positive example of an older sibling was measured by six attitude items that were asked of the target child: that he/she is smart, is a good student, does what parent wants, has friends who do well in school, will do well in life, and likes to be like older sibling. Scores range from 1 to 4, with an alpha coefficient of .82.

More broadly, academic success tells us as much about ongoing and reinforcing social influences as it does about achievement in school. Prosocial friends, for example are more a part of the life of academically successful youth who are enmeshed in a strong family network that often includes an older sibling who provides another stabilizing influence ($r = .38$ vs. .28). An older brother or sister gains special significance as a confidante among successful youth when the school and neighborhood networks of friends and kin are weak ($r = .47$ vs. $-.04$). Older siblings may become a positive influence for youth in an otherwise dysfunctional family.

Problem behavior also tells us more about the quality of friends and older brothers or sisters, and also more about life chances. But only among older boys do we find a substantial subgroup of antisocial youth. Cumulative disadvantages are especially striking among acting-out youth, ages thirteen and fourteen, who are not part of a strong network. Compared with problem boys in strong networks, problem youth in weak networks are more likely to hold a negative view of their life chances ($r = -.47$ vs. $-.37$), not to have access to a supportive older sibling ($r = -.33$ vs. $-.11$), and to associate with friends who get in trouble ($r = .65$ vs. 48). Thus more isolated families that lack the support of close kin and friends tend to amplify the cumulative disadvantage of problem offspring as they reach the age when they spend more time outside the home.

CHAPTER SEVEN

1. We used census tracts because (1) they are the most frequently used unit in the existing literature; (2) our preliminary work comparing tracts with planner's units and block groups uncovered little difference in intraclass correlations, though the planner's conception reduced the sample size to seventeen neighborhoods and block groups, leading to such tiny resident samples per neighborhood that we were not confident we had stably represented a neighborhood; (3) the intermediate sample size of census tracts (averaging about forty-five hundred persons) is large enough to contain many local institutions (which block groups cannot), yet small enough to capture some of the richer social networking that takes place in more local settings; and (4) all other conceptions of neighborhoods have limitations as large as these or larger.

2. It may seem that we could increase the sample size by attaching neighborhood scores to each person's data file and then analyzing the data as though there were 489 neighborhoods, but if families are more similar to one another within neighborhoods than between them, this design effect (Kish 1987) would diminish standard errors and result in too many statistically significant findings. So we decided to analyze the data mostly using hierarchical linear modeling (HLM), since it was designed to correct for this problem (Bryk and Raudenbush 1992). For family management and success measures, where we shall soon see that the clustering was modest, we conducted further analyses using ordinary least-

square (OLS) regression techniques based on the sample size of individuals and not tracts. These resulted in essentially the same results we shall report later using HLM.

3. Inspecting the means and standard deviations for these 436 and comparing them to the 489 reveals no significant differences, and we will shortly see that the individual-level predictors of family management and success variables were the same. Thus we can be confident that the need to create tract aggregates did not bias the sample.

4. We tried three versions of such a composite. In one, the three components were equally weighted and summed; in the second, the social climate measure was triple-weighted to reflect its importance in theories of social disorganization (e.g., Elliott et al. 1996); and in the third, socioeconomic factors from Census Bureau records were added to the social resource measures and aggregated to the tract level. The three resulting measures were so highly intercorrelated (at least .94) that they are virtually interchangeable.

5. The graphs were computed by applying three levels of the individual predictors and two levels of the neighborhood variables to the estimated HLM regression equation, while the other control variables are set at their mean levels.

6. All the explanations we have offered for the relationships in figure 7.2 must be considered speculative and built upon findings that themselves need to be replicated. Replicating statistical interactions is more problematic than replicating simpler relationships, and achieving such replication will not by itself explain why there are such complex associations between family management and individual and neighborhood advantage.

7. When social capital was used as the neighborhood causal agent, the simultaneous effects of the percent white and poverty level were controlled for. However, when the percent white and poverty level were examined as causal agents, social capital was not controlled because it is presumed to be a consequence of tract demography.

CHAPTER EIGHT

1. Trying other cutoffs made little or no substantive difference in the findings.

2. Individuals are categorized as high-risk if they have high demographic, neighborhood, and caregivers' risks, or are high on two measures. Individuals are coded as low-risk if they have low risk in the three areas, or are low on two and moderate on the other. The other individuals are coded as moderate-risk.

CHAPTER NINE

1. We also investigated the extent to which forms of capital were stable over time—that is, whether financial and social resources reported by the families in the survey were reproduced in the in-depth interviews provided by the families several years later. Again, we were impressed by the stability in these very different ways of tapping family assets, especially considering the inevitable error in different measures. Correlations ranged from .24 to .46 (see appendix table 9.1). We correlated those assets, both those reported in 1990 and those reported in 1993, with adolescent outcomes. The relatively modest associations reported

throughout this volume testify to the loose associations between social structure, parenting, and adolescent responses.

2. In one instance, for example, a family sending two children to Catholic school could not afford to pay its electric bill or move out of a deteriorating neighborhood. Their adolescent son's risk score from the survey was relatively high (5), but he was an involved teen at the time of the survey and continued to do relatively well two years later. Several other parents reported that they might have moved out of the city had they not instead been able to send their children to parochial schools.

References

Achenbach, T. M., S. H. McConaughy, and C. T. Howell. 1987. Child/adolescent behavioral and emotional problems: Implications of cross-informant for situational stability. *Psychological Bulletin* 101: 213–232.

Adams, C., D. Bartelt, D. Elesh, I. Goldstein, N. Kleniewski, and W. Yancey. 1991. *Philadelphia: Neighborhoods, division, and conflict in a postindustrial city.* Philadelphia: Temple University Press.

Aldenderfer, M. S., and R. K. Blashfield. 1984. Cluster analysis. Pp. 1–88 in *Sage University paper series on quantitative applications in the social sciences.* Edited by J. L. Sullivan and R. G. Neimi. Beverly Hills: Sage.

Alexander, K. L., S. L. Dauber, and D. R. Entwisle. 1993. First-grade classroom behavior: Its short- and long-term consequences for school performance. *Child Development* 64: 801–803.

Alexander, K. L., D. R. Entwisle, and S. L. Dauber. 1994. *On the success of failure. A reassessment of the effects of retention in the primary grades.* New York: Cambridge University Press.

Anderson, E. 1990. *Streetwise: Race, class, and change in an urban community.* Chicago: University of Chicago Press.

Baldwin, A. L., C. P. Baldwin, T. Kasser, M. Zax, A. Sameroff, and R. Seifer. 1993. Multiple levels of risk for psychopathology in late adolescence. *Development and Psychopathology* 5: 741–761.

Bandura, A., ed. 1995. *Self-efficacy in changing societies.* New York: Cambridge University Press.

———. 1996. *Self-efficacy: The exercise of control.* New York: W. H. Freeman.

Barber, B. K., J. E. Olson, and S. C. Shagle. 1994. Associations between parental psychological and behavioral control and youth internalized and externalized behaviors. *Child Development* 65: 1120–1136.

Baumrind, D. 1989. Rearing competent children. Pp. 349–378 in *Child development today and tomorrow.* Edited by W. Damon. San Francisco: Jossey-Bass.

Behrman, R. E., ed. 1997. *Children and poverty. The Future of Children,* 7: 2. Los

Angeles: Center for Future of Children, The David and Lucille Packard Foundation.

Blank, R. M. 1997. *It takes a nation.* New York: Russell Sage Foundation.

Blashfield, R. K., and M. S. Aldenderfer. 1988. The methods and problems of cluster analysis. Pp. 447–473 in *Handbook of multivariate experimental psychology.* 2d ed. Edited by J. R. Nesselroade and R. B. Catell. New York: Plenum Press.

Bornstein M. H., ed. 1995a. *Handbook of parenting: Children and parenting.* Vol. 1. Mahwah, NJ: Lawrence Erlbaum.

———. 1995b. *Handbook of parenting: Status and social conditions of parenting.* Vol 3. Mahwah, NJ: Lawrence Erlbaum.

Brent, D. A., and G. Moritz. 1997. Developmental pathways to adolescent suicide. Pp. 233–258 in *Adolescence: Opportunities and challenges.* Edited by D. Cicchetti and S. L. Toth. Rochester, NY: University of Rochester Press.

Bronfenbrenner, U. 1979. *The ecology of human development: Experiments by nature and design.* Cambridge: Harvard University Press.

———. 1986. Ecology of family as a context for human development. *Developmental Psychology* 22(6): 732–742.

Brooks-Gunn, J., G. J. Duncan, and J. L. Aber, eds. 1997a. *Neighborhood poverty: Context and consequences for children.* Vol. 1. New York: Russell Sage Foundation.

———. 1997b. *Neighborhood poverty: Policy implications in studying neighborhoods.* Vol. 2. New York: Russell Sage Foundation.

Brooks-Gunn, J., G. J. Duncan, P. K. Klebanov, and N. Sealand. 1993. Do neighborhoods influence child and adolescent development? *American Journal of Sociology* 99 (2): 353–395.

Bryk, A. S., V. E. Lee, and P. B. Holland. 1993. *Catholic schools and the common good.* Cambridge: Harvard University Press.

Bryk, A. S., and S. W. Raudenbush. 1992. *Hierarchical linear models: Applications and data analysis methods.* Newbury Park, CA: Sage Publications.

Bryk, A. S., and Y. M. Thum. 1989. The effects of high school organization of dropping out: An exploratory investigation. *American Educational Research Journal* 26: 353–403.

Bugental, D. B., and J. J. Goodnow. 1998. Socialization processes. Pp. 389–462 in *Handbook of child psychology.* Vol 3. *Social, emotional, and personality development.* 5th ed. Edited by N. Eisenberg. New York: Wiley.

Burton, L. 1990. Teenage childbearing as an alternative life-course strategy in multigenerational black families. *Human Nature* 1: 123–143.

Burton, L. M., D. A. Obeidallah, and K. Allison. 1996. Ethnographic perspectives on social context and adolescent development among inner-city African-American teens. Pp. 394–418 in *Ethnography and human development: Context and meaning in social inquiry.* Edited by D. Jessor, A. Colby, and R. Shweder. Chicago: University of Chicago Press.

Cairns, R. B., and B. Cairns. 1994. *Lifelines and risks: Pathways of youth in our time.* New York: Cambridge University Press.

Carnegie Corporation. 1992. *A matter of time.* New York: Carnegie Corporation.

———. 1995. *Great transformations: Preparing youth for a new century.* New York: Carnegie Corporation.

Cary, L. 1991. *Black ice.* New York: Random House.

Caspi, A., D. J. Bem, and G. H. Elder, Jr. 1989. Continuities and consequences of interactional styles across the life course. *Journal of Personality* 57 (2): 375–406.

Chase-Lansdale, P. L., and J. Brooks-Gunn, eds. 1995. *Escape from poverty: What makes a difference for children?* New York: Cambridge University Press.

Clark, R. 1983. *Family life and school achievement: Why poor black children succeed or fail.* Chicago: University of Chicago Press.

Clausen, J. A. 1993. *American lives: Looking back at the children of the Great Depression.* New York: The Free Press.

Cloward, R. A., and L. E. Ohlin. 1960. *Delinquency and opportunity: A theory of delinquent gangs.* Glencoe, IL: Free Press.

Coleman, J. S. 1961. *The adolescent society.* Westport, CT: Greenwood Press.

———. 1988. Social capital in the creation of human capital. *American Journal of Sociology* 94: S95–S120.

Coleman, J. S., and T. Hoffer. 1987. *Public and private high schools: The impact of communities.* New York: Basic Books.

Coleman, J. S., T. Hoffer, and S. Kilgore. 1982. *High school achievement: Catholic, public, and private schools compared.* New York: Basic Books.

Comer, J. P. 1988. Educating poor minority children. *Scientific American* 256 (11): 42–48

Comer, J. P., and N. M. Haynes. 1991. Parent involvement in schools: An ecological approach. *Elementary School Journal* 91: 271–277.

Condran G. A., and F. F. Furstenberg, Jr. 1994. Are trends in the well-being of children related to changes in the American family? Making a simple question more complex. *Population* 6: 1613–1638.

Conger, R. D., and G. H. Elder, Jr. (in collaboration with F. O. Lorenz, R. L. Simons, and L. B. Whitbeck). 1994. *Families in troubled times: Adapting to change in rural America.* New York: Aldine de Gruyter.

Cook, T. D. 1985. Post-positivist critical multiplism. Pp. 21–62 in *Social science and social policy.* Edited by R. L. Shotland and M. M. Mark. Beverly Hills: Sage.

Cook, T. D., and T. R. Curtin. 1986. The mainstream and the underclass: Why are the differences so salient and the similarities so unobtrusive? Pp. 218–263 in *Social comparison, social justice and relative deprivation: Theoretical, empirical and policy perspectives.* Edited by J. C. Masters and W. P. Smith. Hillsdale, NJ: Lawrence Erlbaum.

Cook, T. D., F. F. Furstenberg, Jr., J. R. Kim, J. O. Teitler, L. M. Geitz, J. S. Eccles, G. H. Elder, Jr., and A. Sameroff. Forthcoming. Neighborhood differences in resources for promoting the positive development of adolescents. Work in progress.

Cook, T. D., D. J. Schleef, L. L. Miller, and B. C. Stockdill. March 1992. Moving as a strategy of family management. Paper presented at the biennial meetings of the Society for Research on Adolescence, Washington, D. C.

Cook, T. D., S. Shagle, S., M. Phillips, R. Settersten, S. Degirmengioglu, and W. S. Chan. Forthcoming. The social worlds of early adolescence: Interconnections among schools, neighborhoods, peers and families. Work in progress.

Cookson, P. W., Jr., and C. H. Persell. 1985. *Preparing for power: America's elite boarding schools.* New York: Basic Books.

Coser, R. L. 1991. *In defense of modernity: Role complexity and individual autonomy.* Stanford: Stanford University Press.

Coser, R. L., and G. Rokoff. 1974. Women in the occupational world: Social disruption and conflict. Pp. 490–511 in *The family: Its structures and functions.* 2d ed. Edited by R. L. Coser. New York: St. Martin's Press.

Crane, J. 1991. The pattern of neighborhood effects on social problems. *American Journal of Sociology* 96: 1226–1259.

Cronbach, L. J. 1951. Coefficient alpha and the internal structures of tests. *Psychometrika* 16: 297–334.

Dance. L. J. 1996. "Hard" like a "Gangsta": The impact of street culture on schooling. Unpublished manuscript. University of Maryland, College Park.

Dornbusch, S. M., P. L. Ritter, P. H. Leiderman, D. F. Roberts, and M. J. Fraleigh. 1987. The relation of parenting style to adolescent school performance. *Child Development* 58: 1244–1257.

Dornbusch, S. M., and K. D. Wood. 1989. Family processes and education achievement. Pp. 66–95 in *Education and the American family.* Edited by W. J. Weston. New York: New York University Press.

Dryfoos, J. G. 1990. *Adolescents at risk: Prevalence and prevention.* Oxford: Oxford University Press.

Duncan, G. J., and J. Brooks-Gunn, eds. 1994. *Consequences of growing up poor.* New York: Russell Sage Foundation.

Eccles (Parsons), J., et al. 1983. Expectancies, values and academic behaviors. Pp. 75–146 in *Achievement and achievement motivation.* Edited by J. Spence. San Francisco: W. H. Freeman.

Eccles, J., and B. Barber. In press. Adolescents' activity involvement: Predictors and longitudinal consequences. *Journal of Adolescent Research.*

Eccles, J. S., C. Buchanan, C. Flanagan, A. Fuligni, C. Midgley, and D. Yee. 1991. Control versus autonomy during adolescence. *Journal of Social Issues* 47 (4): 53–68.

Eccles, J. S., and R. D. Harold. 1993. Parent-school involvement during the early adolescent years. *Teachers College Record,* 94: 568–587.

Eccles, J. S., S. E. Lord, R. W. Roeser, B. L. Barber, and D. M. H. Jozefowicz. 1997. The association of school transitions in early adolescence with developmental trajectories through high school. Pp. 283–320 in *Health risks and developmental transitions during adolescence.* Edited by J. Schulenberg, J. Maggs and K. Hurrelman. New York: Cambridge University Press.

Eccles, J. S., C. Midgley, C. Buchanan, A. Wigfield, D. Reuman, and D. MacIver. 1993. Development during adolescence: The impact of stage/environment fit on young adolescents' experiences in schools and in families. *American Psychologist* 48: 90–101.

Eccles, J. S., A. Wigfield, C. A. Flanagan, C. Miller, D. A. Rellman, and D. Yee. 1989. Self-concepts, domain values, and self-esteem: Relations and changes at early adolescence. *Journal of Personality* 57:283–310.

Eccles, J. S., A. Wigfield, and U. Schiefele. 1998. Motivation to succeed. Pp. 1017–

1095 in *Handbook of child psychology.* Vol. 3. *Social, emotional, and personality development.* 5th ed. Edited by N. Eisenberg. New York: Wiley.

Eckert, P. 1989. *Jocks and burnouts: Social categories and identity in the high school.* New York: Teachers College Press.

Elder, G. H., Jr. 1980. Adolescence in historical perspective. Pp. 3–46 in *Handbook of adolescent psychology.* Edited by J. Adelson. New York: Wiley.

Elder, G. H., Jr., and A. Caspi. 1988. Economic stress in lives: Developmental perspectives. *Journal of Social Issues* 47 (4): 53–69.

Elder, G. H., Jr., and R. D. Conger. In press. *Leaving the land: Rural youth at century's end.* Chicago: University of Chicago Press.

Elder, G. H., Jr., and R. D. Conger. 2000. *Children of the Land: Adversity and Success in Rural America.* Chicago: University of Chicago Press.

Elder, G. H., Jr., J. S. Eccles, M. Ardelt, and S. Lord. 1995. Inner-city parents under economic pressure: Perspectives on the strategies of parenting. *Journal of Marriage and the Family* 57 (3): 771–784.

Elder, G. H., Jr., and A. M. O'Rand. 1995. Adult lives in a changing society. Pp. 452–475 in *Sociological perspectives on social psychology.* Edited by K. S. Cook, G. A., Fine and J. S. House. New York: Allyn and Bacon.

Elliott, D. S. 1983. *Interview schedule, National Youth Survey.* Boulder, CO: Behavioral Research Institute.

Elliott, D. S., D. Huizinga, and S. S. Ageton. 1985. *Explaining delinquency and drug use.* Beverly Hills: Sage.

Elliott, D. S., D. Huizinga, and S. Menard. 1989. *Multiple problem youth: Delinquency, substance use, and mental health problems.* New York: Springer-Verlag.

Elliott, D. S., S. Menard, A. Elliott, B. Rankin, D. Huizinga, and W. J. Wilson. Forthcoming. *Overcoming disadvantage: Successful youth development in high-risk neighborhoods.* Chicago: University of Chicago Press.

Elliott, D. S., W. J. Wilson, D. Huizinga, R. Sampson, A. Elliott, and B. Rankin. 1996. The effects of neighborhood disadvantage on adolescent development. *Journal of Research in Crime and Delinquency* 33: 389–426.

Entwisle, D. R., and K. L. Alexander. 1992. Summer setback: Race, poverty, school composition, and mathematics achievement in the first two years of school. *American Sociological Review* 57: 72–84.

Entwisle, D. R., K. L. Alexander, and L. S. Olson. 1997. *Children, schools, and inequality.* Boulder, CO: Westview Press.

Epstein, J. L. ed. 1981. *The quality of school life.* Lexington, MA: Lexington Books.

Epstein, J. L. 1990. School and family connections: Theory, research, and implications for integrating sociologies of education and families. Pp. 99–126 in *Families and community settings: Interdisciplinary perspectives.* Edited by D. G. Unger and M. B. Sussman. New York: Haworth Press.

Epstein, J. L., and J. M. McPartland. September 1977. Family and school interactions and main effects on affective outcomes. Center for Social Organization of School Reports, John Hopkins University, no. 235.

Erikson, E. 1963. *Childhood and society.* New York: W. W. Norton.

Farber, N. B., and R. R. Iversen. 1998. Family values about education and their transmission among black inner-city young women. Pp. 141–67 in *Competence and Character through Life*. Edited by A. Colby, J. James, and D. Hart. Chicago: University of Chicago Press.

Featherman, D. L., and R. M. Hauser. 1978. *Opportunity and change*. New York: Academic Press.

Feldman, A. F., and G. R. Elliott. 1990. *At the threshold: The developing adolescent*. Cambridge: Harvard University Press.

Flanagan, C. A. April 1989. Adolescents' autonomy at home: Effects on self-consciousness and intrinsic motivation at school. Paper presented at the meeting of the American Educational Research Association, Montreal, Canada.

———. 1990. Change in family work status: Effects on parent-adolescent decision making. *Child Development* 61: 163–177.

Frazier, E. F. 1966. *The Negro family in the United States*. Chicago: University of Chicago Press.

Friedenberg, E. Z. 1964. *The vanishing adolescent*. Boston: Beacon Books.

Furstenberg, F. F., Jr. 1993. How families manage risk and opportunity in dangerous neighborhoods. Pp. 231–258 in *Sociology and the public agenda*. Edited by W. J. Wilson. Newbury Park, CA: Sage.

Furstenberg, F. F., Jr., and M. E. Hughes. 1995. Social capital and successful development among at-risk youth. *Journal of Marriage and the Family* 57 (3): 580–592.

———. 1997. The influence of neighborhoods on children's development: A theoretical perspective and a research agenda. Pp. 23–47 in *Neighborhood poverty: Policy implications in studying neighborhoods*. Vol. 2. Edited by J. Brooks-Gunn, G. Duncan, and J. L. Aber. New York: Russell Sage Foundation.

Gans, H. J. 1990. Deconstructing the underclass: The term's danger as a planning concept. *Journal of the American Planning Association* 56: 271–277.

Garbarino, J. 1992. *Children and families in the social environment*. 2d ed. New York: Aldine de Gruyter.

Garmezy, N. 1985. Stress resistant children: The search for protective factors. Pp. 213–233 in *Recent research in developmental psychopathology*. Edited by J. Stevensen, Jr. Oxford: Pergamon Press.

Gephart, M. A. 1997. Neighborhoods and communities as contexts for development. Pp.1–43 in *Neighborhood poverty: Context and consequences for children*. Vol 1. Edited by J. Brooks-Gunn, G. J. Duncan, and J. L. Aber. New York: Russell Sage Foundation.

Gjerde, P. F., and J. Block. 1996. A developmental perspective on depressive symptoms in adolescence: Gender differences in autocentric-allocentric modes of impulse regulation. Pp. 167–198 in *Adolescence: Opportunities and challenges*. Edited by D. Cicchetti and S. L. Toth. Rochester, NY: University of Rochester Press.

Goode, J., and J. A. Schneider. 1994. *Reshaping ethnic and racial relations in Philadelphia: Immigrants in a divided city*. Philadelphia: Temple University Press.

Granovetter, M. 1973. The strength of weak ties. *American Journal of Sociology* 78: 1360–1380.

Grolnick, W., and R. Ryan. 1989. Parent styles associated with children's self-regulation and competence in school. *Journal of Educational Psychology* 81: 143–154.

Haggerty, R. J., L. R. Sherrod, N. Garmezy, and M. Rutter. 1994. *Stress, risk, and resilience in children and adolescents*. New York: Cambridge University Press.

Hall, G. S. 1904. *Adolescence 1–2*. New York and London: Appleton.

Hamburg, D. A., and R. Takanishi. 1989. Preparing for life: The critical transition of adolescence. *American Psychologist* 44 (5): 825–827.

Hareven, T. K. 1994. Aging and generational relations: A historical and life course perspective. *Annual Review of Sociology* 20: 437–461.

Harter, S. 1983. Developmental perspectives on the self-system. Pp. 275–385 in *Handbook of child psychology*. Vol. 4. *Socialization, personality, and social development*. 4th ed. Edited by E. M. Hetherington. New York: Wiley.

Hayes, C. D., ed. 1987. *Risking the future: Adolescent sexuality, pregnancy, and childbearing*. Washington, DC: National Academy Press.

Hershberg, T. 1991. *At the crossroads: The consequences of economic stability or decline in Philadelphia for the city, region, and commonwealth*. Philadelphia: Center for Greater Philadelphia.

Heyns, B. 1978. *Summer learning and the effects of schooling*. New York: Academic Press.

Hindelang, M. J., T. Hirschi, and J. G. Weiss. 1981. *Measuring delinquency*. Beverly Hills: Sage.

Hochschild, A. R. 1997. *The time bind: When work becomes home and home becomes work*. New York: Metropolitan Books.

Hogan, D. P., and E. Kitagawa. 1985. The impact of social status, family structure, and neighborhood on the family structure of black adolescents. *American Journal of Sociology* 90: 825–855.

Holland, A., and T. Andre. 1987. Participation in extracurricular activities in secondary school: What is known, what needs to be known. *Review of Educational Research* 57: 437–466.

Hughes, M. E., F. F. Furstenberg, Jr., and J. O. Teitler. 1995. The impact of an increase in family planning services on the teenage population of Philadelphia. *Family Planning Perspectives* 27 (2): 60–65, 78.

Huizinga, D., and Elliott, D. S. 1986. Re-assessing the reliability and validity of self-reported delinquency measures. *Journal of Quantitative Criminology* 2 (4): 293–327.

Huston, A. C., ed. 1991. *Children in poverty: Child development and public policy*. New York: Cambridge University Press.

Huston, A. C., V. C. McLoyd, and C. Garcia Coll. 1994. Children and poverty. *Child Development* 65 (special issue): 275–282.

Iversen, R. R. and N. B. Farber. 1996. Transmission of family values, work and welfare among poor urban black women. *Work and Occupations,* 23: 437–60.

Jarrett, R. L. 1992. *A comparative examination of socialization patterns among low-income African-Americans, Chicanos, Puerto Ricans, and Whites: A review of the literature*. Evanston, IL: Northwestern University, Center for Urban Affairs and Public Policy.

Jencks, C., and S. Mayer. 1990. The social consequences of growing up in a poor neighborhood. Pp. 111–186 in *Inner-city poverty in the United States*. Edited by L. E. Lynn and M. G. H. McGeary. Washington, DC: National Academy Press.

Jencks, C., and P. E. Peterson, eds. 1991. *The urban underclass*. Washington, DC: The Brookings Institute.

Jessor, R. 1992. Risk behavior in adolescence: A psychosocial framework for understanding and action. Pp. 19–34 in *Adolescents at risk: Medical-social perspectives*. Edited by D. E. Rogers and E. Ginzburg. Boulder CO: Westview Press.

———, ed. In press. *New perspectives on adolescent risk behavior*. New York: Cambridge University Press.

Jessor, R., A. Colby, and R. A. Shweder, eds. 1996. Ethnography and human development: Context and meaning in social enquiry. Chicago: University of Chicago Press.

Jessor, R., and S. L. Jessor. 1973. The perceived environment in behavioral science. *American Behavioral Scientist* 16 (6): 801–827.

———. 1977. *Problem behavior and psychological development: A longitudinal study of youth*. San Diego: Academic Press.

Johnston, L. D., P. M. O'Malley, and J. G. Bachman. 1993. *National survey results on drug use from the Monitoring the Future Study, 1975–1992*. Washington, DC: U.S. Government Printing Office.

Joreskog, K. G., and Sorbom, D. 1989. *LISREL 7: A guide to the program and applications*. Chicago: SPSS.

Kandel, D. B. 1991. The social demography of drug-use. *Milbank Quarterly* 69 (3): 365–414.

Kasarda, J. D. 1985. Urban change and minority opportunities. Pp. 33–67 in *The new urban reality*. Edited by P. E. Peterson. Washington, DC: The Brookings Institute.

Kazdin, A. 1993. Adolescent mental health: Prevention and treatment programs. *American Psychologist* 48: 127–141.

Kett, J. F. 1977. *Rites of passage: Adolescence in America, 1790 to the present*. New York: Basic Books.

Kinney, D. A. 1993. From nerds to normals: The recovery of identity among adolescents from middle school to high school. *Sociology of Education* 66: 21–40.

Kish, L. 1987. *Statistical design of research*. New York: Wiley.

Kotlowitz, A. 1991. *There are no children here*. New York: Doubleday.

Lancaster, J. B., and B. A. Hamburg. 1986. *School-age pregnancy and parenthood: Biosocial dimensions*. New York: Aldine de Gruyter.

Lareau, A. 1989a. Family-school relationships: A view from the classroom. *Educational Policy* 3 (3): 245–257.

———. 1989b. *Home advantage: Social class and parental intervention in elementary education*. New York: Falmer Press.

Larson, R. 1994. Youth organizations, hobbies, and sports as developmental contexts. Pp. 46–65 in *Adolescence in context*. Edited by R. K. Silbereisen and E. Todt. New York: Springer-Verlag.

Leahy, R. L. 1981. Parental practices and the development of moral judgment and self-image disparity during adolescence. *Developmental Psychology* 17 (5): 580–594.

Lemert, E. M. 1951. *Social pathology: A systematic approach to the theory of sociopathic behavior.* New York: McGraw-Hill.

Lerner, R. M., D. R. Entwisle, and S. T. Hauser. 1994. The crisis among contemporary American adolescents: A call for the integration of research, policies, and programs. *Journal of Research on Adolescence* 4 (1): 1–4.

Lord, S. E., J. S. Eccles, and K. A. McCarthy. 1994. Surviving the junior high school transition: Family processes and self perceptions as protective and risk factors. *Journal of Early Adolescence* 14: 162–199.

Maccoby, E. E., and J. A. Martin. 1983. Socialization in the context of the family: Parent-child interaction. Pp. 1–101 in *Handbook of child psychology,* Vol. 4. *Socialization, personality, and social development.* 4th ed. Edited by E. M. Hetherington. New York: Wiley.

MacLeod, J. 1987. *Ain't no making it: Leveled aspirations in a low-income neighborhood.* Boulder, CO: Westview Press.

Males, M. 1996. *Scapegoat generation.* Monroe, ME: Common Courage Press.

Massey, D. S. 1996. The age of extremes: Concentrated affluence and poverty in the twenty-first century. *Demography* 33 (4): 395–412.

Massey, D. S., and N. A. Denton 1993. *American apartheid: Segregation and the making of the underclass.* Cambridge: Harvard University Press.

McCord, J. 1990. Problem behaviors. Pp. 414–430 in *At the threshold: The developing adolescent.* Edited by S. S. Feldman and G. R. Elliott. Cambridge: Harvard University Press.

McLaughlin, M. W., M. A. Irby, and J. Lanagman. 1994. *Urban sanctuaries: Neighborhood organizations in the lives and futures of inner-city youth.* San Francisco: Jossey-Bass.

McLoyd, V. C. 1990. The impact of economic hardship on black families and children: Psychological distress, parenting and socioemotional development. *Child Development* 61: 311–346.

Mead, M., and M. Wolfenstein, eds. 1955. *Childhood in contemporary cultures.* Chicago: University of Chicago Press.

Medrich, E., J. Roizen, V. Rubin, with S. Buckley. 1982. *The serious business of growing up: A study of children's lives outside of school.* Berkeley: University of California Press.

Merton, R. K. 1968. Social structure and anomie. Pp. 185–214 in *Social theory and social structure.* Edited by R. K. Merton. Enlarged edition. New York: Free Press.

———. 1972. Insiders and outsiders: A chapter in the sociology of knowledge. *American Journal of Sociology* 78 (1): 9–47.

Merton, R. K., M. Fiske, and P. L. Kendall. 1990. *The focused interview: A manual of problems and procedures.* 2d ed. Glencoe, IL: Free Press.

Modell, J. 1989. *Into one's own: From youth to adulthood in the United States, 1920–1975.* Berkeley, CA: University of California Press.

Modell, J., F. F. Furstenberg, Jr., and T. Hershberg. 1976. Social change and transition to adulthood in historical perspective. *Journal of Family History* 1 (1): 7–32.

National Academy of Sciences. 1993. *Losing generations.* Washington, DC: National Academy Press.

National Commission on Children. 1991. *Beyond rhetoric: A new American agenda for children and families.* Washington, DC: U.S. Government Printing Office.

National Research Council. 1990. *Inner-city poverty in the United States.* Washington, DC: National Academy Press.

———. 1993. *Losing generations: Adolescents in high-risk settings.* Washington, DC: National Academy Press.

———. 1996. *Youth development and neighborhood influnces: Challenges and opportunities.* Washington, DC: National Academy Press.

Newman, K. 1996. Working poor: Low wage employment in the lives of Harlem youth. Pp. 323–343 in *Transitions through adolescence: Interpersonal domains and context.* Edited by J. Graber, J. Brooks-Gunn, and A. Petersen. Hillsdale, NJ: Erlbaum Associates.

Otto, L. B., and D. Alwin. 1977. Athletics, aspirations and attainments. *Sociology of Education* 50: 102–113.

Paikoff, R. L., and J. Brooks-Gunn. 1989. Physiological processes: What role do they play during the transition to adolescence? Pp. 63–81 in *Advances in adolescent development.* Vol. 2. *The transition from childhood to adolescence.* Newbury Park, CA: Sage.

———. 1991. Interventions to prevent adolescent pregnancy. Pp. 808–813 in *The encyclopedia of adolescence.* Edited by R. M. Lerner, A. C. Petersen, and J. Brooks-Gunn. New York: Garland Publishing.

Parke, R. D., and R. Buriel. 1998. Socialization in the family: Ethnic and ecological perspectives. Pp. 463–552 in *Handbook of child psychology.* Vol. 3. *Social, emotional, and personality development.* 5th ed. Edited by N. Eisenberg. New York: Wiley.

Parsons, T. 1954. *Certain patterns of aggression in the Western world: Essays in sociological theory.* 2d ed. Glencoe, IL: Free Press.

Patterson, G. R. 1976. The aggressive child: Victim and architect of a coercive system. Pp. 267–316 in *Behavior modification and families.* Vol. 1. *Theory and research.* Edited by E. J. Marsh, L. A. Hamerlynck, and L. C. Handy. New York: Brunner/Mazel.

Patterson, G. R., Capaldi, D. M., and L. Bank. 1991. An early starter model for predicting delinquency. Pp. 139–168 in *The development and treatment of childhood aggression.* Edited by D. J. Pepler and K. H. Rubin. Hillsdale, NJ: Lawrence Erlbaum.

Patterson, G. R., B. D. DeBaryshe, and E. Ramsey. 1989. A developmental perspective on antisocial behavior. *American Psychologist* 44: 329–335.

Patterson, G. R., J. B. Reid, and T. J. Dishion. 1992. *Antisocial boys.* Eugene, OR: Castalia.

Patterson, G. R., and M. Stouthammer-Loeber. 1984. The correlation of family management practices and delinquency. *Child Development* 55: 1299–1307.

Pepler, D. J., and K. H. Rubin, eds. 1991. *The development and treatment of childhood aggression.* Hillsdale, NJ: Lawrence Erlbaum.

Petersen, A. C., B. E. Compas, J. Brooks-Gunn, M. Stemmler, S. Ey, S. Sydney, and K. E. Grant. 1993. Depression in adolescence. *American Psychologist* 48 (2): 155–168.

Petersen, A. C., and B. A. Hamburg. 1986. Adolescence: A developmental approach to problems and psychopathology. *Behavior Therapy* 17 (5): 480–499.

Putnam, R. D. 1995. Bowling alone: America's declining social capital. *Journal of Democracy* 6: 65–78.

Raudenbush, S. W., B. Rowan, and S. J. Kang 1991. Multi-level, multi-variate model for studying school climate with estimation via the EM algorithm for application to U.S. high school data. *Journal of Educational Statistics* 16: 295–330.

Roeser, R., and J. S. Eccles. In press. Academic functioning and mental health in adolescence: Patterns, progressions, and routes from childhood. *Journal of Adolescent Research.*

Roeser, R., J. S. Eccles, and A. Sameroff. In press. Academic and psychological adjustment during early adolescence: Longitudinal relations, patterns, and prediction by experience in middle school. *Developmental Psychopathology.*

Ruble, D. N., and C. L. Martin 1998. Gender development. Pp. 933–1016 in *Handbook of child psychology.* Vol 3. *Social, emotional, and personality development.* 5th ed. Edited by N. Eisenberg. New York: Wiley.

Rutter, M. 1979. Protective factors in children's responses to stress and disadvantage. Pp. 49–74 in *Primary prevention of psychopathology.* Vol. 3. Edited by M. W. Kent and J. E. Rolf. Hanover, NH: University Press of New England.

Rutter, M., ed. 1988. *Studies of psychosocial risk: The power of longitudinal data.* Cambridge, UK: Cambridge University Press.

Rutter, M., and N. Madge. 1976. *Cycles of disadvantage.* London: Heinemann.

Ryan, R. M. 1992. Agency and organization: Intrinsic motivation, autonomy, and the self in psychological development. Pp. 1–56 in *Nebraska Symposium on motivation.* Vol. 40. Edited by J. Jacobs.

Ryan, B. A., G. R. Adams, T. P. Gullota, R. P. Weissberg, and R. L. Hampton. 1995. *The family-school connection: Theory, research, and practice.* Thousand Oaks, CA: Sage.

Sameroff, A. J. 1983. Developmental systems: Contexts and evolution. Pp. 238–294 in *Handbook of child psychology.* Vol. 1. *History, theories, and methods.* 4th ed. Edited by W. Kessen. New York: Wiley.

————. 1995. General systems theories and developmental psychopathology. Pp. 659–695 in *Developmental psychopathology.* Vol. 1. Edited by D. Cicchetti. New York: Wiley.

Sameroff, A. J., and B. H. Fiese. 1992. Family representations of development. Pp. 347–369 in *Parental belief systems: The psychological consequences for children.* 2d ed. Edited by I. E. Sigel, A. V. McGillicuddy-DeLisi, and J. J. Goodnow. Hillsdale, NJ: Lawrence Erlbaum.

Sameroff, A. J., R. Seifer, A. L. Baldwin, and C. A. Baldwin. 1993. Stability of intelligence from preschool to adolescence: The influence of social and family risk factors. *Child Development* 64: 80–97.

Sameroff, A. J., R. Seifer, and W. T. Bartko. 1997. Environmental perspective on adaptation during childhood and adolescence. Pp. 507–526 in *Developmental psychopathology: Perspectives on risk and disorder.* Edited by S. S. Luthar, J. A. Barack, D. Cicchetti, and J. Weisz. Cambridge: Cambridge University Press.

Sameroff, A. J., R. Seifer, M. Zax, and R. B. Barocas. 1987. Early indices of developmental risk: The Rochester longitudinal study. *Schizophrenia Bulletin* 13: 383–394.

Sampson, R. J. 1992. Family management and child development: Insights from social disorganization theory. Pp. 63–93 in *Advances in criminological theory*. Vol. 3. Edited by J. McCord. New Brunswick: Transaction Books.

Sampson, R. J., and J. H. Laub. 1993. *Crime in the making: Pathways and turning points through life*. Cambridge: Harvard University Press.

Sampson, R. J., S. W. Raudenbush, and F. Earls. 1997. Neighborhoods and violent crime: A multilevel study of collective efficacy. *Science,* August 15, 918–924.

Sapir, E. 1927. The unconscious patterning of behavior. Pp. 114–142 in *The unconscious: A symposium*. Edited by C. M. Child, K. Koffka, J. E. Anderson, et al. New York: A. A. Knopf.

Schneider, B., and J. S. Coleman. 1993. *Parents, their children, and schools*. Boulder, CO: Westview Press.

Schorr, L. B. 1997. *Common purpose: Strengthening families and neighborhoods to rebuild America*. New York: Anchor Books, Doubleday.

Shaw, C., and H. McKay. 1942. *Juvenile delinquency and urban areas*. Chicago: University of Chicago Press.

Simcha-Fagan, O., and J. E. Schwartz. 1986. Neighborhood and delinquency: An assessment of contextual effects. *Criminology* 24: 667–704.

Simmons, R. G., and D. A. Blyth. 1987. *Moving into adolescence: The impact of pubertal change and school context*. Hawthorn, NY: Aldine de Gruyter.

Smetana, J. G. 1988. Adolescents' and parents' conceptions of parental authority. *Child Development* 59: 321–335.

Smith, C., A. J. Lizotte, T. P. Thornberry, and M. D. Krone. 1995. Resilient youth: Identifying factors that prevent high-risk youth from engaging in delinquency and drugs. Pp. 217–247 in *Delinquency and disrepute in the life course*. Edited by J. Hagan. Greenwich, CT: JAI Press.

Smith M. B. 1968. Competence and socialization. Pp. 276–320 in *Socialization and society*. Edited by J. A. Clausen. Boston: Little, Brown.

South, S. J., and K. D. Crowder. 1997. Escaping distressed neighborhoods: Individual, community, and metropolitan influences. *American Journal of Sociology* 102: 1040–1084.

Spencer, M. B. and S. M. Dornbusch. 1990. Challenges in studying minority youth. Pp. 123–146 in *At the threshold: The developing adolescent*. Edited by S. S. Feldman and G. R. Elliott. Cambridge: Harvard University Press.

Stack, C. B. 1974. *All our kin*. New York: Harper & Row.

Steinberg, L. 1990. Autonomy, conflict, and harmony in the family relationships. Pp. 225–276 in *At the threshold: The developing adolescent*. Edited by S. S. Feldman and G. R. Elliott. Cambridge: Harvard University Press.

Steinberg, L., N. E. Darling, and A. C. Fletcher. 1995. Authoritative parenting and adolescent adjustment: An ecological journey. Pp. 423–466 in *Examining lives in context: Perspectives on the ecology of human development*. Edited by P. Moen, G. H. Elder, Jr., and K. Luscher. Philadelphia: Temple University Press.

Steinberg, L., S. Lamborn, S. Dornbusch, and N. Darling. 1992. Impact of parenting practices on adolescent achievment: Authoritative parenting, school involvement, and encouragement to succeed. *Child Development* 63: 1266–1281.

Steinberg, L., N. S. Mounts, S. D. Lamborn, and S. M. Dornbusch. 1991. Authoritative parenting and adolescent adjustment across varied ecological niches. *Journal of Research on Adolescence* 1: 19–36.

Sullivan, M. 1989. *Getting paid: Youth crime and work in the inner city.* Ithaca, NY: Cornell University Press.

Sutherland, E. H. 1939. *Principles of criminology.* New York: Lippincott.

Suttles, G. 1968. *The social construction of communities.* Chicago: University of Chicago Press.

Tannenbaum, F. 1938. *Crime and community.* New York: Columbia University Press.

Teitler, J. O. 1996. The impact of neighborhood norms on youth sexual and fertility behavior. Ph.D. diss. University of Pennsylvania.

Thornberry, T. P., D. Huizinga, and R. Loeber. 1995. The prevention of serious delinquency and violence: Implications from the Program of Research on the Causes and Correlates of Delinquency. Pp. 213–237 in *Sourcebook on serious, violent, and chronic juvenile offenders.* Edited by J. C. Howell, B. Krisberg, J. D. Hawkins, and J. J. Wilson. Thousand Oaks, CA: Sage.

Thrasher, F. M. 1927. *The gang.* Chicago: University of Chicago Press.

Tienda, M. 1991. Poor people in poor places: Deciphering neighborhood effects on poverty outcomes. Pp. 244–262 in *Macro-micro links in sociology.* Edited by J. Huber. Newbury Park, CA: Sage.

Walker, K., and F. F. Furstenberg, Jr. August 1994. Neighborhood settings and parental strategies. Paper presented at the annual meetings of the American Sociological Association, Los Angeles, CA.

Waters, M. 1990. *Ethnic options.* Berkeley: University of California Press.

Werner, E. E., and R. S. Smith 1982. *Vulnerable but invincible.* New York: McGraw-Hill.

Weston, W. J., ed. 1989. *Education and the American family.* New York: New York University Press.

Whiting, B. B., and C. P. Edwards. 1988. *Children of different worlds.* Boston: Harvard University Press.

Williams, S., J. Anderson, R. McGee, and P. A. Silva. 1990. Risk factors for behavioral and emotional disorder in preadolescent children. *Journal of the American Academy of Child and Adolescent Psychiatry* 29: 413–419.

Wilson, W. J. 1987. *The truly disadvantaged: The inner-city, the underclass, and public policy.* Chicago: University of Chicago Press.

———. 1991. Studying inner-city social dislocations: The challenge of public agenda research. *American Sociological Review* 56 (1): 1–14.

———. 1996. *When work disappears: The world of the new urban poor.* New York: Knopf.

Wynn, J., H. Richman, R. A. Rubenstein, and J. Littell 1988. *Communities and adolescents: An exploration of reciprocal supports.* Washington, DC: Youth and America's Future: William T. Grant Foundation, Commission on Work, Family and Citizenship.

Yancey, W., and E. P. Ericksen. 1979. The antecedents of community: The economic and institutional structure of urban neighborhoods. *American Sociological Review* 44, 253–263.

Yee, D. K. April 1987. Participation in family decision-making: Parent and child perspectives. Paper presented at the biennial meetings of the Society for Research in Child Development, Baltimore, MD.

Yee, D. K., and C. Flanagan. 1985. Family environments and self-consciousness in early adolescence. *Journal of Early Adolescence* 5: 59–68.

Zill, N., and C. W. Nord. 1994. *Running in place: How American families are faring in a changing economy and an individualistic society.* Washington, DC: Child Trends.

Index

Locators in **boldface** refer to figures and tables.